A Series from
Southern Illinois University Press
Robert A. Schanke
SERIES EDITOR

Women in Turmoil

Women in Turmoil

SIX PLAYS BY

Mercedes de Acosta

Edited and with an Introduction by
Robert A. Schanke

Southern Illinois
University
Press

Carbondale and
Edwardsville

Library of Congress Cataloging-in-Publication Data
Acosta, Mercedes de, 1893–1968
Women in turmoil :
six plays by Mercedes de Acosta / Mercedes de Acosta ;
edited and with an introduction by
Robert A. Schanke.
p. cm. — (Theater in the Americas)
Includes bibliographical references.
1. Women—Drama. I. Schanke, Robert A., 1940–
II. Title. III. Series.
PS3501.C7 A6 2003
812'.52—dc21
2002008821
ISBN 0-8093-2509-8 (cloth : alk. paper)

To Mercedes,
whose voice
is finally
being
heard

Contents

Illustrations

Acknowledgments

My thanks go to the following:

Alice Birney, Literary Manuscript Historian of the Library of Congress, for assisting in the discovery and photocopying of scripts

Elizabeth E. Fuller, librarian at the Rosenbach Museum and Library, Philadelphia, and her staff for assisting in my research and for granting permission to publish materials and photos from the de Acosta collection

Nicholas Scheetz and Scott Taylor of the Manuscripts Division of the Lauringer Library at Georgetown University for providing access to several scripts

the literary executors of the late Sir Cecil Beaton and Hugo Vickers, literary executor, for permission to quote from the letters and diaries of Sir Cecil Beaton, copyright © Estate of Sir Cecil Beaton

Justine D. Tenney for the Estate of Norman Bel Geddes, Edith Lutyens Bel Geddes, Executrix, for permission to publish quotations from letters by Norman Bel Geddes to Mercedes de Acosta as well as the photo of the set design for *Jehanne d'Arc*

Ram Gopal for permission to quote from my interviews with him

Elizabeth Brymer of Southern Illinois University Press for serving as a wise, patient, and gracious editor

Wayne Larsen, a former student of mine at Midland Lutheran College, for his meticulous and careful copyediting for Southern Illinois University Press

Diane Schuring, Central College Campus Services Clerk, for converting the photocopied scripts onto disk format

Introduction

BY 1924, MERCEDES DE ACOSTA, who was then only thirty-one years of age, had clearly established herself as an author on the move. She had published three volumes of poetry—*Moods* (1920), *Archways of Life* (1921), *Streets and Shadows* (1924)—a novel entitled *Wind Chaff* (1920), and a one-act play about World War I called *For France* (1917).[1] The haunting quality of her imagery prompted poet and critic Charles Hanson Towne to declare that her poetry "bears promise of even finer achievement. . . . She may go far."[2] A critic for the *New York Herald* called *Wind Chaff* "an illuminating commentary on modern society."[3] Almost always, her writing was praised for its charm, freshness, sincerity, and frankness. Mercedes gained such prominence and credibility that when Isadora Duncan was writing her autobiography in 1927, Mercedes served as her unofficial agent and arranged for a publisher solely on the basis of her own personal endorsement of the manuscript.

Descended from a noble and proud Spanish family, Mercedes's orphaned mother had traveled at the age of fourteen to the United States, where she fought successfully in the New York Supreme Court for the return of the family fortune that had been stolen by her sinister uncle. Her father had migrated from Spain to Cuba, where he is said to have led a group of revolutionaries in an attempt to overthrow Spanish rule. The story goes that he was arrested but escaped from a firing line and fled to New York, where he eventually met Mercedes's mother. He persuaded his future wife to remain in the United States and marry him rather than return to Spain with her inheritance.

Mercedes, along with her parents and seven siblings, lived in New York City on fashionable Forty-seventh Street, between Fifth and Sixth Avenues, where their neighbors included such personalities as former President Theodore Roosevelt, statesman Joseph Choate, and the William Vanderbilts. Mercedes's parents often took part in the genteel social activities of the neighborhood. The escapades of her beautiful older sister, Rita, were often mentioned in the society sections of the daily newspapers.

When Mercedes was about four years old, her nanny began taking her to daily Mass at St. Patrick's Cathedral, where she always made faces and stuck out her tongue at one particular parishioner in a pew behind her. Charmed by the precocious little girl, the elderly man went to the mother superior of the orphanage next to the church and asked whether he might adopt her. Since she always sat next to the orphan children, he had assumed she was one of them. When he persisted even after the mother superior identified Mercedes, a meeting between him and Mercedes's mother was arranged. In the end, it was agreed that this kindly gentleman, who was none other than the famous theater producer Augustin Daly, could fetch Mercedes every Sunday afternoon so she could spend the day with him. He did not take Mercedes home, however. Instead, unbeknownst to Mercedes's mother, he would steal her off to the home of actress Ada Rehan where the three of them would create a world of little toy stages and reenact a delightful mix of plays.

When Mercedes's mother learned where her daughter was spending Sunday afternoons, the visits came to a halt. Mercedes was allowed, however, to go backstage with Daly during matinees at his theater. Sometimes she would sit on his lap and watch a rehearsal; other times, he carried her around on his shoulders and told people that Mercedes was going to become a great actress one day. Needless to say, her visits to the theater left a strong stamp on the impressionable young girl.

> *I remember distinctly being perched on Mr. Daly's shoulder in the wings and listening to the overture. I remember the excitement of the curtain going up and the hush that fell over everyone in the wings. Mr. Daly would put his finger to his lips to make sure I would be quiet. I remember the footlights and the 'spots' and the smell of grease paint and the continual coming and going of actors and actresses in strange costumes.*[4]

Enthralled by the world of the theater, the young Mercedes walked along Fifth Avenue to catch glimpses of her favorite actors, swooning if she saw John or Ethel Barrymore. She "had a mania for going to the theatre. On the sly," she attended matinees when her parents thought she was "out exercising in the air."[5] Particularly exciting was a performance of Maude Adams, who lived nearby. In 1905, when Mercedes was twelve, Adams created the role of Barrie's Peter Pan, probably her most popular performance. "Every child was hysterical about her as the little boy who never grew up and I was no exception," Mercedes confessed. "To me she *was* Peter Pan and when I saw her in the part I was thrown into a state of ecstasy."[6]

It was through her sister Rita, who moved in the artistic and literary circles of the day, that Mercedes eventually met Bessie Marbury, one of the first women theatrical agents and producers in the country. Marbury, in turn, introduced Mercedes to actress Alla Nazimova in 1916. A romantic relationship quickly developed between them, possibly the first lesbian relationship for both Mercedes and Alla. A year later,

Mercedes established a longtime liaison with Isadora Duncan, whom she had seen dancing "with a terrible fierce joy"[7] at the Metropolitan Opera House.

Inspired by these romantic relationships with both Nazimova and Duncan, Mercedes contemplated a career in the theater as a playwright. Encouraging her were the recent successes of other female playwrights. Prior to this time, women had written plays, but as historian Sherry Engle has pointed out, "a 'worldly' stigma associated with the theatre . . . discouraged all but the most determined and venturesome from seeking careers in the theatre."[8] Following the example set by such trailblazers as Rachel Crothers and Zoë Akins, however, the "number of women dramatists who were produced in New York City alone soared."[9] In February 1917, the magazine *Every Week* featured photographs of women who were aglow with their royalty checks. One article describes Rachel Crothers "riding on Fifth Avenue, New York, in a white automobile, with a chauffeur dressed in white."[10]

For Mercedes, the financial possibilities lit a fire. Although accustomed to wealth and a life of leisure, the de Acosta household had recently fallen on hard times. The U.S. economy had taken a major downturn in 1906 that led to a stock market collapse, a run on banks, and a recession. Jobs disappeared, and many solvent businesses went under. The dwindling family fortune undoubtedly contributed to her father's suicide in 1907. The family was left in financial jeopardy, forcing Mercedes's mother to move to a more modest home and eventually move in with one of her daughters. Success on Broadway could reverse all this.

Before moving to Hollywood in 1931 with the hope of becoming a screenwriter, Mercedes wrote ten plays, one musical, and an English translation of a French comedy. Several of these scripts have been excluded from this collection for various reasons. *For France* (1917) and *Sandro Botticelli* (1923) have been published and are readily available through interlibrary loan.[11] Others were disregarded owing to space limitations. *Loneliness* (1916) is an antiwar one-act similar in content to *For France*. *They That Walk Enchained* (1916) and *The Better Life* (1925) were revised after their original compositions, so included here are the revisions and not the originals. Since only the book and lyrics of *What Next!* (1920) are extant and not the music, the value of publishing this play is minimal, especially since it is not representative of Mercedes's work. *The Moon Flower* (1920) is an unwieldy, experimental, Strindbergian play and is hardly representative. Finally, *Himself* (1930) is a translation of a French play and not an original script by Mercedes.

Four of her plays were actually produced. *What Next!*, a musical that launched the acting career of Hope Williams, was performed at the intimate Princess Theatre. *Jehanne d'Arc* (1922), which starred Mercedes's lover at the time, Eva Le Gallienne, was designed by Norman Bel Geddes and premiered in Paris in 1925. *Sandro Botticelli* also starred Eva Le Gallienne and played for a limited engagement at the Provincetown Theater.

Her most successful production was of *Jacob Slovak* (1923), a drama portraying rampant anti-Semitism in a little New England town. It opened at a theater in Brooklyn in March 1927 with the title *Closed Doors* and starred Florence Eldridge and Jose Ruben. Directed by Edward Goodman and produced by Joseph P. Bickerton, Jr., it was such a success that it was transferred to the Greenwich Village Theatre six months later.[12] Though Eldridge and Ruben reprised their roles, James Light became the director and Cleon Throckmorton the designer. Just ten days after the off-Broadway tryout, the Shubert brothers moved the play to a major Broadway house, changing the title to *Conflict*. The following year, the Arts Theatre Club in London presented the play, casting John Gielgud and Ralph Richardson in leading roles and once again changing the title, this time to *Prejudice*.

In 1920, at the same time that Mercedes was actively pursuing her career as a playwright, she was also contemplating marriage to Abram Poole. When he proposed, however, she balked. "I couldn't make up my mind," she wrote in her autobiography. "As a matter of fact I was in a strange turmoil about world affairs, my own writing, suffrage, sex, and my inner spiritual development."[13] Undoubtedly a contribution to her turmoil was her introduction to the young, attractive, and ambitious actress Eva Le Gallienne just three days before Mercedes's marriage. Soon after her honeymoon, she began a five-year romantic relationship with the actress. The women that Mercedes created in these plays are also in turmoil, struggling over issues of unhappy marriages, divorce, sexual desire, identity, and self-recognition.

In the first scene of *Jehanne d'Arc,* Jehanne begs her uncle for help "to escape this marriage that my mother and father are planning for me." Throughout the play, Jehanne is jeered at and spat upon for dressing in men's clothes and cutting her hair like a man's. Voices in the crowd call her "a woman trying to be a man" and "a sexless woman." At one point, Jehanne argues, "We are each one of us chained to something. Each one of us in a different way. I have my battles, too."[14]

In *Jacob Slovak,* Myra Flint confesses that even though her preacher warned her about the evil of sexual passion, she could not resist sneaking to Jacob's lodging for sex. "Somehow I jest had ter have yer," she confesses. "I had ter. I had ter." But in spite of her love for Jacob, she cannot marry a Jew. "I can't go against everythin'. . . . I've been taught all my life ter hate yer race," she argues. "I can't go against the way I've ben brought up."

The Mother of Christ (1924) does not dramatize issues of marriage or sexual desire but continues Mercedes's preoccupation with strong-willed women who are fighting for a cause and for self-realization. The play is a long one-act written originally for the internationally famous actress Eleonora Duse, who had agreed to star in it before she died. Several other actresses—Jeanne Eagels, Lillian Gish, Marjorie Moss—also hoped to star in productions. Igor Stravinsky contemplated composing a score, and Norman Bel Geddes and Gladys Calthrop offered designs. Max Reinhardt considered a production in Germany.

It opens with Mary deciding that she must offer her life to Pontius Pilate in exchange for her son's. When she ultimately fails and Jesus is crucified, Mary "suddenly becomes the wildly enraged mother fighting for her child. . . . She is like a tortured, cornered animal, fighting her last fight with her back against the wall." In the final scene, she sits outside the sepulcher and prays for the time when people will appreciate how her son embraced "compassion, tolerance, understanding and forgiveness." Suddenly she knows why she alone realizes his importance. A revelation comes to her: "Because I am—the—Mother—of—Christ."

Several years before *World Without End* begins, Romola Charrington had been accused unjustly of promiscuity. Now, however, she confesses that when she had learned of her husband's infidelities, she retaliated and nurtured an affair with one of their mutual friends, who wrote her love letters and even stayed overnight in their home. During the course of the play, when she is reintroduced to her estranged son, who idolizes her, she must decide whether to confess to him her own shady past. When she does, he runs from the room and commits suicide.

Svanhild in *The Dark Light* is passionately in love with her twin brother, Ivar, a struggling poet. She pretends to destroy his new poems, hoping it will force him to admit that they were written for her rather than for the woman he is about to marry. When he does, "Svanhild drops her arms to her side and lowers her head. For a full second they look at each other. When Ivar speaks again, his voice is hardly audible" as he says, "Love you." Ecstatic, Svanhild replies, "And I love you—love you—have always loved you." They then kiss on the lips "deeply, violently, passionately—clinging to one another." Finally triumphant in achieving the love of her brother, Svanhild rushes out of the room and throws herself from the top of an adjoining lighthouse and is killed instantly.

When Hunt proposes marriage to Maggie in *Illusion*, she accepts. Although the match is an unlikely one from the start—she is a prostitute in a waterfront bar and he is from a wealthy and established family—Maggie yearns for a better life. Reality soon sets in. Maggie learns that her sister-in-law, who is engaged to be married, is having a secret affair with one of Maggie's former customers at the brothel. Disillusioned with high society people who "conceal what they are most of the time from other people," Maggie decides to return to her former life where people "live openly what they are."

An examination of two of her scripts reveals Mercedes's efforts not only to improve and grow as a playwright but also to strengthen her theme of women in turmoil. She completed *World Without End* in 1925 —nine years after finishing the original version. Initially, Mercedes had ended act 1 safely with the entrance of a young man whom Romola suspects is her long-lost son. The later ending to act 1 is much more provocative. Her son comes out of her house to tell Romola that dinner is being served. When he picks up a small lantern, "she takes it from him and impulsively holds it up to his face. She gazes intensely and longingly at him. He drops his eyes and breathes hard. Suddenly she casts the lantern aside—seizes him in her arms and kisses him." This erotic relationship is seen again in act 3. Her son sits at her feet. As she strokes his hair, he takes her fingers and kisses them. He puts his arms around her and then kisses her shoulder, her arm, and her hand, exclaiming, "I must keep kissing you to make sure you are really here." The incestuous suggestion not only added eroticism to the drama but also created more motivation for the son's eventual suicide.

Likewise, the 1923 copyrighted script for *Jacob Slovak* located at the Library of Congress is considerably different from the one used for both the 1927 and 1928 productions. In the original copyrighted version, Jacob begs Myra, his employer's daughter, to join him one evening in his room above the shop. Act 2 began with a scene between Jacob and Myra in this room. Nervous and embarrassed, Myra remembers her minister warning her that "love making is wicked." To relax her, Jacob plays a Chopin prelude. When he finishes and takes her in his arms, Myra protests and pushes him away. Undeterred, Jacob "tears down her bodice" and kisses her passionately before he carries her into his bedroom. In the next scene, Myra insists she will never marry him. Regretting that she "gave in to the lust of the flesh," Myra rushes out, slamming the door behind her.

In Mercedes's revision, Jacob is surprised when he sees Myra standing outside his bedroom window. She confesses that she has walked past his room many times in the past but "never quite dared to come in before."

Jacob blurts out sharply, "Go home, Myra, I can't stand having you here any longer—you're driving me mad—go home." Ultimately, he seizes her in his arms. Myra does not refuse him, does not push him away as in the original version, and says that she loves him. Whereas Jacob's actions in the original script could have been described as sexual harassment and possibly even acquaintance rape, in the final version, Myra becomes much more culpable. She does not run from him at the end of the act. Instead, she tries to explain her love for him.

> *I used ter lay in bed night after night and think about this—my body hot. The branches of the trees knockin' against the winder—I'd think it's a man—a man knockin' there—tryin' ter git in. It never was a special man. . . . And then yer came, and my man's body got a face— yer face. It got yer face because I loved yer—from the very first time I saw yer. After that I used ter think it was yer voice in the wind callin' me. . . . I had ter have yer or go crazy—that's all.*

As Jacob tries to persuade her to marry him, Myra suddenly "flings her arms around him and with all the passion of her nature she desperately holds him to her. Then she pushes him violently away." She rushes out of the room as Jacob cries out, "I'll come back for you—I'll come back!" Whereas in the original version Myra had pushed him away from her and threatened to spit on him if he followed her, Myra now reveals her passionate love for Jacob and how she is struggling with her decision to reject his proposal or to accept and thereby renounce her family.

The original final act takes place two months later. Jacob, who has been run out of town for being a Jew, has returned for Myra. She is pregnant with his child but tells him that she gave herself to another man who wanted to marry her in order to make him think it was his child. She says, however, that after the marriage, she will persuade her husband to give Jacob a job in the store so that "we—you can be close to me again." Jacob refuses. With suppressed hatred, he yells out,

> *And the child. Do you think I would let another man bring up my child?. . . . No, my child is a Jew. A Jew, I tell you! Go call them all in. Call in the whole village—everyone. Call them all in! Tell them you are carrying a Jew child in your womb!*

When Myra screams, "I hate you—you dirty Jew!" Jacob pulls out a revolver and kills her. The family tries to subdue him, but Jacob grabs a large bread knife from the table and plunges it into his heart.

The final pages of this earlier draft reinforce the town's prejudice. Jacob's body is not allowed in the church because he is a Jew. A servant girl who questions the decision kneels and places a crucifix on Jacob's chest as the curtain descends. Setting the play in New England, the site of traditional American values, and ending it with such damning and obvious indictment of the church and of the smug, provincial, intolerant attitudes of the villagers, Mercedes clearly illustrated her personal views of Americans who also rejected her own uniqueness.

The revised ending is much less blatant and melodramatic. Though tempted, Jacob cannot reveal Myra's lie to her future husband and the rest of the town. Before he leaves, he warns Myra, "I'll come back over and over again in your child. You think you can turn me out, but you can't. . . . Another man may bring up that child, but it will be my child and my race. My race that will come in here and go on." Rather than end the play with murder, suicide, and hatred for Jacob, Mercedes, by shaping a finale that revealed his defiance and determination, created more sympathy and compassion for the victim of prejudice.

Both *Jehanne d'Arc* and *Jacob Slovak* received extensive coverage by the press. When *Jehanne d'Arc* opened in Paris on June 12, 1925, the theater world was bustling with excitement. American newspapers in such far-flung corners as Walla Walla, Washington; Grand Forks, North Dakota; and Duluth, Minnesota, proclaimed the opening. *Theatre Magazine* ran photos of the sets along with detailed descriptions.[15] The French press had capitalized on the novelty of an American author and actress presenting, in French, a play about one of the French heroes. Front-page headlines of the Paris edition of the *Chicago Tribune* read, "Eva Le Gallienne to Play *Jehanne d'Arc*."[16] Opening night dignitaries included Elsie de Wolfe, Elsa Maxwell, Arthur Rubenstein, Mrs. Vincent Astor, Condé Nast, the Cole Porters, Ivor Novello, Dorothy Parker, Zoë Akins, and Constance Collier.

The French critics were impressed with the spectacle. As a critic for *Le Matin* concluded, "It is a 'great show' for the eyes, and nothing at all for the brain and spirit."[17] Unfortunately, the contribution of Mercedes suffered from all the dazzle. Sometimes, as the pageantry was unfolding, ten minutes would pass before a word of dialogue was uttered. At least it was enough of a success for the press to report that *Jehanne d'Arc* would move to London later in the summer and to Broadway in the fall of the year. Neither plan materialized, however.

If Mercedes had reservations about her future as a playwright after *Jehanne d'Arc*, she undoubtedly thought she had proven herself when *Jacob Slovak* opened on October 5, 1927. The *New York Times* called it "an honest and interesting play . . . with fine emotional and touching scenes," and a critic for the *New York World* praised Mercedes's originality and conviction and described the play as an "interesting study of prejudice and desire under the eternal elms." *Billboard* thought it was "strong meat . . . an excellently written play presented with real skill and under-standing."[18] Just ten days after the off-Broadway tryout, the Shuberts moved *Jacob Slovak* to Broadway.

The critics were equally enthusiastic when the play opened in London on June 17, 1928. The *Daily Sketch* called it "a remarkable and powerful religious play," and the *Evening Standard* stressed that Mercedes had "a sense of character and of writing for the stage, and she avoids mincing matters, sometimes to the verge of brutal frankness." Other critics said it was "a moving play . . . finely acted," and that it went "far to restore one's faith in the London theatre."[19]

It is shortsighted to conclude that her contribution might be dismissed with a simple shrug since most of her plays were never produced. Mercedes fully recognized that she faced an uphill battle. After receiving comments that her dialogue in *Sandro Botticelli* was artificial, stilted, and "so flowery . . . that it resemble[d] a seed catalogue,"[20] Mercedes came to the conclusion that

> [i]n New York at this time, if an artist rose from the gutter the crit-ics were all out to give him a break, but if he had background and wealth it was assumed from the start that he was an untalented idiot. Usually the critics either demolished him without fair criticism or completely ignored him.[21]

Mercedes was doubly dealt—she had both background and a history of wealth working against her.

There were other barriers to success. Her good friend of thirty years, Indian dancer Ram Gopal, confided in a recent interview that "when she met men who ran the theaters, they did not want to work with a strong woman who loved women. Men found her too overpowering."[22] Cecil Beaton described her in one of his diaries as "one of the most rebellious & brazen of Lesbians."[23] In another diary entry, he recorded that when he accompanied Mercedes to a Broadway theater performance in 1930, he felt embarrassed when people saw him walking with "that furious lesbian."[24] Even though she had married in 1920, Mercedes had refused to camouflage her desire for other women. As historian Felicia Londré has pointed out, even with the improved status of women in the theater, it remained important "to show how a woman drama-tist's essential femininity—her attractive appearance, her social posi-tion as a wife, her ability to run a household, her maternal devotion, and so forth—had not been impaired by her writing career."[25]

Indeed, the career of Rachel Crothers shows how a lesbian could succeed on Broadway. Unlike Mercedes, Crothers never married. Although she failed to fulfill the role of a wife, she carefully "scripted a public identity of herself . . . that not only explained away the lack of a husband and children, but to some degree even celebrated her lack of conformity to a traditionally feminine, domestic role." The press always portrayed her "as married to her work and too busy for a social or personal life." As historian J. K. Curry points out, Crothers clearly felt "compelled to limit the subject matter of her plays in order to maintain public approval and commercial appeal."[26]

When suggestions were offered to Mercedes on how to make her scripts more commercial, "she would say, 'To hell with them.'" Mercedes "did not give a damn for the men in power," Ram insisted. "She was just herself and would not hide and conceal herself. She would not pander to anyone's taste. Because she insisted on being the dominant person in any production, interest always fell apart."[27] Not much had improved since a few years earlier when playwright Marion Fairfax had argued, "The best and first thing for an aspiring playwright to do is to be born a man."[28]

Though a New Yorker by birth, Mercedes moved in 1931 to Hollywood, where she hoped she would be more successful as a screenwriter. Soon after her first film script, *East River,* was rejected as a vehicle for Pola Negri, she began a lifelong infatuation with Greta Garbo. From 1931, when they met, until she died thirty-seven years later, Mercedes's life was forever linked with Garbo's. They vacationed, sunbathed in the nude, and even lived together for a time in 1932. The relationship, however, was unpredictable and stormy. Sometimes Garbo would scatter blossoms on the threshold when Mercedes entered her home and then usher her to the bedroom. Other times she would refuse to acknowledge Mercedes's presence.

The first film Mercedes penned for Garbo was *Desperate.* Irving Thalberg, head of production at Metro-Goldwyn-Mayer, stopped the project when he learned that Garbo would be dressed as a boy for more than half the film: "We have been building Garbo up for years as a great glamorous actress, and now you come along and try to put her into pants and make a monkey out of her."[29] This decision brought an abrupt end to Mercedes's dreams of film writing.

For the next thirty-some years, Mercedes's life and career were a series of disappointments and rejections. Although she received no official credit for her work, she assisted on Garbo's *Queen Christina* (1933) and *Camille* (1937), primarily because she hoped for Garbo to star in her revision of *Jehanne d'Arc.* In 1932, when Garbo was being particularly aloof and quarrelsome, she engaged in a love affair with still another screen goddess—Marlene Dietrich.

In 1935, Mercedes's husband of fifteen years finally sued for divorce.

"That we could no longer make a success of our sexual life seemed to me no reason to separate," she argued. "I was too European to feel, as Americans do, that the moment the sex relation is over one must fly to the divorce courts."[30] Once again she felt rejected: "It was as though my father or some close friend had written to me that he wanted me out of his life."[31]

In an effort to alleviate her depression, Mercedes took off for Italy where she spent time meditating with twelve nuns.[32] She had grown up as a devout Roman Catholic, often kneeling in prayer for hours at a time. Once, she even put nails and stones in her shoes as a kind of penance. Later, she rejected Catholicism to embrace the teachings of Kahlil Gibran and Jiddu Krishnamurti. In 1938, she flew to India and met with gurus Sri Meher Baba and Ramana Maharshi.

From the 1940s until the late 1960s, Mercedes's health deteriorated dramatically. After three of her close acquaintances committed suicide —Eleanora von Mendelssohn in 1949, Ona Munson in 1955, and William McCarthy in 1965—she suffered a breakdown, fell into a severe state of depression, and contemplated suicide herself.

Through these bleak years, however, she continued to write. When she learned that the Office of War Information was publishing a propaganda magazine called *Victory,* she moved back to New York and joined the editorial staff in 1942. Two years later, she embarked on a tour for the National Concert and Artists Corporation, lecturing on "The Challenge of a Changing World," "New Trends in Art and Literature," and "Friends and Celebrities." Other lecturers on the circuit included Lee Simonson, Lillian Gish, and Guthrie McClintic. For more than a decade, she and Natacha Rambova worked together on a play called *The Leader,* which was an adaptation of Mercedes's earlier *The Mother of Christ.*

Her major focus at that time was her autobiography. When *Here Lies the Heart* finally appeared in 1960, reaction was mixed. Her close friends praised the book. Cecil Beaton wrote her that "there is so much good stuff in it & I have enjoyed it a lot."[33] Alice B. Toklas was another fan: "Your book has left me breathless—excited and very happy. I curtsy before your tremendous accomplishment."[34]

Her early, unpublished chapters of the book contain coded accounts of Mercedes's lesbian relationships. Although the finished book discusses all of her female friends without reference to their sexual orientation, many readers were outraged by the mere implications. In 1960, the subject of lesbianism was still quite unpopular. The book's publication should have excited Mercedes, but instead it threw her into a deeper depression, especially now that she was living a threadbare existence.

Her only visitors in the end were "Les Girls," young women hoping they would be introduced to Garbo. Although she had been damned as "star-struck," a "lover to the stars," and, more outrageously, as "the greatest starfucker ever,"[35] she had been deserted by them all, whispering to one of the few friends who still visited her, "I'm sitting here all alone."[36] She pointed to the autographed photographs in her room signed "To Dearest Mercedes," "To the One and Only Mercedes," and others, and admitted that she had been forgotten by all the famous personalities in her past now that she was penniless. "I don't think it's made me bitter—just damned bewildered. And I'm not ashamed to say I'm lonely."[37] She died on May 9, 1968.

The twelve years between 1916 and 1928 had been extremely productive for Mercedes: three books of poetry, two novels, four produced plays—two Off-Broadway, another in Paris, and a fourth both on Broadway and in London—and several unproduced plays. However, with the exception of her 1960 autobiography, her last forty years produced very little. The early promise she had shown as a poet, novelist, and playwright never materialized. In the pantheon of theater history, she is now virtually unknown.

Probably my most thrilling discovery during preparation of a book-length biography of Mercedes, *"That Furious Lesbian": The Story of Mercedes de Acosta* (2003), occurred in August 2000 during the national convention of the Association for Theatre in Higher Education in Washington, D.C. At one session, a panelist who represented the Manuscript Division of the Library of Congress happened to mention that plans were being made to destroy or to convert to microfilm the contents of several cardboard boxes of old, copyrighted plays. He noted that in one of the boxes were plays by a woman named Mercedes de Acosta. As far as he knew, nobody was aware that these scripts existed. I was not at that presentation, but as the gods have it, my dear friend and colleague Kim Marra was, knew I was working on this biography, and shot down the hall to find me minutes after the session ended. Immediately, I connected with the Library of Congress and arranged a meeting with Alice Birney, Literary Manuscript Historian of the Library of Congress. With her assistance, I was able to photocopy every one of the plays before I left the city.

I had originally written a detailed synopsis of these unpublished plays in the biography, since none of them were available to the public. Because Southern Illinois University Press decided to publish this collection, however, I have only summarized them in the biography. The plays have been edited extremely lightly to reflect their archival nature and retain a bit of Mercedes's personality. Errors in spelling, as well as those that affect meaning, have been corrected. Hopefully, these two books will correct certain myths about Mercedes de Acosta and will help in finally restoring her name to its proper place in history.

Notes

1. *Moods* (New York: Moffat, Yard, 1919); *Archways of Life* (New York: Moffat, Yard, 1921); *Streets and Shadows* (New York: Moffat, Yard, 1924); *Wind Chaff* (New York: Moffat, Yard, 1920); *For France, Outlook* (July 25, 1917): 482–83.

2. *Moods,* 2.

3. "Many Women of Society Win Fame in the World of Literature and Art," *New York Herald* [1920?].

4. Mercedes de Acosta, "Here Lies the Heart," typescript with corrections, n.d., de Acosta collection, folder 03:01, 11, Rosenbach Museum and Library, Philadelphia.

5. Mercedes de Acosta, *Here Lies the Heart* (New York: William Morrow, 1960), 43.

6. *Here Lies the Heart,* 17.

7. Isadora Duncan, *My Life* (New York: Liveright Publishing, 1927), 239.

8. Sherry Engle, "An 'Interruption of Women Dramatists': The Rise of America's Woman Playwright, 1890–1920," *New England Theatre Journal* 12 (2001): 28. For more discussion of the growth of women dramatists in this period, see Felicia Hardison Londré, "Money Without Glory: Turn of the Century America's Women Playwrights," in *The American Stage,* ed. Ron Engle and Tice L. Miller's (New York: Cambridge University Press, 1993), 131–40.

9. Ibid.

10. "Mrs. Shakespeares," *Every Week* 26 (February 1917): 11.

11. *For France* was published in *Outlook* (1917) and *Sandro Botticelli* by Moffat and Yard (New York, 1923). The dates provided here are when the plays were copyrighted at the Library of Congress. *Illusion* is a renamed revision of *The Better Life. World Without End* is a revision of *They That Walk Enchained.*

12. In Philip Hoare, *Noel Coward* (Chicago: University of Chicago Press, 1998), 151, the author refers to Bickerton as the "sometime lover of Mercedes de Acosta." Such a relationship is highly unlikely. A committed lesbian, she was never romantically linked with any man except her husband, Abram Poole.

13. *Here Lies the Heart,* 109.

14. Mercedes de Acosta, *Jehanne d'Arc* typescript, Rosenbach Museum and Library, Philadelphia.

15. *Theatre Magazine* (May 1925).

16. *Chicago Tribune* (Paris edition), June 11, 1925.

17. *L'Action Française* (Paris), June 18, 1925.

18. *New York Times,* October 6, 1927; *New York World,* October 6, 1927; Barclay V. McCarty, *Billboard,* [October 6, 1927?].

19. *Daily Sketch,* June 18, 1928; *Evening Standard,* June 18, 1928; *Morning Post,* June 18, 1928; *Western Morning News and Mercury* (Plymouth), June 19, 1928.

20. Percy Hammond, "The Theaters," *New York Tribune,* March 27, 1923; Heywood Broun, *Democrat Chronicle,* April 1, 1923; Gordon Whyte, *Billboard,* April 7, 1923.

21. Typescript with corrections, folder 02:02, 101, Rosenbach Museum and Library, Philadelphia.

22. Ram Gopal, interview by author, Norbury Hall, Norbury, England, November 4, 2001.

23. Cecil Beaton, unpublished diary entry, May 1968, quoted in Hugo Vickers, *Loving Garbo: The Story of Greta Garbo, Cecil Beaton, and Mercedes de Acosta* (New York: Random House, 1994), 281.

24. Cecil Beaton, unpublished diary entry, February 3, 1930. The unpublished diaries are in the possession of Hugo Vickers, literary executor of the Cecil Beaton estate.

25. Londré, "Money Without Glory," 131.

26. See J. K. Curry, "Rachel Crothers: An Exceptional Woman in a Man's World," in *Staging Desire: Queer Readings of American Theater History,* ed. Kim Marra and Robert A. Schanke (Ann Arbor: University of Michigan Press, 2002), 55–80.

27. Ram Gopal, interview.

28. *Cleveland Plain Dealer,* July 23, 1911.

29. *Here Lies the Heart,* 233.

30. *Here Lies the Heart,* 261.

31. "First Writing," folder 02:05, 419, Rosenbach Museum and Library, Philadelphia.

32. Mercedes de Acosta, "Study in Sainthood," *Tomorrow* (May 1942): 37–40.

33. Cecil Beaton to Mercedes, March 26, 1960; Rosenbach Museum and Library, Philadelphia.

34. Quoted in *Staying On Alone—The Letters of Alice B. Toklas,* ed. Edward Burns (New York: Random House, 1974), 380.

35. These descriptions are from the dust jacket of Diana McLellan's *The Girls: Sappho Goes to Hollywood* (New York: St. Martin's Press, 2000) and from an interview of Gavin Lambert by Ron Hogan in 1997, retrieved June 20, 2002, <www.beatrice.com/interviews/lambert/index.html>.

36. Kieran Tunney, *Interrupted Autobiography and Aurora* (London: Quartet Books, 1989), 37; Wilder Luke Burnap to Hugo Vickers, September 30, 1992, quoted in Vickers, *Loving Garbo,* 280.

37. Quoted in Tunney, 37.

Women in Turmoil

Jehanne d'Arc
A Tragedy in Two Parts

The Characters

JEHANNE D'ARC
JACQUES D'ARC, *father of Jehanne*
ISABELLETTE D'ARC, *mother of Jehanne*
DURAND-LAXART, *uncle of Jehanne*
PIERRE
PIERRE'S FATHER
JEAN DE METZ, *a soldier of fortune*
GASTON, *a soldier*
CAPTAIN BAUDRICOURT, *Seigneur of Vaucouleurs*
CURÉ OF VAUCOULEURS
LA TRÉMOUILLE, *favorite at the court*
DUKE OF ALENÇON
THE DAUPHIN, *afterwards* KING CHARLES VII OF FRANCE
MARÉCHAL DE BOUSSAC
CAPTAIN DE RAIS
CAPTAIN DE LA HIRE
CAPTAIN DE XAINTRAILLES
A BOURGONDIAN SOLDIER *in disguise*
MAYOR OF ORLÉANS
CONSTABLE OF FRANCE
JEAN DE LUXEMBOURG
DUKE OF BEDFORD
EARL OF WARWICK
ARCHBISHOP CAUCHON
EARL OF STAFFORD
ARCHBISHOP OF RHEIMS
SOLDIERS, PEASANTS, PAGES,
LADIES-IN-WAITING,
COURTIERS, MONKS

Part 1

Place: *Outside the home of* JEHANNE D'ARC, *Domrémy, Lorraine*
Time: *Spring in 1428*
There is no scenery in this play. A glorious blue cyclorama is used through-out the entire play regardless of the change of properties. The stage is built

Library of Congress Copyright, March 3, 1922. Registration number 60141.

architecturally upon planes or inclines, upstage being the highest of all. This remains as a permanent structure during the entire play and is painted, together with the floor, the same color blue as the cyclorama. Different scenes are played upon different planes. An old, primitive well is upstage to left; a wooden bench to right upstage.

When the curtain rises, JEHANNE *is alone on the stage. She is distinctly a peasant girl, rather large hands and feet, but with a strange beauty in her face and almost terrifying frankness and sincerity in her eyes and gesture. Her hair is brushed straight back off her face and worn in a small knot at her neck. Her eyes are blue and set wide apart; she is dressed in ordinary peasant costume. She is sitting on the bench with a wooden bowl on her lap and a basket filled with carrots at her feet. She is cutting the carrots into the bowl. She works steadily but occasionally she stops and sits motionlessly as though something were troubling her, then she resumes her work again. She continues it for as long as it can be sustained. Then she pauses again; she seems puzzled—as though something were trying to force its way and break through her consciousness. She goes to the well and draws water in a wooden pail; she returns to the bench and washes the remaining carrots, which she has not yet cut. Finally she drops her work, rises, and comes forward. She places her hand to her breast and seems to breathe hard; her exalted expression shows that she is in contact with something supernatural, as the sound of tiny bells, tinkling softly as though from another world, can be heard. A great shaft of brilliant white light pours down upon the ground beside her.* JEHANNE *raises her head and listens; she seems conscious of voices addressing her. She advances into the light and drops upon her knees, extending her arms. After a short silence she speaks.*

JEHANNE: Yes, yes, I hear—I'm listening. *(With exaltation and joy)* It's you, Saint Catherine, it's you! A command for me? *(She humbly lowers her head as though receiving a command. She breathes with difficulty and speaks in a low voice.)* I—save France? I can do nothing—not even carry a bucket or guard sheep.

(She slowly raises her head; the sound of bells becomes louder as larger ones join in. There is a long silence. JEHANNE *rises; she lifts her arms as though receiving strength. From the timid clumsy peasant girl she visually becomes confident. She seems to grow taller, carries herself straighter and remains quivering, awaiting the commands.)*

JEHANNE: Yes, yes, Saint Marguerite, Saint Michael, I hear—I'm listening. You will give me the power. My body will be filled with strength and my heart with courage—this mission would not be given me if the King of Kings were not near me to guide me on my way. Yes, I promise. I pledge myself to Him alone and to no other. I give my heart to Him and to no other; He of all the world will never forsake me . . . Go to the house of Captain Baudricourt, tell him of your commands and from him I will obtain an escort to the Dauphin . . . *(She speaks all these words in a low voice and as though repeating word for word what she has been told.)* Yes, yes, I understand, I understand! *(She lowers her head an instant, then raises it high.)* You will be with me to help me,—to guide me. Save France! Save France! *(Chimes join the bells.)* I pledge myself, I pledge myself, but I am not worthy! *(A divine light radiates from her face.)* Yes, Strength and Faith . . .

(Large cathedral bells of deeper tone join the others. JEHANNE *staggers, and as one spent by some terrific emotion, she sinks down breathing and trembling. She remains like this when suddenly* DURAND-LAXART *comes out of the house.)*

DURAND-LAXART: *(Seeing* JEHANNE *and rushing toward her)* Jehanne! *(All bells cease ringing suddenly.)* Jehanne, are you ill?

JEHANNE: *(Struggling and trying to find words)* No—Uncle—do—not—call—anyone. It has happened before. What I have told you of once before.

DURAND-LAXART: *(Putting his arms around* JEHANNE *)* The voices? You mean the voices? You heard the voices again?

JEHANNE: Yes.

DURAND-LAXART: *(Becoming agitated himself)* What did they say? What did they say?

JEHANNE: That I was to go to Captain Baudricourt and tell him of my visions, and from him I would obtain an escort to the Dauphin.

DURAND-LAXART: *(Breathless)* To the Dauphin! Why child, what are you talking about? *(With intense interest in spite of himself)* But what then? What then? What else did they say?

JEHANNE: *(Rising to her feet)* And then—then I shall save France!

DURAND-LAXART: *(He looks at her and draws back, amazed at the change he sees in her.)* Jehanne! *(In a whisper)* You are altered. Some terrific change has come to you.

JEHANNE: I have spoken with the messengers of the King!

DURAND-LAXART: *(Convinced)* You *are* changed. *(Pause)* Has anything happened about Pierre? What of him?

JEHANNE: Uncle, you must help me. You *must* help me—not only to go to Captain Baudricourt but also to escape this marriage that my mother and father are planning for me. I cannot marry Pierre.

DURAND-LAXART: Don't be foolish, Jehanne. You know very well they are inside the house now discussing your marriage. You can't change your mind for any better reason than these—these voices. Other people won't believe in them, no matter how real they may seem to you. Besides, your mother and father will never consent to your refusing Pierre—you know yourself that every other girl in the village wants him—he could marry any one of them, and you, you are the envy of them all. It's only you he wants.

JEHANNE: No matter—I cannot marry.

DURAND-LAXART: *(Distressed)* I don't know what to say. Pierre and his father came today only for your answer.

JEHANNE: I know. They left me alone out here so that I might decide.

DURAND-LAXART: The decision is already made as far as they are concerned. Reflect, Jehanne—don't be hasty. No girl can afford to throw away a chance like this.

JEHANNE: *(Distressed but determined)* No matter, Uncle, I've made up my mind.

DURAND-LAXART: *(He looks to right.)* Here comes Pierre now. Don't be hasty, Jehanne, I beg of you! *(At that moment PIERRE appears.)*

PIERRE: *(Happily and confidently)* Well, have you decided on the day, Jehanne? *(JEHANNE does not answer. PIERRE looks at LAXART and reads something amiss in his face.)* You both look strange. What is the matter? You've surely decided—haven't you?

JEHANNE: Yes, Pierre—I've decided—I've—

PIERRE: *(Enthusiastically breaking in)* When is it to be?

JEHANNE: *(Sadly)* Never.

PIERRE: What do you mean? *(Laughing)* You're joking, of course.

JEHANNE: *(Slowly and with difficulty)* I am pledged. It's—more—difficult—than—you—will—believe.

PIERRE: *(Suddenly serious)* Pledged? I don't know what you mean.

JEHANNE: I am pledged to another.

PIERRE: Pledged to another—you're not serious—

JEHANNE: *(Passionately and pathetically extending her hand to* PIERRE, *which he ignores)* Can't you understand Pierre—can't you understand it's stronger than I? Don't you see I would have wanted to marry you—I, too, want a home and love—like—like the other girls that want you, too—but this pledge is greater—bigger than I am—bigger than you. *(Helplessly)* Understand, Pierre—help me . . .

PIERRE: *(Frantically and beside himself)* I don't know what you are saying—I don't know what you are talking about—

JEHANNE: And I don't know how to explain. I hoped you might understand—

PIERRE: You are really serious? This is final?

JEHANNE: Final.

PIERRE: *(Angrily)* You have deceived and tricked me? Led me on and lied to me?

JEHANNE: No! No, Pierre, not that!

PIERRE: Yes, lied!—and tricked me! Father! Jacques d'Arc! *(He rushes into the house, calling.)* Listen to what Jehanne has told me. She doesn't want to marry me! She won't marry me! *(*JACQUES D'ARC, ISABELLETTE D'ARC, *and* PIERRE'S FATHER *all come out, led by* PIERRE.*)* She has tricked me! She has fooled me! She is pledged to another!

JACQUES D'ARC: What is this? Are you raving, Jehanne?

JEHANNE: *(Determined and firm)* He is right. I am pledged to another.

JACQUES D'ARC: *(In a thundering voice)* To whom, I should like to know? To whom?

PIERRE'S FATHER: Yes—to whom?

JEHANNE: *(Proudly)* To my King.

JACQUES D'ARC: *(Stepping back)* She is mad! Surely she is mad.

JEHANNE: No. Today I leave your house never to return. *(As they have been speaking, twilight slowly falls.)*

JACQUES D'ARC: You are mad. I shall lock you up. *(He advances toward her, but* JEHANNE *raises her hand and he suddenly stops.)*

JEHANNE: No, father. You are so used to seeing me obey you that today you don't understand when I cannot. Parents never understand the day when their children cease to obey them. But that day must always come.

JACQUES D'ARC: You have no reason to leave your home. Your mother and I have done everything we could for you.

JEHANNE: I must be about my King's business.

JACQUES D'ARC: You will not leave this house. I command you to remain!

JEHANNE: *(Calmly)* Uncle, will you lead the way to Vaucouleurs? *(*DURAND-LAXART *starts off to right. As* JEHANNE *follows him,* JACQUES D'ARC *and* PIERRE *throw themselves before her in an effort to block her way.* JEHANNE *continues forward as one in a trance, and as though faced by some unearthly power, they both fall back and let her pass, compelled to make way for her; the others also slowly fall back.* JEHANNE *takes a few steps, and then suddenly turns with an outstretched gesture of love and agony toward her mother. In her prophetic soul is the knowledge that this is a parting forever.)*

ISABELLETTE D'ARC: *(With outstretched arms)* I will come with you, Jehanne!

JEHANNE: No, mother, I must do this work alone. *(*JEHANNE *takes a step forward, then turning, flings her arms about her mother. They hold each other in passionate, agonized embrace.* JEHANNE *breaks away, for an instant bewildered.)*

ISABELLETTE D'ARC: *(Weeping)* You will not return! You will not return!

(After a moment JEHANNE *rouses herself and starts forward slowly.* ISABELLETTE D'ARC, JACQUES D'ARC, PIERRE *and his* FATHER, *huddled together, their eyes fixed on* JEHANNE, *slowly back offstage to right.* JEHANNE *walks with her head thrown back as one tremendously exalted, while a strange radiance glows on her face. The wall and bench have disappeared.* CHILDREN *enter and gather around* JEHANNE. *As she does not apparently perceive them, they are silenced by her mood and fall back from her. Gradually the stage fills with* PEASANTS. *They are wonderful types of old and young and are symbolic of all peasants of the world. As* JEHANNE *walks in their midst they show incredulous surprise and intense curiosity. They crowd about her a trifle timidly, as though if she moved quickly they would disband and run away. One or two of the older ones touch* JEHANNE, *then quickly run back forming little groups*

and discussing her. Their voices keep up a low mumble; occasionally they can be understood speaking.)

A YOUNG WOMAN: Someone should lead her home.

A YOUNG MAN: Perhaps she is mad or walking in her sleep.

AN OLD WOMAN: *(Steps forward and speaks.)* I have known her since she was a child. I used to see her praying in the fields.

A CHILD: She would stop playing to pray.

AN OLD MAN: I remember her, too. They laughed at her, but she has always been an earnest and serious girl.

A YOUNG PEASANT WOMAN: She has asked an audience with Seigneur Baudricourt.

SEVERAL VOICES: *(With surprise)* No? Impossible!

OLD WOMAN: The idea of a peasant girl wishing to talk to one of so high a rank.

A YOUNG PEASANT MAN: Baudricourt will have other use for her! *(Laughter)*

YOUNG WOMAN: She's not a bad girl, I know.

A CHILD: She dreams of saving France.

OLD MAN: *(Repeating himself)* They laughed at her, but she has always been an earnest and serious girl.

A YOUNG WOMAN: Too earnest—it's gone to her head! *(Louder laughter)*

A YOUNG MAN: Someone has put crazy notions into her head—she's really not a bad girl.

ANOTHER OLD WOMAN: It may bring bad luck to laugh at her. I've heard it said a maid would be born in this place who would do great deeds and save France.

ANOTHER YOUNG MAN: Another crazy one! They're all going mad! *(More laughter)*

A CHILD: *(Poking* JEHANNE*)* She pretends not to see us. *(More* CHILDREN *gather round her. They make fun and laugh at her. The older* PEASANTS *snicker among themselves and join in the laughter.)*

JEHANNE: *(She turns toward them with extended arms and deep supplication in her voice.)* Peasants—people of the soil—I need your aid.

(They slowly back away from her as though in terror of anything she would ask them and as though they consider her mad. JEHANNE *turns sadly from them; she attempts to go forward in the opposite direction when suddenly a great tall* GUARD *in armor bars her way with extended arms. She tries to pass him but cannot. She should give the impression of pushing against him without being able to move him. In despair, she beats upon his chest as though beating upon a closed door, but he remains unmoved.*

She turns from him but gives no sign of losing courage. At that moment from among the PEASANTS, *her* UNCLE *approaches with an old* CURÉ. *The* CURÉ *steps forward and stretches out his hand.* JEHANNE *takes it.)*

CURÉ: I will take you to Baudricourt, Jehanne d'Arc. *(They move a few steps forward, but still the* GUARD *bars the way.)* Let us pass. I believe in this girl. *(The* CURÉ *also makes an effort to pass the* GUARD, *who continues oblivious of them both.)*

OLD PEASANT: She will never be allowed even to see Seigneur Baudricourt.

CURÉ: *(Indignant)* But I insist—

*(*BAUDRICOURT *enters from behind the* GUARD; *he flings him aside as though throwing back and opening wide a door.* BAUDRICOURT *is a middle-aged man; he is dressed elaborately but with distinction. In the dim light and while the* PEASANTS *are crowding in the scene, a chest is placed on the stage. When* BAUDRICOURT *enters, a* SOLDIER *pushes the chest in evidence. It denotes the house of* BAUDRICOURT. *The lights come up and grow bright.)*

BAUDRICOURT: *(With a great deal of manner)* What is this noise? What do the people want?

(The CURÉ *stands with* JEHANNE *and her* UNCLE *close behind him and the* VILLAGERS *crowding about.* JEAN DE METZ, *a soldier of fortune, and* GASTON, *another soldier, have followed* BAUDRICOURT *at a distance.)*

CURÉ: *(Removing his hat)* A thousand pardons, Seigneur Baudricourt, but I have taken the liberty to bring a very remarkable and strange girl to you.

BAUDRICOURT: Indeed. *(To the* GUARD) Disperse that gaping crowd. *(The* GUARD *makes a gesture and the* MOB *withdraws.)*

BAUDRICOURT: *(To the* CURÉ) And now what is this story? What is all this that I have been hearing about this girl?

CURÉ: I would prefer that she should tell you herself. I would only like to say that I think she is sincere and good, and if I am not wrong, I think she is inspired.

BAUDRICOURT: *(To* JEHANNE *with curiosity)* Go on. Go on with your story.

JEHANNE: *(She seems more spiritual and her whole presence gives out a conviction of exaltation and inspiration.)* For a long time, Seigneur, I have heard voices—

BAUDRICOURT: Voices?

JEHANNE: Yes, while I was working in the fields I heard them— sometimes at twilight or at early dawn they spoke to me—as plainly as you spoke now—as plainly as any voice speaking here.

These voices, my lord, these heaven-sent voices directed me to
come to you and ask you to equip me, and send me to Chinon,
where I may be escorted into the presence of our Dauphin.

BAUDRICOURT: *(Thunderstruck for a moment, tongue tied.)* And for
what reason?

JEHANNE: That I may tell him the voices have appointed me and
that he should put me in command of his forces—that I may lead
his soldiers to victory and the saving of France.

BAUDRICOURT: *(Bursts into laughter)* You expect me to believe this?
A girl lead soldiers! This is madness.

CURÉ: *(Timidly)* I think it would be well to obey her voices. She has
given me many signs and proofs.

BAUDRICOURT: If I send her to the Dauphin and she turns out to be
a fool—which I suspect her of being already—it will be I who will
be made a fool of at court and held up to ridicule. No, I thank
you; I am not sufficiently in favor to take any such risk as that.

CURÉ: Let her give you a sign as she did me.

BAUDRICOURT: I'm afraid I'm not as easily taken in by signs as
you—soldiers are not quite as partial to signs and visions as priests.

CURÉ: It might be for your own good to ask a sign of this girl. At
any rate it couldn't in any way harm you.

BAUDRICOURT: No—no, I suppose not. It might even be interesting
or amusing. *(Shrugs his shoulders incredulously.)* Let me see. *(Hesitates a moment, thinks.)* Ah, I have it—this will be a test! *(Goes to
chest, takes a key out of his pocket, and unlocks it, holding his hand
over the lid.)* I have something in here which belonged to a friend
I loved, who was killed many years ago in battle. Since I put it in
there no one has opened this chest or knows what is in it. Can you
tell me what it is?

*(*JEHANNE *closes her eyes, clasps her hands and seems to pray. There is a
moment of intense suspense while everyone holds their breath.)*

JEHANNE: *(Slowly, distinctly, but with some effort)* It is a heavy silver
sword. The hilt is heavily engraved with a large ruby on the top.
Inside the hilt is written, "For country and honor." *(*BAUDRICOURT
*is stunned. He takes out a sword which answers to description. The
others step back in amazement.)*

CURÉ: *(Triumphantly)* What did I tell you?

BAUDRICOURT: *(Pausing, perplexed)* Well done, my girl—still,
I don't care to take the responsibility of sending you to the
Dauphin. There may be some trick in this after all.

JEAN DE METZ: *(Profoundly impressed, stepping forward with animation and enthusiasm)* Why not let me take her, Seigneur? I'm a sol-

dier of fortune and used to risks. *(*BAUDRICOURT *is confused. Looks at* CURÉ.*)*

CURÉ: Yes, yes, let him take her.

BAUDRICOURT: *(To* JEHANNE*)* Do you think you can really do what you say?

JEHANNE: Yes, I am sure of it.

BAUDRICOURT: *(To the others)* It's true I find no fault in this girl.

JEAN DE METZ: No, my lord. I think you may safely let us go. *(A* PAGE *steps forward with a bowl of water.)*

BAUDRICOURT: Very well, let her have her way. But remember, I assume no responsibility one way or another. There may be trickery in all this, or witchcraft. I will not attempt to judge this girl, I will not judge whether she is right or wrong, and see *(He dips his hands into the bowl of water.)* I wash my hands of her, although in a way, I wish her well.

JEAN DE METZ: I'll give her a horse and ride with her to Chinon.

DURAND-LAXART: *(To* JEHANNE*)* How can you ride in such clothes?

JEHANNE: I'll put on a soldier's uniform.

BAUDRICOURT: What, dress yourself in men's clothes?

JEHANNE: A soldier should wear a soldier's uniform.

CURÉ: That's a reasonable answer.

BAUDRICOURT: *(Laughing)* But a soldier with long hair.

JEHANNE: I'll cut it.

BAUDRICOURT: Well, God speed you, de Metz. *(Claps* DE METZ *on the shoulder.)* You are a brave fellow. Sometimes a soldier is braver out of battle than in it.

CURÉ: Good-bye, my lord. *(He turns to* DE METZ *and* JEHANNE.*)* I'll bless these children. *(They bow their heads as he blesses them. He goes out followed by* DURAND-LAXART.*)*

JEAN DE METZ: Come, Jehanne d'Arc.

(He gives JEHANNE *his hand, and they move forward. The* VILLAGERS *crowd around them. The great shaft of light enveloping* JEHANNE *follows her off.)*

BAUDRICOURT: *(Calling after her)* Whatever your mission may be, may it bring you luck. *(To* GASTON, *who has remained silent, standing through the whole scene)* That soldier of fortune is a little—*(Taps his finger to his brain, then goes off.* GASTON *remains, looking after the crowd, then he goes out. The* POPULACE *laments her dangerous and doubtful mission. They call after her. A* CHILD *cries. It is growing darker.)*

PEASANTS: She will never get there.
    The way is filled with danger and crime.
    The journey is too long.
    She'll lose courage and turn back.
    Where has she gone?
    Ah, she is doomed!
    See how dark it grows!
    It seems unusually dark for so early.
    She will lose her way in such darkness.
    She is doomed!
    Doomed! Doomed!
    It serves her right for her arrogance.
    She thinks she can do more than anyone else.
    Perhaps we shouldn't judge one who is mad.
    She's surely mad.
    Then she should be locked up.
    Mad people should not be allowed at large.
    But the Curé believed in her—
    Yes, and Seigneur Baudricourt, too.
    Nonsense—he only wanted to get rid of her.
    He passed the responsibility on to de Metz, that's what he did.
    A fool could see that.
    He would not have dared to have taken it upon himself. Hush!
    We may get in trouble.
    No one can hear. Baudricourt has already gone.
    By now he has forgotten about the girl.
    When she fails or is killed he will say, "I told you so."
    He will not care.
    Only her parents will care.
    Only her mother will *really* care.

(Gradually they dissolve. Some go off left. Others, shaking their heads, go off right. The lights become very dim. Vaguely, like shadows, FIGURES *carrying tall poles mount the levels from both sides, they unroll on their poles great banners of brocade, which fall clear to the floor and form walls of gold. This should give the effect of a solid gold background. Two* PAGES *enter carrying a dais, which they place to the right and place the throne upon it. A great procession of* PAGES *enters carrying torches. With their entrance, the stage becomes brilliantly lighted.* LA TRÉMOUILLE, *a thin man with a shrewd, sly face and distrustful manner enters. He is very polished and polite. With him is the* DUKE OF ALENÇON, *who holds himself straight and shows at once by his manner and bearing that he is a soldier.)*

LA TRÉMOUILLE: You see everything is quite ready.

DUKE OF ALENÇON: Then you think the Dauphin is going to receive this girl?

LA TRÉMOUILLE: I know it's absurd that he should, but what can one do with him? It's the fault of all these gossiping people coming to him with foolish stories about the extraordinary things she has been doing in the town.

DUKE OF ALENÇON: But it appears they are true. Her fame has spread everywhere and the people already believe she will save France. So, of course, the Dauphin has to receive her.

LA TRÉMOUILLE: Well, let him receive her. She will soon find out we are not all fools. I've arranged a snare that she will easily fall into. Save France, indeed! He had better go back to his luxuries and his women. France is all right as she is.

DUKE OF ALENÇON: How strangely you talk. If I did not know in what great favor you stand with our Dauphin, I should almost think you were against him.

LA TRÉMOUILLE: Not against him, my dear Duke, oh, dear, no—for him. I am for him. I want him to be amused and not thinking of such unhappy things as war.

DUKE OF ALENÇON: What is this snare you speak of?

LA TRÉMOUILLE: You shall see. *(Clapping his hands. A* PAGE *comes forward.)* Tell the Chancellor to give orders that the Court may attend at once. *(The* PAGE *withdraws to left.* LA TRÉMOUILLE *rubs his hands together.)* I have a great jest. *(The* PAGE *reappears, followed by other* PAGES.*)*

1ST PAGE: The Court.

(Enter from the left, MARÉCHAL OF BOUSSAC, CAPTAIN DE RAIS, CAPTAIN DE LA HIRE, CAPTAIN DE XAINTRAILLES, *followed by elaborately robed* NOBLES, *thin-faced* YOUTHS, LADIES-IN-WAITING, COURTIERS, AMBASSADORS, *etc. They are dressed in gorgeous costumes of brilliant colors. They all crowd in, elbowing and pushing each other. A* DIGNITARY *manages affairs. All take their places across the center of the stage, allowing a clear aisle in front from the entrance at the left to the throne on the right. When they appear, there is an incessant hum of conversation, much of which may be distinguished; the rest remains soft murmuring among themselves. There should, however, be much action and agitation among the whole* COURT.*)*

A NOBLE: *(To a* LADY-IN-WAITING*)* We've seen many strange things in our day, but this is the strangest of all. A girl proclaiming that she can save France!

LADY-IN-WAITING: A peasant at that! If she had even been of noble birth one might feel a little more confident.

A COURTIER: *(Overhearing the conversation and joining in. Sarcastically)* You forget that she has taken care of sheep; that, of course, must surely give her great experience in managing an army! *(Laughter)*

ANOTHER NOBLE: Or in managing us. Perhaps she thinks of us as sheep. *(They all laugh.)*

A LADY: She has cut her hair, she must be a sight to behold.

A DANDY: *(Stepping forward)* And if you please she is wearing a common soldier's tunic, and will dare to present herself here looking like that.

A KNIGHT: She might have asked you to lend her an elaborate costume. You could well spare one! *(Laughter from the CROWD)*

A GENTLEMAN: At any rate it will be interesting to see her; it appears the whole town is in a state of agitation concerning her appearance and the things she claims herself capable of doing.

CAPTAIN DE RAIS: I must say she has journeyed far to make her claims.

DUKE OF ALENÇON: It must have taken great courage for a girl to ride that long distance—we should grant her that.

CAPTAIN DE LA HIRE: It seems a mad, young soldier-of-fortune came with her.

A LADY-IN-WAITING: It is difficult to see why the Dauphin should waste his time with just a bold peasant girl. Judging by her audacity she is perhaps mad. I think something should be done to protect him from her as long as he won't listen to reason.

ANOTHER VOICE: Someone should protect him against himself.

LA TRÉMOUILLE: *(Rubbing his hands together enthusiastically and smiling slyly, he turns and addresses the assembly.)* Let me tell you something. I have a great jest to recount to you all.

THE CROWD: *(Gathering round him)* A jest!
What is it, La Trémouille?
Tell us what it is if it will cheer us.

LA TRÉMOUILLE: You were just saying someone should protect the Dauphin against this girl and himself—and, of course, I agree with you. In fact, I agree so much with you that I have taken it into my own hands—to—to accomplish this protection. You see she has never seen the Dauphin, so it occurred to me that I might put on his cloak and take his place upon the throne; at the same time, His Majesty, very simply attired, will stand among you—

you must try and conceal him. This Jehanne d'Arc will, of course, show at once that she is not as clever as she pretends to be. She will naturally take me for His Majesty and then we can show what a fraud the whole thing is. I was able to get His Majesty to agree with me in doing this so if we all act our parts well it will be amusing as well as revealing. *(The* CROWD *laughs uproariously.)*

VOICES IN THE CROWD: Wonderful, La Trémouille.

    Wonderfully clever of you.

    An amusing and sly idea.

(Everyone laughs and joins in the general amusement except D'ALENÇON, *who remains serious.* LA TRÉMOUILLE *notices his expression.)*

LA TRÉMOUILLE: D'Alençon, you seem to miss the joke. Is your sense of humor asleep today or have you already seen this wonderful girl and fallen under her spell?

DUKE OF ALENÇON: Perhaps my sense of humor is not as keen as yours; it is hard for me to laugh at what seems to me merely a child.

LA TRÉMOUILLE: *(Gayly)* Well, that will not prevent *us* from laughing!

A NUMBER OF VOICES: No, indeed.

    This is really amusing.

    A clever ruse and worthy of La Trémouille.

(Sound of trumpets without. Two PAGES *enter, taking their places at either side of the throne.* CHIEF PAGE *steps forward.)*

CHIEF PAGE: The Dauphin of France!

(The DAUPHIN *enters from the left, followed by* PERSONAL ATTEN- DANTS, KNIGHTS, SOLDIERS AND PAGES. *His face is amazingly weak —almost giving the impression of feeble mindedness. He enters craftily, bending slightly and slyly eyeing the assembly. He advances hesitatingly with furtive glances to right and left—as one followed and haunted by some underlying fear. He is dressed simply. A* PAGE *follows carrying an elaborate cloak.* CHIEF PAGE *retires.)*

THE DAUPHIN: *(To the* SOLDIERS *and* PAGES*)* Go stand by the throne where La Trémouille will sit. Where is he? Where is La Trémouille?

LA TRÉMOUILLE: I am here, Sire. *(*LA TRÉMOUILLE *steps forward.)*

THE DAUPHIN: *(Impatiently to the* PAGE*)* Where is the cloak? Where is the cloak, you idiot?

PAGE: *(Kneeling)* It is here, your Majesty. *(He holds forth the cloak.)*

THE DAUPHIN: Take this cloak, La Trémouille—put it on at once— *(*PAGES *place the cloak on* LA TRÉMOUILLE*.)* ascend the throne. *(Laughing and rubbing his hands)* We'll have a joke yet—one way

or the other. The jest will be either against the girl or against you,
La Trémouille.

LA TRÉMOUILLE: Not against me, Sire—she will surely not be able
to find you, I'm confident of that.

THE DAUPHIN: *(Still chuckling)* We shall see—we shall see. I must
hide now—let me see—*(He pauses, then quickly darts and hides
behind* COURTIERS. *They close in round him; he peeks from behind
them, laughing maliciously.)* Let's see if heaven-sent voices can
cope with my cunning! *(Roars of laughter from everyone)* Where is
the girl? *(Impatiently)* Bring her in at once! *(Mockingly and still
laughing)* And be sure and sound trumpets for her—she must enter in state. (CHIEF PAGE *goes quickly out. Sound of trumpets without. The* CROWD *grows to left and right. Two* PAGES *enter and
stand either side in center stage.* CHIEF PAGE *steps forward.)*

CHIEF PAGE: Jehanne d' Arc.

*(There is a murmur in the crowd, and all bend forward. There is a glow
of light; suddenly* JEHANNE *appears. A great column of gold light surrounds her, she stands in its midst, when she moves it moves with her. She
is dressed in a blue soldier's tunic with a brown girdle of leather. She wears
tan hose of the period and long, pointed black velvet shoes. Her hair is
cut short. She advances slowly to center of the stage, turns, looks at* LA
TRÉMOUILLE, *then takes a step toward him.)*

LA TRÉMOUILLE: *(Leaning forward off the throne)* What can I do for
you, Jehanne d' Arc!

JEHANNE: *(In a clear voice)* You can do nothing for me. I have come
to see the King of France.

(She hesitates an instant, then quickly divides the CROWD *behind which
the* DAUPHIN *is hiding. She drops on her knees before him. A hushed
murmur goes up from the* CROWD.*)*

THE DAUPHIN: You are wrong, my child, I am not he.

JEHANNE: No—my Dauphin, but you soon will be. Have confidence
in me and I will make you so.

THE DAUPHIN: Have you such power in yourself!

JEHANNE: No—but I have power in the King who guides me.

THE CROWD: She means you—Sire.

JEHANNE: No, I mean the King who rules all kings.

DUKE OF ALENÇON: I think in recognizing you, Sire, she has shown
guidance of some kind. Should we not listen to her about saving
France? *(The* CROWD *murmurs assent.)*

LA TRÉMOUILLE: *(Stepping down quickly)* Let us try her again—
after all, what can a girl know about an army?

THE DAUPHIN: *(Angrily)* You grow tiresome, La Trémouille, with your proofs; it seems to me she has already proved a point in her favor by recognizing me—a very great point, I should say.

LA TRÉMOUILLE: *(Bowing and with a great manner)* A thousand pardons, Sire. I am merely anxious for your welfare. Of course, if you wish to place your trust in a—a person like this and a woman in the bargain—I—I can say no more. No doubt you are a better judge of these matters than I. I only pray that France and you may not suffer by—let us say—a too hasty judgment in the matter.

THE DAUPHIN: But you told me she would not recognize me and then she did. It is quite natural that I should grow impatient with your disbelief. However, and to be on the safe side, we will ask her one more question. You can put the question to her yourself, but be quick about it.

LA TRÉMOUILLE: Very well—I will ask her a question. *(He pauses.)* Let me see—Ah, I have it! *(To JEHANNE)* If you were leading the army of France, what would be the first thing you would do?

JEHANNE: Strengthen the artillery and fight more with it.

DUKE OF ALENÇON: She is right—She is right. It is what I have always said.

THE DAUPHIN: *(Excited beyond words)* She is more than right. She is indeed inspired. Your sword, Trémouille! Give me your sword. *(He seizes LA TRÉMOUILLE's sword from him)* Take this sword, Jehanne—you have proved your right to carry one. Take it and may you save France!

JEHANNE: No, sire. I would only carry the sword that will be found buried under the altar in the Church of St. Katherine.

THE DAUPHIN: You shall have it. A page, a soldier, go for it at once. *(Two PAGES rush out.)*

DUKE OF ALENÇON: Strange that she should know of this sword.

LA TRÉMOUILLE: She must have been told of it before and she pretends it to be inspiration.

THE DAUPHIN: *(Angrily to LA TRÉMOUILLE)* What have you against this girl that you are not willing to trust anything she says?

LA TRÉMOUILLE: It is only because I fear for your safety, my lord! After all, we are all grown up people and it hardly seems reasonable to me to put the safekeeping of France into the hands of a girl you had not seen an hour ago. I can only appeal to these ladies and gentlemen to say in justice to me whether I am right or not. *(A murmur of agreement from the CROWD)*

CAPTAIN DE LA HIRE: La Trémouille is right. It is not safe to be too hasty in one's judgment.

LA TRÉMOUILLE: *(Encouraged by being agreed with)* Besides, why should we speak of such odious things as war, when life can be so gay with so many beautiful women desiring only the pleasure of your Majesty.

JEHANNE: *(With courage and force)* It is just such flattering phrases as these that you are always listening to, Sire—Phrases that prevent you from hearing the real needs and true words of France. *(A murmur of astonishment from the crowd.* LA TRÉMOUILLE *steps forward, enraged.)*

LA TRÉMOUILLE: Sire, you can't allow this girl to address you in this manner. *(Turning to* JEHANNE*)* Take care! You may bring grave punishment upon yourself.

A VOICE IN THE CROWD: She's too bold.

CROWD: Yes—yes.

> Far too bold!
> How dare a peasant talk this way!
> She presumes too much!

THE DAUPHIN: *(Stepping forward, pushing* LA TRÉMOUILLE *aside and gazing at* JEHANNE *with a fixed and hypnotized glance)* There's something in the eyes of this girl that tells me I should listen to her.

JEHANNE: Imprisonment or death would be a small thing compared to the destruction of France. I am not afraid of your punishments —I who have listened to voices that have more power than all the soldiers of Christendom. It is those voices I have heeded; fighting and struggling to make my way here to your side, to warn you to throw off the frivolity and sin of the life you are leading, to plead for France before it is too late. *(The* CROWD *draws in closer around her not knowing quite what may happen next.)*

DUKE OF ALENÇON: She speaks with courage and not as one wrongly inspired or foolishly guided.

JEHANNE: What one of you here wants to live under the yoke of England?

CROWD: None—none.

JEHANNE: And yet at this minute, while you feast and laugh, the blood of France is flowing from out strong young hearts, while the soldiers of England advance over their bodies. At this very hour a messenger is arriving with word of a great English victory.

LA TRÉMOUILLE: It is not true—it is not true.

THE DAUPHIN: Send someone to verify it! *(The* DUKE OF ALENÇON *rushes out followed by a* PAGE. JEHANNE *stands resolute.)*

JEHANNE: It's not too late, Sire. There's still time.

THE DAUPHIN: We will see if what you said is true.

LA TRÉMOUILLE: *(Scoffingly)* Of course it isn't true.

A VOICE IN THE CROWD: Yet if it were true, it would be extraordinary.

ANOTHER GIRL: Extraordinary for this girl—extraordinary proof of her judgment but terrible for France!

ANOTHER VOICE: France can't afford any more defeats!

LA TRÉMOUILLE: No fear of another defeat. To hear all this nonsense one might think this absurd peasant girl was divine. I can't be so easily deluded.

A COURTIER: If she has not spoken the truth now, there will be no reason to believe anything else she says in the future.

VOICES IN THE CROWD: Of course not. Certainly not.

THE DAUPHIN: *(In a highly excitable state)* We shall see for ourselves. We shall see! We shall see! After all, she called me King.

A KNIGHT: *(Looking toward the door)* D'Alençon is coming now. *(He goes to the door.)* Yes, here he is. *(Everyone looks and crowds toward the entrance except JEHANNE.)*

CROWD: D'Alençon! D'Alençon! Is there a defeat? Is it true?

DUKE OF ALENÇON: *(D'ALENÇON enters breaking through the* CROWD. *He rushes to the* DAUPHIN. *Excitedly)* It is true! A messenger has just ridden up with news of a great loss for France. Just this second they were outside the door, about to come in and inform your Majesty.

CROWD: Another defeat!
A loss for France!
She was right.
She's not a liar after all!
It shows us we should listen to her!
After this proof it would be stupid and foolhardy to disregard her advice! *(They show a decided swing in JEHANNE'S favor.)*

LA TRÉMOUILLE: *(Aside to the* DAUPHIN*)* Sire, don't be so easily taken in by her. Think what is at stake. This all may be only chance. Try her with something that no one knows.

THE DAUPHIN: *(The* DAUPHIN *hesitates, then drags* JEHANNE *aside, dropping his voice. He is almost beside himself and beats his hands upon hers.)* Listen—Listen, Jehanne. If you can tell me this, for once and for all you will convince me. If you can answer me this, I will give you anything you wish—you shall have gold—fine clothes—I—I will make you a lady-in-waiting and no one shall laugh at you, I will see to that.

JEHANNE: I have no wish for any of these things. I only want to accomplish and fulfill my mission. But tell me just the same, what you want to know.

THE DAUPHIN: *(With terror)* I am haunted by a fear, Jehanne— night and day—day and night—a ghastly fear following me like a cold hand always on my shoulder. Can you tell me what that fear is? Can you wipe that fear away?

JEHANNE: You fear that you are not lawfully born and so not the rightful heir to the throne.

THE DAUPHIN: *(Trembling and shaking)* That's it! That's it! You have guessed it. *(Seizing her hand)* Softly, Jehanne—softly. Don't let anyone hear us. But what of my fear—tell me of that.

JEHANNE: Don't tremble, Sire—you mustn't be afraid because you are the lawful heir to France.

THE DAUPHIN: *(Frantically and like a maniac, almost dropping on his knees)* I am convinced by you. Thank God, thank God! Thank God for this day and you! *(He turns wildly to the crowd.)* Listen all of you. All of you who have scoffed at this girl. She has convinced me of her truth—she has read the tormenting secret of my heart that none of you has known. She has answered that secret, and now I fear none of you. I fear nothing more! *(His voice raises to a shriek.)* Jehanne d'Arc has lifted my fear! *(He falls to the ground.)*

LA TRÉMOUILLE: *(Shrugging his shoulders)* Another one of these tantrums to put up with.

(A PAGE *enters with the sword. It is rusty and has five crosses on it. The* DAUPHIN *staggers to his feet and seizes the sword. Everyone crowds around him in tense excitement.)*

THE DAUPHIN: *(Holding high the sword)* This is your sword, Jehanne, upon it I pledge the rallying to arms and the defense of France.

CROWD: *(Pressing close with excitement)* Yes—yes, to arms!

THE DAUPHIN: *(The* DAUPHIN *touches* JEHANNE *with the sword.)* With this sword I appoint you, Jehanne d'Arc, Commander-in-Chief of the Armies of France! *(The* CROWD *is tense with mad excitement.* JEHANNE *kneels on one knee, makes a sign of the cross and accepts the sword.)* And you, Duke of Alençon, I appoint you to be her lieutenant and Chief of Staff, to furnish her with men and horses, to see that she receives any uniform she desires to wear. Let this decree be known over all the realm of France. And you, Maréchal de Boussac, and Captain de Rais, de la Hire and de Xaintrailles *(All four step forward.)* I appoint that you shall serve her also and pledge you to her command. *(They all drop on their knees before* JEHANNE.*)*

ALL FOUR: *(With extended hands)* Until Death! Until Death!

THE DAUPHIN: Let the trumpets sound forth.

(A PAGE sounds a trumpet, which is taken up and repeated by two trumpets offstage. The four CAPTAINS rise to their feet and in one impulsive spontaneous gesture they rush and surround JEHANNE, who at the same moment raises her sword. Suddenly they lift her high on their shoulders, the crowd massing about and JEHANNE forming a pyramid high up.)

CROWD: Vive Jehanne d'Arc! Vive Jehanne d'Arc!

JEHANNE: *(JEHANNE holding her sword high)* And now to Orléans and the aid of France!

(They carry her out followed by the excited crowd cheering. The column of gold light follows JEHANNE, leaving the stage with only the torches burning. The voices of the crowd can be heard dying away fainter and fainter.)

CROWD: Orléans! Orléans! To Orléans!

Vive Jehanne d' Arc! Vive Jehanne d'Arc! Vive Jehanne d'Arc! Vive Jehanne d'Arc! Vive Jehanne d' Arc! Jehanne d'Arc! Jehanne d'Arc! Jehanne d'Arc!

(Their voices die away fainter and fainter. The stage is left empty except for LA TRÉMOUILLE, who remains behind pacing the floor furiously. He beats his hands behind his back.)

Curtain

Part 2

A square in Orléans.

A happy, excited CROWD *is surging back and forth in a state of expectancy. A seething mass of poor village people and peasantry. The* MAYOR *and* IMPORTANT CITIZENS *are also gathered together waiting.* OLD PEOPLE, YOUNG PEOPLE *and* CHILDREN *press forward talking, laughing, shouting. They mount and form groups on various levels. They express their joy by waving flags and throwing their hats in the air. The volume of voices increases as the stage grows lighter.*

VOICES IN THE CROWD: Jehanne d'Arc! Jehanne d'Arc! Jehanne d'Arc! Jehanne d'Arc! Vive Jehanne d' Arc! Vive! Vive! Vive! Vive Jehanne d'Arc! Jehanne d' Arc is coming this way! She is coming this way! *(Trumpets sound some distance off. They press wildly forward.)* She is coming this way. Can you see her? Not yet! She will soon be here! She will come. She will not fail us. She has delivered us after eight months! She is our Savior! We want her blessing upon our children.

A CHILD: *(Running in)* She is almost here. She is beautiful like an angel! *(The light is full up.)*

VOICES OF THE CROWD: Blessed Jehanne d'Arc! Savior Jehanne d'Arc!

(*They all crowd forward trying to see, pushing each other and becoming impatient. A general confusion follows, shared with the tenseness of a waiting crowd held in check only because of intense anticipation. La Trémouille enters followed by a* SOLDIER.)

LA TRÉMOUILLE: She will soon come this way.

SOLDIER: The populace is mad with happiness.

LA TRÉMOUILLE: A tiresome mob. I am glad you showed me the sign or else I never would have known you were a Bourgondian.

SOLDIER: So I feared, Seigneur.

LA TRÉMOUILLE: Listen to this carefully. Tell your master, Jean de Luxembourg, that at present I can do nothing. Of course the Dauphin will be made King—it is then that I am counting on his wearying of war and wishing to return to his pleasures, which I shall make more enticing for him. I'm then sure Jehanne d'Arc will march on Paris; but before she arrives there I will tell the King things are going badly in Compiègne and persuade him to recall her. The retreat will dishearten the soldiers and when they arrive at Compiègne they'll not fight well. Then, and then only tell your master to be ready.

SOLDIER: Yes, Seigneur, I understand.

LA TRÉMOUILLE: Go your way and not a word.

SOLDIER: Yes, Seigneur.

(*They separate. At that moment a great* CROWD *is heard and martial music in the distance.* CROWDS *of poor children and women come on the stage strewing flowers, waving banners and calling, "Vive Jehanne d'Arc." They crowd in as the procession approaches and finally* MEN-AT-ARMS *make way for heralds with trumpets who sound them.*)

CROWD: She has come at last! Let me see her! Let me touch her! Make way! Make way! I can see her now! I see her, too. Her eyes shine like stars! She gives out a radiance like one from another world! She is beautiful! Beautiful! Beautiful! She has delivered us from our long suffering! God be praised! Christ be praised! Jehanne d'Arc be praised! Jehanne d'Arc be praised! Viva Jehanne d'Arc! Praise this wonderful day! She rides like one guided by an angel! She is an angel herself! She is an angel! An angel! An angel! Viva Jehanne d'Arc! She gazes forward like one who sees far! She sees where we cannot see! Hush! Hush! She is here!

(*There is a sudden and intense silence. The* CROWD *kneels as* JEHANNE *enters. She is dressed in a gorgeous costume. She holds her sword, which seems like a sword of flames, before her. A sublime look shines on her face, which at the same time is always sorrowful.)*

JEHANNE: Thank you. Thank you, people of Orléans. In the name of Christ, I thank you. *(The* MAYOR OF ORLÉANS *steps forward.)*

THE MAYOR: And I, Jehanne d' Arc, the Mayor of Orléans, thank you in the name of all the population. For eight months our city has been surrounded, the spirit of our people crushed and discouraged, and in eight days you have raised the siege.

JEHANNE: Don't thank me. Thank rather the Divine Power that guided me. A power that like a great burning star guided my way. I—I am helpless without that Power.

THE MAYOR: But it is you we love—what can we do for you to show our everlasting gratitude? *(A strange sad look passes over* JEHANNE's *face as though for a single instant her vision penetrates the future.)*

JEHANNE: *(sadly)* Everlasting? Did you say everlasting?

THE MAYOR: Why yes—everlasting I said. Why?

JEHANNE: *(With a gesture of dismissal)* Nothing—no matter. May I have a few minutes alone with the Constable of France? I'm told he is here in Orléans.

THE MAYOR: Certainly. I'll send for him.

(He goes out. JEHANNE *moves forward. The* PEOPLE *rise to their feet. Some of them rush forward to touch her. They look at her with love and veneration. They cannot withdraw their eyes away from her.* CHILDREN *try to kiss* JEHANNE's *hand. A* WOMAN *with an infant tries to draw closer to her.* LA TRÉMOUILLE *suddenly comes forward and pushes them all roughly away.)*

JEHANNE: *(Stopping him)* Don't do that, La Trémouille. You are pushing aside the future of France. *(Sadly)* A future I will never see.

LA TRÉMOUILLE: Why should you say that? You are only a child and will see many long years.

JEHANNE: A child, perhaps, but one whose soul sees with the eyes of a thousand centuries. No, La Trémouille, Jehanne d'Arc must work quickly for France. Her time is closing in rapidly. *(A* SOLDIER *comes onstage and salutes.)*

SOLDIER: The Constable is coming, as you wished.

(Throughout, the hum of the crowd's low voices can be heard. The CONSTABLE OF FRANCE *enters. He drops on his knee to* JEHANNE. MEN-AT-ARMS *push the* CROWD *back, gradually they fade back at a distance, leaving only* SOLDIERS *and* KNIGHTS *near* JEHANNE. *They also gradually move away.)*

JEHANNE: Don't kneel to me, Constable. What is this sorrow I see in your heart?

CONSTABLE: *(Surprised and rising)* You know I have a sorrow? How did you know?

JEHANNE: There are few hearts without some sorrow. But I seem to see in yours something connected with France.

CONSTABLE: You're right. My love of France is so great, but because of the anger which the Dauphin bears me I cannot serve France as I would wish to. That is my sorrow.

JEHANNE: That must not be. Soon I'll pass and France will then have need of you. *(At that moment a* COURIER *enters and kneels to* JEHANNE *handing her a letter. She tears the seal and makes a gesture that she is unable to read. She hands the letter back.)* Read it for me.

COURIER: *(Reading)* "Greetings to Jehanne d'Arc, Commander-in-Chief of the Armies of France, from her Lord and Dauphin with gratitude and thanks for raising the siege of the city of Orléans and a prayer that he may be permitted to grant her any wish that is in his power and that she may desire."

(The COURIER *ceases reading; he gives the letter back to* JEHANNE *who places it in her belt.)*

JEHANNE: Return with this messenger, Constable—and you, Courier—give this message to my lord, the Dauphin. Say that it is my wish that he reconcile himself with the Constable of France—that he welcome the Constable in his presence again and receive him warmly as a loyal friend, which I know him to be. *(To the* CONSTABLE*)* Wait while the Courier delivers this word. I know then the Dauphin will receive you.

Constable: Oh, thank you, thank you, God be with you. *(He kneels and kisses her hand.* JEHANNE *raises him up.)* Farewell and Christ be with you.

(He departs. JEHANNE *remains standing alone. Suddenly her mood changes. She puts her hand to her brow and shivers slightly. Out of the shadows the same* WOMAN *with the infant in her arms approaches timidly. She takes one or two steps forward; as* JEHANNE *does not perceive her, she speaks.)*

WOMAN: *(Shyly and awkwardly)* Jehanne d' Arc.

*(*JEHANNE *turns. On seeing the* WOMAN *and the child she half smiles, takes a step forward then also pauses awkwardly. Each one is conscious of some existing elemental comparison between them.* JEHANNE *gazes a trifle sadly and wistfully at the child; the* WOMAN *gazes a trifle enviously,*

yet with burning admiration at JEHANNE, *at her sword, at her splendor and sense of freedom. The* WOMAN *breaks the silence holding forth the child.)*

WOMAN: I thought it would bring my child luck and courage all her life to have your blessing. I waited until you would be alone.

JEHANNE: *(Sadly)* My blessing could bring her nothing. I have nothing to offer her—*you* have everything.

WOMAN: I? What?

JEHANNE: *(With infinite tenderness and wistfulness)* Your love—your milk with which to nourish her—your dreams—

WOMAN: Dreams that she will never fulfill. I dream that she might be like you, having your courage, your freedom, your daring. Remaining unburdened by the low domestic things of life; free from slavery and the breeding of children. *(There is a pause.* JEHANNE *does not answer and looks sadly away. The* WOMAN *continues passionately.)* You have everything—honor, glory, triumph, admiration, victory! You do not know the hardship of domestic servitude —the slavery of those chains—you are free—free.

JEHANNE: We are each one of us chained to something. Each one of us in a different way. I have my battles, too.

WOMAN: Yes, yes! Glorious exciting battles with a shining sword in your hand, leading men forward with the heat of victory in your eyes.

JEHANNE: What is that? What is facing a battle compared to having a child torn from out your womb? *(Another pause)* Yet you have something I have not.

WOMAN: *(Incredulously)* I? What?

JEHANNE: *(Pathetically—longingly)* That child.

WOMAN: *(Bitterly)* This child.

JEHANNE: *(Tenderly and childishly. She smiles, bending over the child.)* She's so little. Her hands are so little. She must be warm and wonderful to hold. I—I would hardly dare hold her.

WOMAN: You may if you like.

JEHANNE: *(*JEHANNE *awkwardly and clumsily takes the child in her arms. She holds her as one unaccustomed to children.)* Is she afraid of me?

WOMAN: I hope not. I said I wanted her to be like you.

JEHANNE: She's so little—it's frightening. She's warm and soft like the tiny new-born lambs. I used to hold them in my arms when I guarded the sheep in the fields. I knew how to hold *them (laughing)* even though they had long straight legs that waved about. It's harder to hold a child.

WOMAN: *(Smiling)* I see it is. I'll take her back. *(She takes the child again in her arms.)* I have five more at home. Five more to dress, to slave for, to hear their unceasing shrill voices; five more, whom when they grow up will abandon me when I am old and need them most.

JEHANNE: Perhaps all things must abandon us when we need them most. It may be, that only through utter and desperate loneliness we can reach something—something that we are seeking—something we want so much but do not know what it is. Do you feel like that?

WOMAN: I don't think about it—I miss something, often—but I don't think about it.

JEHANNE: *(Pensively and with a flash of vision)* Loneliness may be the only way to the Divine Heart.

WOMAN: You can't really long for children. If you did, you would not have chosen this—*this* path.

JEHANNE: I didn't choose this path, it was chosen for me. It is difficult to explain—even to myself. Something that came in here and here—*(She puts her hand to her heart and brow.)* that made me do things quite simply that before I couldn't do. I have wanted children; there are moments when every woman wants a child—but there was something stronger, bigger, more far-reaching than any small desire of mine—that carried me on, that brought me here. Voices that shut out human longings. It is only when I do not hear those voices—when I lose those voices, that the longings return— and then—and then—*(Childishly, bewilderedly and almost fearfully)* I'm very lonely. You speak of triumph and victory. What are they? What am I? Only a small thing obeying something over which I have no control—some power that flashes through me like the swift flight of birds—then afterwards darkness and silence for me . . . but you, you will live in this child—some fragment of your thoughts, of your hopes, will be passed on and may live five hundred years from now. No one will remember me. Jehanne d'Arc will be forgotten then.

(Suddenly the WOMAN looks at JEHANNE. It is as though in her soul there dawned a flash of prophetic vision.)

WOMAN: Jehanne d'Arc will live after any blood of mine—long, long and forever—in the hearts of all those to come. (JEHANNE *shakes her head sadly in negative. The* woman *drops on her knees, holding the child up to* JEHANNE.) Bless my child and me—we need your blessing.

(JEHANNE *bends tenderly over them, touching them both. For a brief in-*

stant she gathers the child in her arms and holds it passionately to her. The WOMAN *rises to her feet,* JEHANNE *gives her back the child and quickly turns away as though the emotion was too poignant for her. The woman goes quickly off leaving* JEHANNE *alone. She sighs, then puts her hand to her heart.)*

JEHANNE: *(Sadly)* Oh, my voices—where are you now? Jehanne is weary—lonely—and has need of you. And you, Domrémy, little village of quiet pastures, will Jehanne d'Arc ever sleep in your green fields again?

(She comes wearily to the center of the stage. Everything falls into darkness except for the column of light in which she stands. For a moment she bows her head, then she straightens up and makes the sign of the cross. A PAGE *appears beside her with a pure white tunic with fleur-de-lys embroidered all over it in gold. He places it on her shoulders. Another* PAGE *appears with a white banner, which* JEHANNE *takes in her hand. The* PAGES *back off and* JEHANNE *kneels alone in prayer.)*

JEHANNE: *(Praying)* Give also to me, O Divine Power, the light of splendid vision, the strength of untiring agility, the clarity of penetrating subtlety, the courage of strong impossibility.

(Very faintly comes the mellow music of a sacred organ. Gradually the sound comes nearer. A PRIEST *enters carrying a large candle and stands behind* JEHANNE. *Three* PRIESTS *also carrying candles come from each side and take various positions in the shadowed area beyond the row of candles. From each side come more figures, each carrying a tall gold object suggestive of a reliquary or shrine. They walk to the center, turn, and in pairs go upstage where they group themselves at the top of the incline. The seven* PRIESTS *come together in the center, turn about and walk upstage where they stand holding the candles at the altar. They group themselves on various planes. Their combined composition suggests the high altar at Rheims. A great procession of* ALTAR BOYS *carrying candles enters from the left back of where* JEHANNE *stands. With their entrance the stage becomes lighted. The* ALTAR BOYS *are followed by* INCENSE BEARERS, PRIESTS, MONKS *and finally the* ARCHBISHOP OF RHEIMS, *who is followed by the* KING *dressed in the royal "blue as the sky flowered with lilies of gold." Following the* KING *comes* LA TRÉMOUILLE, *the* DUKE OF ALENÇON, MARÉCHAL DE BOUSSAC, *the* CONSTABLE OF FRANCE, CAPTAIN DE RAIS, CAPTAIN DE LA HIRE, CAPTAIN DE XAINTRAILLES, JEAN DE METZ *and* LADIES AND GENTLEMEN OF THE COURT. *They are all richly and gorgeously attired and should give an effect of great massing of color. The populace surges in and stands to the back. The* ARCHBISHOP *goes to the altar and turns. The* KING *kneels at his feet surrounded by his* COURTIERS *and the* COURT *who*

take their places according to rank. The PRIESTS, MONKS *and* ALTAR
BOYS *form groups back of the altar. In the back, eight* PAGES *stand with
trumpets. As the lights come fully on, the* CONSTABLE OF FRANCE *steps
forward and leads* JEHANNE *to the altar. She kneels below the* KING,
leaning upon her banner. The organ stops playing and the ARCHBISHOP
holds the crown with both hands over the KING'*s head.)*

THE ARCHBISHOP: By the grace of God and with this crown I
    name you King of France.

(The circle of PEERS *stretches forth their arms and touch the crown. The*
ARCHBISHOP *places it on the* KING'*s head. The* CHIEF KNIGHT *steps
forward and cries,* "Long live the King of France!" *As he does so a mighty
shout rings out, the* PAGES *all together sound their trumpets and the organ peals forth. The* KING *rises and faces the people.* JEHANNE *remains
kneeling with bowed head, the column of light streams down upon her.
The* KING *steps down and touches* JEHANNE.*)*

KING: Rise, Jehanne d'Arc. It is to you France owes its King. *(More
    cheers from the* CROWD*)* Speak—require anything—demand any-
    thing. Whatever you ask, I'll grant it to you, even if I beggar my
    whole kingdom to meet your wish.

JEHANNE: *(*JEHANNE *rises, steps back with a look of intense exalta-
    tion.)* The command of my Master is accomplished; that I should
    guide you to Rheims and bestow on you your rightful crown. My
    work is now finished; give me your blessing—let me return to my
    mother who is poor and growing old; she has need of me.

LA TRÉMOUILLE: *(Stepping forward)* Return home before your work
    is ended—before you have marched on Paris and Compiègne!

THE KING: *(Raises his hand and silences him.)* Silence, La Tré-
    mouille. *(To* JEHANNE*)* No, my child, I can't grant you this.

JEHANNE: But you said you would grant me any wish and this is the
    one I most want. I can help France no further.

THE KING: Nonsense, child. There may be still much for you to do.
    We shall see. Now that I am King things may go better. Ask me
    something else.

JEHANNE: Then I ask that my village of Domrémy will never again
    be taxed.

THE KING: *(Surprised)* That shall be granted; it is an unselfish and
    noble wish—Ask something for yourself, Jehanne.

JEHANNE: There is nothing, Sire. Nothing I wish. I have had all my
    wish today in seeing you wear that crown.

THE KING: Very well, then, I have granted your wish. We must go
    now; the people are waiting. Are you coming, too?

JEHANNE: With your leave, I will remain here, Sire.

THE KING: Alone in this gloomy church?

JEHANNE: For a little while.

THE KING: Very well—as you wish. Each one to his own taste. *(To the* KNIGHTS *and* PEOPLE*)* Proceed!

(The bugles sound again, the organ peals forth and the KING *walks out followed by* KNIGHTS, PAGES, *all the* COURT, *and finally the* PEOPLE. *No one is left on the stage except* JEHANNE, *and the church is left in utter silence.* JEHANNE *faces the audience. She puts her arm up and with the back of her hand covers her eyes. An* OLD MONK *totters on the stage and with a long candle extinguisher puts out the altar candles one by one. As he does so, the* PRIESTS *that form the altar disappear. The stage is left in darkness except for the light on* JEHANNE. JEHANNE *drops her hand, pauses, then slowly advances toward the altar. As she does, the* OLD MONK *stops and looks at her.)*

OLD MONK: Why should you be sad when today of all days you have fulfilled your wish? You should be gay, too.

JEHANNE: Gay?

OLD MONK: Yes—in your hour of triumph.

JEHANNE: My hour is over—no one has even remained to watch with me. My voices—they have left me, too.

OLD MONK: *(Sympathetically)* You are tired—worn out. One forgets that you are still a child. You need rest.

JEHANNE: *(Beseechingly)* You, who for so many years in the darkness of this church have lighted the flame of so many candles—surely you must be wise. Tell me, is there no rest in rest? Only rest in struggle? Not the struggle of arms in battle—the futility of that must dawn one day. I have served my hour of battle with a sword in hand, because the shortsightedness of men could only understand a sword. I have served the hour of battle, so that the hour of peace might be greater. Peace born of struggle, of ingratitude, of loneliness, of death; so that higher, far higher along at the end, struggle may be peace—peace everlasting. But you, you with your wisdom gathered from long watching the flame of so many straight, white, burning candles—you with the wisdom of so much light—tell me, are peace and struggle the same? Can one only be arrived at through the other, like the night to reach the day and the day to reach the night?

(The OLD MONK *shakes his head sadly and with hopeless non-comprehension. He pauses an instant, then slowly totters off.* JEHANNE *kneels, covers her face with her hands as one in despair. Then finally she flings her whole body down prostrate on the altar steps. She remains like this, mo-*

tionless. The great cathedral bells begin to ring. In the distance, soft chanting can be heard coming from a nearby chapel; it swells its tempo, becoming faster and wilder; it gradually and almost imperceptibly turns into a war song. JEHANNE *rises. Two* KNIGHTS *step forward, one bearing her armor. The other tears off her coronation costume. They dress her in full armor ready for battle. The great bells sound like pagan gongs. The war song has begun. The light on* JEHANNE *has become red. Gongs and cymbals finally merge into the sound of clashing steel. This merges into the tramp of marching feet. Masses of* SOLDIERS *pass.* JEHANNE *picks up her banner and urges her men forward. She stands in the center and above them. They surround her with their lances, the points of which glow in her red light, like tongues of flame. In silhouette and dimly, black masses of the* ENEMY *with swords break through her* SOLDIERS. *They fight off her* SOLDIERS, *who retreat, leaving* JEHANNE *surrounded by the* ENEMY. *The* ENEMY *then presses her further and further back, and higher and higher upon each plane, until finally she is high above them and they are gathered like a great black mass below her. Suddenly* JEHANNE*'s banner is wrested from her; the light on her wavers and becomes almost extinguished. The sound of steel clashing furiously is heard; it ceases but a curious tremor like vibrating beats of a muffled drum continues.* JEHANNE *is roughly dragged down by the* SOLDIERS. *They tear off her armor and all vestiges of her soldiery as the Roman soldiers tore off the garments of Christ. She stands with bowed head in her simple tunic. The* SOLDIERS *go off and disappear in the darkness.* JEHANNE *sinks to her knees, then finally falls to the ground. The* VOICE OF A SOLDIER *nearby can be heard calling. The call is taken up by* OTHER VOICES *until it swells into hundreds of voices, until it sounds as if the whole world vibrated and resounded with the hideous cry.)*

A VOICE: Jehanne d'Arc has been captured!

OTHER VOICES: Jehanne d'Arc has been captured! Jehanne d' Arc has been captured! Jehanne d'Arc has been captured! Jehanne d'Arc has been captured! Jehanne d'Arc has been captured!

(The VOICES *repeat themselves like echoes finally dying away as though vanishing in the distance. A plaintive but soft wail goes up from everywhere more like the wind than humanity. Dark figures of* WOMEN *enter and kneel with outstretched arms as in anguish from the death of a beloved one. They rock to and fro on their knees. Dark shawls are pulled over their heads. They sob quietly, like those who have suffered long. Far off, the toll of a great, deep bell can be heard. A scream of a woman rends the air. The scarcely visible form of* JEHANNE *in the faint light writhes and then lies motionless. The dark shadows of the* WOMEN *circle about her prostrate*

form. They choke back their sobs of terror and begin to pray. Faster and faster they pray. They gather over JEHANNE *so that she cannot be seen at all. They form a dark black mass.)*

PRAYING WOMEN: Out of the depths we cry to Thee . . .
  Jesus, hear our prayer!
  From the temptations of Life
  Deliver us—
  Jesus, hear our prayer!
  At the hour of our death
  Be thou near us—
  Jesus, hear our prayer!
  From agony and despair
  Save us—
  Jesus, hear our prayer!
  From darkness and desolation
  Show us the Light,
  From shadow to radiance
  Lead through the Night.
  Lead through the night all—
  Who carry a Cross.
  Lead through the night all—
  Who are nailed to a Cross.
  Lead through the night all
  Whose vision is far—
  Lead through the night all
  Who follow a star.
  Jesus, hear our prayer!

(The tolling bell is louder. The sound of a mallet rapping loudly on a wooden table silences the WOMEN. *The stage is left in utter and complete darkness. Out of the darkness but far off, another deep bell can be heard ringing and a voice cries out.)*

VOICE: Places for the trial! Places for the trial! *(The bell stops tolling. In the darkness a slight shuffling can be heard.)*

VOICE ON STAGE: Bring in the prisoner.

(Suddenly a bright light, which is now violet in color, streams down on JEHANNE, *who stands in a witness box such as used by the clergy. A bible is placed beside her in the center of the stage with her face turned full toward the audience. The rest of the stage, all through the scene, is kept in absolute and complete darkness. The audience should merely feel the existence of menacing faces enveloped in the blackness, and surrounding* JEHANNE. JEHANNE *is dressed in a soldier's tunic such as worn under*

armor. It is dirty and torn. Her hair is unkempt and still short although longer than in previous scenes. Her face is ghastly white and shows signs of laboring under a terrific mental and spiritual strain. She seems completely exhausted, but from time to time she makes superhuman efforts, answering with great spirit. She never lacks courage but has moments of appearing thoroughly dazed and as though she already belonged to another world. The voices of PIERRE CAUCHON *and the other men who try Jehanne are heard from out of the darkness which surrounds her. Their voices come thick and fast from all sides. The whole scene gives the quality of a nightmare.)*

VOICE OF PIERRE CAUCHON: Once more I, Pierre Cauchon, Archbishop of Beauvais, must draw the prisoner's attention, on this the last day of her trial, to her duty to speak the truth. Aided by Jean Le Maistre of the Order of the Dominicans, Magistrate and Inquisitor of France; by Jean Graverent, Grand Inquisitor of France; by Robert Le Barbier, master of Arts; by Jean de Luxembourg, Seigneur of Beaurevoir; by Jean, Duke of Bedford; by Pierre Maurice, professor of sacred theology; by Jean Toutmouillé of the order of the Preaching Fathers and by the Reverent Fathers Nicolas Midi, Jean Beaupere, Jacques de Touraine and others, all masters, professors and doctors of theology, we must again question you, Jehanne d'Arc, as to the veracity of your previous statements during these five months of trial; to the truth of your claimed visions, and to determine whether or not you shall be burned at the stake as a liar, witch, invocator of the devil, idolater, infidel and heretic. According to the position of my office, I must ask you, Jehanne, to consider our questions, to place your hands on the Holy Bible and swear to tell the truth.

(During this speech JEHANNE *stands perfectly rigid, staring before her. As the* VOICE OF CAUCHON *dies away, she makes an effort to come out of her trance-like condition.)*

VOICE OF CAUCHON: Swear, Jehanne!

JEHANNE: *(Recovering herself)* I don't know what more you wish of me.

VOICE OF CAUCHON: Swear to tell the truth!

JEHANNE: I'll swear no more. For five months and twice a day I have sworn for you. I'll swear no more.

2ND VOICE: You don't wish to swear because you don't intend to tell the truth.

JEHANNE: More people have been hung for telling the truth than for telling lies.

3RD VOICE: Ha! We know you, and how you have wished to lie!

JEHANNE: If you know me and all I am, there is no cause for me to answer your questions.

VOICE OF CAUCHON: Order! Order! Jehanne, I command you tell the truth.

JEHANNE: If you ask me something of which I can tell the truth, I'll tell the truth. If you ask me something of which I can't tell the truth, I'll not tell the truth.

VOICE OF CAUCHON: Pass on, Pass on!

5TH VOICE: In what manner have you borne yourself since yesterday's trial?

JEHANNE: I've borne myself as well as I could.

VOICE OF CAUCHON: We will go back, Jehanne, for the last time. Do you still claim to have heard voices and to have been directed by them when you were living at home with your parents?

JEHANNE: *(Wearily)* I have already answered that question a hundred times.

VOICE OF CAUCHON: Is it true?

JEHANNE: Yes.

3RD VOICE: *(Sharply)* Then why did you deny your voices the other day?

JEHANNE: I don't remember denying them. If I did, it was when I was ill and you described the torture flames. I don't deny them now.

2ND VOICE: Have you more fear of our flames or the flames of hell?

JEHANNE: Of your flames.

1ST Voice: Why?

JEHANNE: I am sure of your flames, I am not sure of the flames of hell.

VOICE OF CAUCHON: *(Quickly)* You are denying there is a hell?

JEHANNE: I didn't say so.

3RD VOICE: You said you are not sure of the flames of hell.

JEHANNE: I meant I am sure of the forgiveness and compassion of God.

3RD Voice: Is it true that you wished to escape?

JEHANNE: Yes. I still wish it. It's natural that a prisoner should wish to escape.

2ND VOICE: *(Sarcastically)* I suppose it is also natural that a woman should wear men's clothes and defame herself before Heaven.

JEHANNE: Heaven doesn't concern itself with clothes.

4TH VOICE: Yet you claim you were advised by your visions to wear men's clothes.

JEHANNE: Yes—they have directed me in small things as well as big.

VOICE OF CAUCHON: Tell as again how many times in your life you have seen the visions and heard the voices. Tell us in detail of the countrysides you passed through after you left your home on the way to the Dauphin.

JEHANNE: *(Wearily and spent. Places her hand to her brow)* I—cannot—remember.

2ND VOICE: *(Sarcastically)* Tell your voices to help you.

VOICE OF CAUCHON: We are your judges, be careful of your answers.

JEHANNE: *(suddenly and fiercely)* You say you are my judges, take care then what you do with me. I have been sent by God and you are putting yourselves in great danger!

1ST VOICE: She blasphemes!!

2ND VOICE: She lies about God!

3RD VOICE: She is arrogant and lacks the fear of God!

VOICE OF CAUCHON: Order! Order! Jehanne d'Arc, do you dare say God will save you?

JEHANNE: Surely it will not be men who will save me. *(A murmur from the darkness)*

VOICES: She deserves to be burned! Witch! Heretic!

VOICE OF CAUCHON: Order! Order! Prisoner Jehanne. Are you in a state of grace?

JEHANNE: If I am not, may God put me in it; if I am, may He keep me in it.

4TH VOICE: Did your saints speak clearly? Could you understand them?

JEHANNE: Yes.

5TH VOICE: Did they speak to you in French?

JEHANNE: Yes—otherwise how could I understand them?

6TH VOICE: Do they speak French perfectly?

JEHANNE: Better than you, my lord.

VOICE OF CAUCHON: *(Thundering)* Don't answer in that manner.

JEHANNE: You commanded me to tell the truth.

VOICE OF CAUCHON: Pass on! Pass on!

5TH VOICE: Do you ever wish to wear women's clothes again?

JEHANNE: Give them to me and I will leave in them and go home. Otherwise, I'll keep on these since God is pleased that I should wear them.

3RD Voice: She speaks insolently of God.

VOICE OF CAUCHON: Isn't it true that a girl who leaves her mother's roof, who abandons her family, is unnatural and cruel?

JEHANNE: How can any of you know of the sorrow that I had in leaving my mother? (JEHANNE *again places her hand to her brow. Her voice quivers.*)

VOICE OF CAUCHON: Do you claim it was by your hand that the Dauphin was crowned King of France?

JEHANNE: I was only the instrument which worked for a greater hand.

3RD VOICE: Do you claim to be inspired?

JEHANNE: I make no claims.

4TH VOICE: Do you think you are inspired?

JEHANNE: (*Impatiently but dazed*) Pass on! I have answered that question too often before. I told you I have only done what God commanded me. I listened to my voices because they came from Him and they gave me counsel that you could neither hear nor understand.

VOICE OF CAUCHON: Is it true that you used to place your sword on the altar wishing for good fortune?

JEHANNE: What one amongst you has not wished for good fortune?

3RD VOICE: Were you not at first given a French sword?

JEHANNE: Yes.

3RD VOICE: Then why when you were captured did you have a Bourgondian one?

JEHANNE: Because it was more beautiful than a French one.

4TH VOICE: Do you think then that swords should be beautiful?

JEHANNE: If possible, why should not everything be beautiful?

3RD Voice: Are your saints beautiful?

JEHANNE: That depends on your idea of beauty, my lord.

6TH VOICE: What were your conversations with the King of France? (JEHANNE *does not answer.*)

VOICE OF CAUCHON: What were your conversations? (JEHANNE *does not answer.*) Answer!

JEHANNE: If it had been necessary that you should hear them, it would have been arranged by God that you could hear them.

4TH VOICE: (*Angrily*) You speak too lightly of God.

7TH VOICE: Do you know that you are wicked and a liar?

JEHANNE: (*Sadly*) If I am, it is as it should be. I have already told you, I have done nothing that God has not directed.

VOICE OF CAUCHON: Admit you are a liar!

6TH VOICE: Swear you are a liar! (JEHANNE *sways and seems spent, her courage seems to snap.*)

5TH VOICE: You are a traitor and a liar and shall be punished.

3RD VOICE: Who will save you in this hour of trial?

JEHANNE: *(weakly)* My King.

VOICE OF CAUCHON: Your King thinks nothing of you. He has forgotten you already. All France has forgotten you already. *(At these words,* JEHANNE *puts her hands over her eyes.)* Admit your lies and we may yet be spared a burning.

JEHANNE: *(Slowly and through her hands)* His will be done.

4TH VOICE: Why don't your voices release you from prison? *(*JEHANNE *does not answer.)*

VOICE OF CAUCHON: Answer! Why do not your voices release you from prison?

JEHANNE: *(*JEHANNE *slowly, and as though dragging the words out of herself.)* If—I—were—to—question—I—might—ask—why—they—put—me—into—prison.

6TH VOICE: Do you not question them?

JEHANNE: *(Simply)* I am a soldier.

VOICE OF CAUCHON: What has that to do with it?

JEHANNE: I obey orders and don't question.

4TH VOICE: If you are inspired, Jehanne d'Arc, tell us who is the true Pope.

JEHANNE: *(Simply)* The Pope.

VOICE OF CAUCHON: *(Furiously)* Which is the true one?

JEHANNE: I did not know there was more than one.

VOICE OF CAUCHON: Pass on!

4TH VOICE: Tell us of the King of France.

JEHANNE: *(Still swaying)* I told you I will not speak of him.

VOICE OF CAUCHON: Through these five months of trial you have proven stubborn and a liar. Today is your last chance. If sentence is passed against you, tomorrow you will be burned alive. *(*JEHANNE *again places her hands over her eyes.)*

7TH VOICE: Is it not against you that you have no friend, that not a hand has been lifted to save you?

6TH VOICE: She is not worth the saving.

JEHANNE: *(Looking before her with mystic beauty lighting her face)* My Friend is so great that I have not needed the friendship of men. *(Sadly and childishly)* Only sometimes I have longed a little for it.

4TH VOICE: Even your mother has deserted you.

JEHANNE: *(Violently and in a rage)* Don't mention my mother. You have no right to mention my mother. She believes in me no matter what you say. *(Her voice breaks.)*

3RD VOICE: She believes so much in you that she has not sent one word to intercede for you.

2ND VOICE: She is ashamed of you.

JEHANNE: *(Passionately and sobbing)* Leave my mother out of this! *(Tears stream down her face.)*

VOICE OF CAUCHON: Admit your lies. Admit your voices are only lies. Tell the truth for once, Jehanne d'Arc.

JEHANNE: *(Fiercely)* I will answer you no more. For five months you have tortured me, imprisoned me, chained me to a stake like a dog, where all the populace could enter and mock at me. You have starved me; confused my brain; tried to make me fall in with your schemes; tried to make me into the liar you have so easily accused me of being; tried to trap me and break my spirit. *(Sobbing)* But I will tell you this, I will tell you this. *(Fiercely)* There is a power greater and stronger, more divine and compassionate than you could ever know, that stands back of Jehanne d'Arc. Ask her from whom she has received her courage these five long, endless months. She will answer from that Power. Ask her who has fed her soul while you have starved her body. Ask her who has lighted her cell when you have left it in darkness. Ask her who has given her the scent of flowers, when you have filled her cell with vileness and dirt. *(Tenderly, showing the palms of her hands with great cuts in them)* Ask her who has cared for her wounds when your cords have bound them. Ask her who has given her sleep, with the prom- ise of a long, joyous sleep soon to come. Ask her these questions, you judges who cannot judge, and her answer will be *(Raising her voice and pointing)* that Power that will one day judge you!

(JEHANNE sways. She clutches the railing to steady herself, breathing heavily and closing her eyes. After her speech there is a sudden hush and silence, then from out the darkness on all sides, from the left, from the right, from back and front, come the VOICES speaking one by one, rapidly and threateningly.)

VOICES: You have proved you are a liar. You are a witch. The curse of the Church upon you! No wonder France makes no effort to save you. Inspired, indeed! Much talk of the King. No King would look at you. A woman trying to be a man. A sexless woman. Answer our questions, Jehanne d'Arc.

(At this, JEHANNE opens her eyes. As their questions start thick and fast she does not answer but only raises her hands as though to ward off blows and hold their voices back.)

VOICES: How dare you speak of God? How many sheep had you in your field? Who killed Jean de Metz? How many leagues was it from your home to Chinon? Who measured the leagues? Where were you christened? What secrets did you tell the King? Did you pray for the defeat of the English Army? Do you hate the English? Why did you carry a white banner? How dared you wear men's clothes? Who taught you how to fight? Are you a virgin? Will you swear you are a virgin? Have your Saints wings? Where did you leave your sword? Did you drink with your soldiers? Did you curse before children? Are you in league with the devil? Have you sold your soul to the devil? (JEHANNE *holds her hands over her ears. All the* VOICES *cry out together and loudly.*) Infidel! Witch! Liar! Profaner! Despised of God!

(CAUCHON *begins to speak. During his speech,* JEHANNE *drops her hands and stands looking directly before her as though her spirit was far away.*)

VOICE OF CAUCHON: You are all these things, Jehanne d'Arc. For five months we have tried you and found you to be a lying, deceitful girl. The devil is your accomplice. You wear men's clothes as only a harlot would and in spite of all kind persuasion you still persist in your unnatural story of seeing visions and hearing voices. You have sinned against God, your mother, the Church and all men. You have been a traitor to your country and a disgrace to the name of womanhood. You will go back to your cell and await your sentence! (*There is a long pause, then slowly* JEHANNE *speaks.*)

JEHANNE: The hour of my deliverance is near.

(*The light fades; there is utter darkness, then slowly it comes up again. Shadows of heavy bars flood in and cross the light, which is now blue. The walls of a solid prison press in on* JEHANNE *from three sides. A crude bed upon which is dirty straw and a table with a lighted candle on it are within the prison walls.* JEHANNE *stands within the walls. Her hands are tied. Her face is ghastly white. The heavy iron door is opened by a* GUARD *and* CAUCHON *enters with* BEDFORD, STAFFORD, WARWICK, JEAN DE LUXEMBOURG *and two* SOLDIERS.)

BEDFORD: We have come to tell you the verdict of your sentence, Jehanne d'Arc, but there is still time for you to repent—if you will but acknowledge that you have lied and that your voices are of the devil.

JEHANNE: (JEHANNE *turns slowly and looks at him.*) I have not lied.

CAUCHON: Very well, then. (*Taking out a paper and reading*) This verdict reads that unless you admit your lies, tomorrow you shall be burned alive at the stake in the public square of the town. (*At his words,* JEHANNE *shrinks, then makes an effort to recover herself.*)

JEHANNE: *(Bitterly and passionately)* You know that no matter what I admit—lies or no lies—you will kill me just the same. *(Her voice breaks.)*

JEAN DE LUXEMBOURG: If your voices were divine have them save you now!

JEHANNE: Do not mock the messengers of God!

CAUCHON: Well, we cannot tire ourselves anymore with you. We will meet tomorrow before your burning!

(JEHANNE shrinks a trifle—then recovers herself. He goes out followed by STAFFORD, LUXEMBOURG, WARWICK, BEDFORD and the GUARD. The GUARD turns and spits at JEHANNE.)

GUARD: Savior of France! Ha—ha—ha! *(He laughs in a coarse horrible way, then goes out banging and locking the door behind him.)*

JEHANNE: *(In terrified voice)* St. Katherine, St. Katherine, where are you? Deliver me, deliver me. I cannot face this. Oh, my Jesus, oh my King, help me, help me.

(She wrings her hands frantically, then goes to the door, she beats on it and sinks on her knees. On the top step she seems to visualize flames of her approaching torture and feels them drawing closer and leaping up about her. She shrinks in agony and despair.)

JEHANNE: Help me! Help me! I am alone—abandoned—My voices— voices—voices—I can't hear you—*I can't hear you*—darkness— darkness—night. What have I done? Where am I? I tried to serve . . . answer me—hear me . . . don't forsake me . . . I'm afraid—afraid. . . . Everything is closing; round me . . . everything has left me . . . Emptiness—blackness—*(There is a moment's silence; then suddenly she cries out with a heartbreaking cry.)* Mary, help me—keep me from the flames. *(She shudders, then rising to her feet, stands with her arms out in the form of a cross.)* My God, my God, why have you forsaken me?

(She sways, then plunges forward down the steps. She drags herself across the floor on her knees and puts her hands to her eyes. She flings herself on the bed and her body shakes with convulsed sobs. The cell is left in darkness except for a streak of blue light which shines across the bed on JEHANNE. She has ceased sobbing but her hands twist convulsively. Gradually the light vanishes; the cell is left in darkness. A deep tremor like the sound of the vox humana on the organ starts vibrating. It gradually merges into the low murmur of voices. Shadowy forms of many PEOPLE move across stage from left to right. A faint light like early dawn, shows PEOPLE moving, speaking, peering in a tense expectant manner. They elbow each other. As the CROWD increases, some climb on higher levels until every space is

*filled. A mixture of sympathy and indifference. They are bored and restless
from waiting a long time. A tremendous* MOB *inundates the stage, many
of them walking backwards as they watch the approaching procession.*)

AN OLD MAN: There is something terrifying about the dawn today. It is like the shadow of a dark angel dragging his hand across
the sky.

A WOMAN: It seems strange to me, too—the light is so late in coming and the sky is so dark.

ANOTHER WOMAN: Later the flames will make it seem blood red.
(A small GROUP *gathering together)*
A VOICE: There can be no doubt, she is a witch. Anyone could know
that.
ANOTHER VOICE: I am glad an event like this doesn't take place
every day—it will surely upset my business.
ANOTHER VOICE: And certainly mine! You forget my shop is on the
square.
A WOMAN: No one will be able to cross the square today. At first the
crowd will prevent it; after, it will be the dying heat of the faggots.
A MAN: What does it matter? Today should be considered as a
holiday.
MORE PEOPLE COMING ON: Let us get through the crowd here!
I'm tired of waiting! The only hope of finding a place was to come
early. It seems to me we have been here for hours! It seems to me
we have been waiting a lifetime. I'm already hungry. Here comes a
woman selling fruit. *(An* OLD WOMAN *approaches with a basket of
fruit. A small* CROWD *gathers round her and buys her fruit.)* What
delicious fruit. It is well to have something to eat for fear we will
have to remain here hours before the burning. It's an outrage.
They have no right to keep us waiting like this. They should start
these things earlier! They should start them at the promised hour,
but you will see they won't. They should run things on schedule!
Bah! Has anything official ever been run on schedule. They should
think more of the people. They count too much on our patience.
If it were not so interesting to see this girl burned, I would have
gone home long ago! It is too great an event to miss! I am anxious
to see her face. They say she strangely resembles the devil. Some
people say she is beautiful. There are different ideas of beauty. I
am anxious to see how she will look when the flames begin to lick
about her! She will scream and beg for pardon! I'm not so sure.
They say she has shown very little fear up to now. But she did
deny her voices so that she might be pardoned. Afterwards, she
reclaimed them again!
A ROUGH-LOOKING MAN: Like all women she doesn't know her
own mind! *(Laughter from the* CROWD*)*
A WOMAN'S VOICE: Maybe none of us would know our own minds
after five months of torture such as she has endured.
THE MAN AGAIN: *(Mockingly)* Ah! Sympathy for a witch from the
tender heart of the fairer sex! *(More laughter)*
A CHILD: *(Frenziedly and pushing through the* CROWD*)* The procession has started! They are already coming this way.

VOICES IN THE CROWD: They have started! It will still take them long to reach here through that mass of people. The soldiers will clear the way! They will trample over people if they do not make way. Even so it will take them some minutes to reach here! They say Cauchon is hysterical with nerves! Secretly he is afraid of the power of Jehanne d'Arc! *(Bursts of laughter)* She has not shown much power these days. Even her friend, the devil, has forsaken her! She has sold her soul but the devil has cheated her in the bargain! Her name will go down in history as infamous and diabolic! If she is remembered at all, it will only be as an example of wickedness and conceit! In ten years her name will be forgotten! History will not fill its pages with a girl of that kind! Had she been worth anything, the church would have recognized it! The church has disclaimed her so there can be no good in her! They gave her a chance but she would not repent. It is too late now. Forever more her soul will be outside of the church! She has missed the chance of joining the angels and the Saints in heaven. She will be cursed forever!

A VERY OLD MAN: *(Exaltedly and with a prophetic note in his voice)* Christ, too, was cursed and crucified but His name has lived! *(Wild laughter and jeering at the* OLD MAN. *More* PEOPLE *push through the* CROWD.*)*

VOICES: Hurry, hurry, we will be late. The square is nearly full. It must be nearly time. We must not miss the burning. Have they brought her yet? They are coming—hear the drums? They say she is much altered. The drums are drawing nearer. Clear the way. They are bringing her now. She walks forward like one guided by the devil. They say she is controlled by the evil one. I think we should not let the children see her. She will bring harm to our children! It's what comes from a woman wearing men's clothes. Burning is too good for her! Her arrogance is punished at last! It's the justice of heaven! We must keep out of her evil spell! Keep the children from her evil spell! Here she comes now! Make room! Make room! Keep back from her evil path! Do not let her look upon the children! She is looking at no one. She gazes before her! She is in a trance of the evil one! Yes—yes—that's it! Make way! Make way!

*(*DRUMMERS *enter beating at a slow monotonous rhythm. The* PEOPLE *are frantic with excitement.* MEN-AT-ARMS *clear the way, pushing the* CROWD *back. A group of* SOLDIERS *and two* MONKS *enter. The* SOLDIERS *are leading* JEHANNE, *who is in their midst. The light which surrounds her is a very pale clear blue. She is dressed in simple improvised*

dress made of rough sacking. A coarse cord is tied around her waist, and a soiled, purple cloak hangs from her shoulders. Her hands are tied and her face is sorrowful, but she is calm and again has an expression of exaltation. Two SOLDIERS *step forward and strike her with branches and reeds they have pulled off trees on their march. They also place a paper crown on her head, which has inscribed on it, "Heretic," "Infidel," "Liar," "Witch," etc. She stumbles, falling on her knees as Christ did while carrying His cross.)*

1ST SOLDIER: The witch's reign is over and not a voice to help her— ha-ha. *(All join in and laugh.)*

2ND SOLDIER: How do you like being struck with these beautiful reeds of a country you have tried to save?

JEHANNE: I am proud to be struck with reeds since my King was also struck with them.

SOLDIER: She is mad. My girl, your King is safe and very comfortable I am sure.

JEHANNE: My King is waiting for me. *(Laughter from the* CROWD *and* SOLDIERS. *A group of* JUDGES, *including* CAUCHON, *enters. The* CROWD *quiets.)*

CAUCHON: What is the delay? What is this? *(He removes the paper crown from off* JEHANNE*'s head.)* What is this nonsense? *(He reads the inscription on it.)* "Heretic—Infidel—Liar—Witch." *(Tosses crown aside.)* Advance!

JEHANNE: May I not have a crucifix?

(A SOLDIER *breaks two sticks and ties them together in the form of a cross. He hands it to* JEHANNE, *as she reaches for it he pulls it away amidst shrieks of laughter from the* CROWD.*)*

CAUCHON: Pass on! Pass on! Disperse the mob!

(A MONK *steps forward and timidly stretches out a crucifix to* JEHANNE, *the* CROWD *brushes him aside before she has a chance to grasp it. She raises her hands high and clasped before her as though she had taken it—as though she held it in her hands. They move on,* JEHANNE *with extended arms, her eyes riveted upon an imaginary crucifix and seeming to follow it. The light upon her becomes dazzling white. A* YOUNG MAN *tries to kneel to her. He tries to kiss her dress. The* MOB *jeers and flings him to the ground. They laugh wildly. A moment later she can hardly be seen in the frantic mob which engulfs her, shouting themselves hoarse.)*

CAUCHON: No more delays! Advance!

(Then once again JEHANNE *is seen in the inhuman* MOB, *the light upon her is blindingly white, she still holds her hands up, as she goes out. She should still give the illusion of holding a crucifix. The* CROWD *continues pushing and elbowing in an effort to see her.)*

Voices in the Crowd: There is no use trying to break through that mob. We will see better here. The crowds are too dense out there. It is impossible to move forward. The way is blocked. Everyone is frantic to see. It's almost impossible to see. We should have come earlier. If we had come earlier, we could have had places out on the square. Not even the soldiers can get through.

(The sound of the Crowd *is a confused roar. Their voices grow louder and wilder. A shabby, white-faced* Maniac *has climbed onto a prominence in the midst of the* Crowd. *He roars with mocking laugher. A* woman *slaps his face. All stare at him and then begin to laugh. The laughter is taken up until the whole* mob *vibrates with it.)*

Maniac: That's right, burn her! Burn—

(The woman *leaps at him, scratching and biting him. Together they fall into the* Crowd—*fighting desperately. The tenseness of the* Crowd *increases. They lash themselves into a frenzy of excitement.)*

Voices in the Crowd: Poor wretch. Wretch, indeed! She deserves it.

A Woman: *(Hysterically)* They must not burn her. They must not! She is so beautiful. Her eyes were so beautiful. They looked at me once. Save—

Crowd: She is climbing up to the stake. She is at the stake. They are chaining her to the stake. She is fastened. Look how beautiful she is. *(Stillness begins to come over the* Crowd.*)* But she's a witch. Who can be sure? Listen to the crowd. Cauchon must be reading the death sentence. Sssh! Listen. There is a terrible silence out there. They are lighting the faggots. What is she doing? Can you see the smoke? She is holding high a crucifix. She seems to be praying. The smoke is rising. I see flames! *(In tense excitement)* What now? What now? Her hands are free. The flame has burnt the cords that bind her hands. She has raised them high to heaven. The flames are terrible. *(It grows darker. There is a faint rumble of thunder.)* I never saw flames come so fast. They give the smoke no chance to smother her. It is terrible! Flames! Smoke! The smoke is enveloping her now. I can hardly see her. Great flames are leaping toward the sky.

(While this is going on, the stage grows darker and darker and finally thunder is heard in the distance. Three frantic monks *with their hands to their ears rush onto the stage from the right. They seem dazed.)*

One of the Monks: I would that my soul were, where I believe the soul of that woman soon to be.

(They stagger out to left. The attitude of the mob *begins to change. They*

look at one another questioningly. They have become hushed. The silence becomes ghastly. Suddenly, JEHANNE*'s voice is heard. At first clearly, then agonizingly, and finally faintly. She cries six times.)*

JEHANNE: Jesus—Jesus—Jesus—Jesus—Jesus—Jesus! *(As her cries die down, voices of the* MOB *can be heard in terror—a flash of lightning and finally a terrific crash of thunder.)*

CROWD: The stake has collapsed. I can see her no more. *(Their voices are full of terror.)* She has gone. She has gone! Forever! Forever!

(Another terrible crash of thunder. The MOB *is terrified and panic stricken. Their* VOICES *are heard in terror, and finally one voice cries out with a blood curdling and piercing screech followed by another voice, and another, and another.)*

VOICES: We have burned a Saint! We have burned a Saint! We have burned a Saint! We have burned a Saint! We have burned a Saint! We have burned a Saint!

God help us!
God help us!
God help us!
God help us!

(The MOB *from the square breaks onto the stage like a great wild tide. They all rush off to the left, fleeing in panic and terror. The stage becomes almost dark. There is a terrific and momentous silence; then off in the distance the thunder can be heard rumbling.)*

Curtain

Jacob Slovak

The Characters

JOSIAH FLINT, *important citizen*
SARAH FLINT, *his wife*
MYRA FLINT, *their daughter*
LOLA FLINT, *another daughter of eleven*
JACOB SLOVAK, *a Polish Jew*
REV. EZRA HALE, *minister of the town*
THEOPHILUS BRENT, *important man and sheriff*
HEZEKIAH BRENT, *his son*
KITTY, *the hired girl*
SAMUEL JONES, *assistant sheriff*

Act 1

A small town in New England. The first act takes place in the parlor-dining room in the New England farm house of JOSIAH FLINT. *It is about five o'clock of a Sunday afternoon in winter. Upstage, slightly to the right of the center, the front door is placed. Right of door there is a mirror and some pegs with coats, caps, and mufflers hanging from them. Directly to the right side of the stage there is a door leading to the kitchen. This door is closed. To the left of the front door the wall runs along about six feet then breaks going back into a bay window. Directly to the left there is another window. From all the windows lace wash curtains hang. In the bay window there is a seat with pillows piled on it, and a canary sits in a gilded wire cage. Between the bay window and the front door a faded picture of George Washington crossing the Delaware is hanging; above it a picture of a Roman chariot race. The wall paper around the room is brown with yellow flowers on it. It is faded in spots. To the left of the stage a table is placed with a red tablecloth hanging from it. A lighted oil lamp with a green shade, a velvet bible, newspapers, and family photograph and books are on the table. A plush chair and two straight ones are grouped about it. At the window to the left green ferns stand on the ledge and a small table with sewing things strewn on it is placed in the corner. Directly to the right a stove pipe runs out connecting with a stove. Attached to the wall above the stove another lighted lamp stands on a little ledge. A figured red carpet spreads on the floor and a rocking chair is placed in the middle of the stage.*

Library of Congress Copyright, February 20, 1923. Registration number 63687. The version of the play printed here is from the 1927 New York stage manager's script located at the Rosenbach Museum and Library rather than from the copyrighted script. This version was also used for the 1928 London production.

As the Curtain rises JOSIAH FLINT *is sitting by the stove smoking and reading a newspaper.* REV. EZRA HALE *has just entered.* JOSIAH FLINT *is a man about sixty. He is thin and bony, his eyebrows heavy and shaggy.* REV. EZRA HALE *is a small quick little man not unkindly but weak and afraid. He is bundled in a heavy coat and fur cap.*

JOSIAH FLINT: *(Looking up)* Glad ter see yer, Ezra. Lay off yer things. *(*EZRA HALE *takes off his cap and coat and lays them on the chair near the table.)* Sit down. *(*EZRA HALE *pulls a chair near the stove.)*

EZRA HALE: Thanks. I'm glad you're alone. *(Sits on chair.)* I'm worried, Josiah.

JOSIAH FLINT: What's on your mind?

EZRA HALE: It's about Jacob. I suppose I can at least be frank with you about it, seeing it was you that brought him to this town. I'm scared and I'm in a bad hole. I need your help.

JOSIAH FLINT: What's up?

EZRA HALE: You know I wasn't to blame for having Jacob play the organ in the church. When Miss Rivers gave up playing the organ and moved away, I felt it my solemn duty to fill her place. I knew that without music my congregation would not be inclined to come to church—so when you told me Jacob could play the organ and I could get no one else, I naturally took him. It's true, of course, I kept his playing secret because I knew they wouldn't stand for a Jew coming into the house of Christ. I think that deception might be forgiven, seeing I did it for the sake of my church—I might more readily say for the sake of the Lord.

JOSIAH FLINT: Well—I know all that and I hain't kickin' as ter his playin' in the church. I thought yer were mighty lucky ter git him and him mighty fine ter play for yer for nothin'. 'Specially when he ain't got no credit for it.

EZRA HALE: Now, you were the only one that knew of it.

JOSIAH FLINT: I hain't spilled the beans.

EZRA HALE: I know that—but just the same there is a rumor going around about it and if it becomes definitely known that I took a Jew in the church, you can see what a terrible position I'll be in.

JOSIAH FLINT: It'll make yer look like some kind of liar—all right, all right. What do yer want me ter do?

EZRA HALE: I had an idea that if you dismissed him from your store—

JOSIAH FLINT: *(Interrupting)* Kick him out of my store after all he's done ter put it on its feet!

EZRA HALE: Well—*(His sentence is broken in upon by the entrance of*

SAMUEL JONES, *who is a young man about thirty. A New England farmer, shrewd, a busybody and a gossip.*)

JOSIAH FLINT: Hello, Sam—come in.

SAMUEL JONES: *(Brings chair forward.)* Hain't interruptin' I hope. Jest blew down from the village. Things are sort of hot there. Thought I'd drop in, Josiah, and put yer a little wise.

JOSIAH FLINT: What about? (SAMUEL JONES *looks uneasily at Ezra Hale.*)

SAMUEL JONES: Well—maybe I hadn't ought ter say—

EZRA HALE: Go ahead if it's what they're saying down in the village.

SAMUEL JONES: *(Sitting)* I hain't sayin' it's true, Rev. Ezra, but it 'pears there's some gossip that it's that Jew playin' in the church. There's a mighty lot of feelin' against him. I thought I'd tell yer, Josiah, because maybe it will stop folks goin' ter yer store if yer keep Jacob on. Hurt yer business.

REV. EZRA HALE: *(Quickly)* That's just what I say!

JOSIAH FLINT: That's all very well, but Jacob's a might fine feller, and it's him that got my store a-payin'. I hain't a goin' against him jest 'cause Ezra's gotten in hot water.

SAMUEL JONES: It'll be hot fer yer, too. No one will buy at yer store if yer keep Jacob. I've heard the boys talkin' in the village. Theophilus hain't goin' ter stand for it neither—with the things he's ben hearin'.

JOSIAH FLINT: What has Theophilus ter do with it?

SAMUEL JONES: He has alright. He's comin' ter see yer, and wants a word with yer, too, Reverent. *(The door opens and* THEOPHILUS BRENT *enters. He is a large man with important manner, red face and bald head. He wears a large brown hat and is conscious of his position as sheriff.)*

THEOPHILUS BRENT: Ah, here yer be, Ezra. I missed yer at yer house. I've come ter see yer both, 'bout all this kick up 'bout Jacob.

SAMUEL JONES: Jest told 'em yer was comin'.

THEOPHILUS BRENT: *(To* JOSIAH FLINT, *seating himself)* What gits me is how yer ever come ter bring him ter this here town. Yer have always ben pretty smart about keepin' it ter yerself.

SAMUEL JONES: I'll say yer've ben mighty sharp. It looks now like some one's done and killed the goose that's laid the golden egg.

JOSIAH FLINT: I hain't so sure about that gentlemen. When all is said and done, he's done a lot for this here town and her citizens.

THEOPHILUS BRENT: Sure! Yes, but the citizens hain't goin' ter admit that no Jew has helped the progress of this here—their town.

JOSIAH FLINT: Them that deserves credit should git it. Jacob's got more brains than most of these farmers put ter-gether, and I hain't yet seen the reason why everyone should be so sour on him.

Samuel Jones: *(Rises.)* Fine talk, but why should us farmers let a Jew come in and ruin our shootin' matches? Much less our gals!

Josiah Flint: *(Good-naturedly)* He hain't ruinin' our gals. None of our gals would git stuck on a Jew. They'd have better sense than that. Yer jealous, Sam.

Samuel Jones: Wel, all of them are sweet on him. Jest because he looks romantic like, they all go around with sick faces for him. It gives a regular farmer a pain! *(Sits.)*

Theophilus Brent: If it hain't that I knew Myra's goin' ter marry Hezekiah—I'd worry some myself, Josiah, about her an Jacob. It 'pears they see a lot of each other.

Josiah Flint: Why, I know that, Theophilus. Myra sees him in the store, but yer hain't sayin' a grand gal like Myra would look at Jacob except ter be friendly like. I like ter see them friends. Jacob's a nice boy outside of what he is—and he's taught Myra a lot of readin' and how ter run the store.

Theophilus Brent: Whatever made yer bring that feller ter this here town, Josiah? What put the idea in yer head?

Josiah Flint: Yer hain't sayin' I wasn't pretty smart in gittin' him, are yer?

Theophilus Brent: I don't know.

Josiah Flint: *(Puts paper on floor.)* Wel—I 'xpect I might jest as wel make a clean breast of it. I heard tell so many times of the sharpness of Jews. About three months ago I up and finds my store hain't even payin', the business pretty near goin' ter pot.

Samuel Jones: Andy Sharp down in Jerrytown was gittin' a bit too prosperous fer yer!

Josiah Flint: It 'pears most everyone was leavin' me and goin' ter him 'cause his store was newer. I was pretty near sick with worry when the idea comes ter me that maybe if I could git a Jew ter come ter this here town and keep him kinda in the background, he might be sharp and outwit Andy. So I wrote a friend of mine in Boston and says, "Ship a sharp but honest Jew" and the next day he sends Jacob up.

Theophilus Brent: So—yer sent fer him yerself?

Josiah Flint: At first I thought he wasn't so sharp on business as I'd expected him ter be. Right away he begins ter say yer store hain't pretty, naggin' fer ter put curtains like around and paint the place fresh. "The women will come ter it," he says. The business was so bad anyway, I thought I might as wel take a chance with them artistic and what-not ideas of his, and before long all the women comes runnin' ter us.

SAMUEL JONES: He knows what they want, I'll bet yer!

JACOB FLINT: It was him that got in all those pretty signs and got me even ter sellin' fancy wash rags and high smellin' soap with a label on the box "From Paris."

THEOPHILUS BRENT: He hain't done bad fer not havin' a good business head!

JOSIAH FLINT: In six weeks everyone begins ter leave Andy's store fer mine, and in three months—here I am—makin' money hand over fist.

SAMUEL JONES: Yer kept gittin' him mighty secret.

JOSIAH FLINT: Wel, I thought as it might go against my reputation. That's why I tried ter keep him—kinda in the background. Didn't even say he was a Jew until it leaked out by Lola snoopin' round and gittin' wind of it.

THEOPHILUS BRENT: That kid's smart!

JOSIAH FLINT: Wel, anyway, if it hadn't ben for Jacob helpin' yer, Ezra, playin' the organ so wonderful, not a soul would have raised a word against him.

THEOPHILUS BRENT: (*Turning to* EZRA) That's what I wanted ter git at. As Sheriff, I want ter know how this fuss started?

JOSIAH FLINT: Wel—when Jacob first come I gave him the two rooms over the store ter sleep in and I told him I didn't want him seen too much. Jacob says he didn't care how much he stays cooped up so long as he has a pianner.

THEOPHILUS BRENT: A pianner!

JOSIAH FLINT: I was kinda taken back at the idea at first, a strong grown man playin' the pianner—but when I figured it would keep him in, I hired one. That Sunday after service I went back to see Ezra about a little business—

THEOPHILUS BRENT: (*To* EZRA, *pretending to be severe*) Ho, ho— what business?

JOSIAH FLINT: I hadn't oughta give a minister of the Lord away— and on a Sunday afternoon—what do you think, Ezra?

THEOPHILUS BRENT: O, come—Amongst friends!

JOSIAH FLINT: I had promised him a keg of my strongest apple-jack.

THEOPHILUS BRENT: So our good preacher likes apple-jack and likes it strong! (*They all laugh.*)

JOSIAH FLINT: Wel, sir, I went back ter see Ezra—

EZRA HALE: (*Jumping in*) I was terribly worried because Miss Rivers was moving away to get an education.

SAMUEL JONES: Always wantn' somethin' more—these women.

JOSIAH FLINT: Ezra was in an awful state 'cause he felt folks wouldn't stand for no music in the church on Sundays—

EZRA HALE: So Josiah passed Jacob on to me.

THEOPHILUS BRENT: *(To* EZRA*)* Did yer know he was a Jew?

JOSIAH FLINT: I told him that confidential, the same time I told yer.

THEOPHILUS BRENT: Wel, you've started a great uproar.

SAMUEL JONES: And right, too. These foreigners are dangerous anyway.

THEOPHILUS BRENT: Wel, we got ter think what ter do about it.

EZRA HALE: I have no desire to harm any of God's creatures, but if Slovak stays on here we are all going to get in a lot of trouble.

JOSIAH FLINT: Yer mean yer are, Ezra—not none of us.

EZRA HALE: If the people discover that a Jew played the organ in the house of Christ, they will, of course,—not understanding the unselfish position I took—blame me. But they will blame even more the man who brought him to this town; who let him go into our library and fix our books. I was thinking of you wishing to run for Selectman next Fall and wondering how much this would hurt you. And you, Theophilus, I don't think they will be overzealous to believe their sheriff backed one of that race neither.

THEOPHILUS BRENT: I hahn't thought of that!

EZRA HALE: My idea would be for us important citizens to sign a letter asking him nicely and kindly to leave the town. I can see no other way.

JOSIAH FLINT: It seems ter me we're lettin' ourselves git scared bout nothin'.

THEOPHILUS BRENT: The trouble is if we give Jacob his walkin' papers he may git sore and hand out that we were in on it all the time.

EZRA HALE: Not Slovak. He won't put up a fight—too much of a dreamer. As for telling—why the only house he ever comes to is yours, Josiah.

SAMUEL JONES: And that's on account of Myra. *(*THEOPHILUS BRENT *starts.)*

JOSIAH FLINT: What has Myra got ter do with his comin'?

SAMUEL JONES: *(Rises.)* Wel, if yer want the truth—Myra and Jacob are stuck on each other.

EZRA HALE: *(Rises.)* Careful, Samuel.

THEOPHILUS BRENT: *(Rises.)* Why in hell should he be careful? I'm sorry, Josiah, but I'll have ter consider my boy. Go ahead, Sam.

JOSIAH FLINT: It's damn nonsense, I tell yer—if yer wasn't under my roof, Sam, I'd call it a damn lie!

SAMUEL JONES: Wel, yer can call it what yer like, on the way here I seen them walkin' in the woods arm and arm.

JOSIAH FLINT: *(Rises, enraged.)* Myra and Jacob! Why, Myra went to see her aunt!

SAMUEL JONES: Um!

THEOPHILUS BRENT: And Hezekiah was comin' today ter ask Myra ter marry him. If she's goin' around with a feller like that—

JOSIAH FLINT: There's some mistake, Theophilus. Jacob is comin' this evenin' ter look over some stuff from Boston down ter the barn. Yer'll see they won't come in together.

SAMUEL JONES: No, they hain't so stupid as that.

JOSIAH FLINT: *(Angrily to* SAMUEL*)* You will have ter prove this!

EZRA HALE: *(Between* SAMUEL JONES *and* JOSIAH FLINT*)* Gentlemen, gentlemen, calm yourselves. After all, no harm is done. If you do as I say, in three days Slovak will be out of this town. And as for Myra, she will forget all about him, that is, if she's thought of him at all. He just seems romantic to her because he's a foreigner and can play the piano and spout poetry. *(They all calm down a little.)* But no harm is done and I'll warrant you she'll be accepting Hezekiah this evening or whenever he asks her.

THEOPHILUS BRENT: Ezra's right. No harm is done so far, Josiah. But yer had better sack him.

JOSIAH FLINT: By golly, I will! If that's the sort of thing he's pullin' around here. He's got nerve if he thinks he can look at Myra.

THEOPHILUS BRENT: Yer write the letter, Ezra. If that don't work we'll try stronger measures.

EZRA HALE: *(Takes his coat and hat, puts them on.)* I'll run along now. I'm late already. *(At that moment* LOLA, *a little girl of eleven, comes in from the kitchen. She is small for her size, with her hair parted in the middle and braided and large spectacles on her eyes. In manner she is spoiled and old for her age. Her voice is high and disagreeable.)*

LOLA: Say, Paw, Maw wants ter know how many for supper.

EZRA HALE: Hello, Lola. Been a good girl?

LOLA: *(Ignoring the question and looking sourly at the* REV. HALE*)* How many, Paw?

JOSIAH FLINT: Yer'll stay, Theophilus, won't yer, and yer Sam?

THEOPHILUS BRENT: I'd like a bite.

SAMUEL JONES: I'll stay jest ter look on but I won't eat.

JOSIAH FLINT: *(Counting on his fingers)* Me and Maw, Jacob, Myra, Theophilus and Lola. What about Hezekiah?

THEOPHILUS BRENT: He'll come later.

JOSIAH FLINT: Six, Lola.

LOLA: *(*LOLA *puts her hands to her mouth and yells out in a piercing voice.)* Six, Maw!

MRS. FLINT: *(Offstage)* All right, dearie. *(All three men shrink when* LOLA *yells. She goes into the bay window and during the following scene she teases the canary.)*

EZRA HALE: We must be careful not to let Jacob suspect anything. We mustn't let him know how we feel.

JOSIAH FLINT: I hain't goin' ter bother hidin' nothin'—I'll find out a thing or two 'bout *him.*

THEOPHILUS BRENT: Yer should have done that long ago, afore yer took him in.

SAMUEL JONES: Yer can't tell what he may be. He's slick enough ter hide his real self all right.

EZRA HALE: Nevertheless, it's wiser to be polite to him and act as if nothing had happened. Especially you, Josiah, if he's under your roof.

JOSIAH FLINT: I'll be as slick as him.

EZRA HALE: Well, I'll be going along. *(He sighs.)* Seems to be trouble to hire for me and my fold.

THEOPHILUS BRENT: We'll straighten it out or I hain't callin' myself sheriff.

SAMUEL JONES: It'll straighten as soon as we get that kike walkin' on his way.

EZRA HALE: *(*EZRA HALE *walks to the door.)* Good bye, everyone.

THEOPHILUS BRENT: Good bye. *(*REV. EZRA HALE *goes out.)*

JOSIAH FLINT: Not a word about this ter anyone. *(Two men nod their heads in acquiescence.)*

(At that moment MRS. FLINT *enters. She is a thin woman, a busy house-wife of the virago type. During all of the following scene she removes things from the table, spreads a white tablecloth and sets the table for six, going back and forth into the kitchen, bringing bread, etc.)*

MRS. FLINT: How'dy, Theophilus. How'dy, Sam. *(Both men say "How'dy.")*

THEOPHILUS BRENT: *(Changing the subject as* MRS. FLINT *returns.)* John Adams' two cows both had calves last night. I passed by this mornin' and he was pretty nearly all tucked out after havin' ben up all night.

MRS. FLINT: *(Placing the plates with a crash on the table)* Wel, that's more than he did for his wife when Sally was born. He slept right through the whole thing. But I suppose cows is more important than wives.

THEOPHILUS BRENT: O come, Sarah. We hain't sayin' that.

MRS. FLINT: But that's what yer all think, jest the same. A woman like me don't live and drudge for nothin', not ter find that out.

JOSIAH FLINT: Yer make it 'pear as though I maltreated yer, Maw.

MRS. FLINT: O, I hain't sayin' yer. But there's a dozen men round this countryside I'm meanin' and John Adams is one of them. (*She places the water decanter down with a thud.*) And I wish yer men would stop smokin' in this here room. It never gits a breath of air.

THEOPHILUS BRENT: (THEOPHILUS BRENT *puts out his cigar. He winks to* JOSIAH *and as* MRS. FLINT *leaves the room he remarks.*) The wife's on the war path today.

JOSIAH FLINT: She always gits excited when there's company. (MRS. FLINT *returns again.* JOSIAH FLINT *turns to* LOLA.) I wish yer'd stop teasin' that canary, Lola; it don't like bein' poked.

LOLA: I won't stop.

JOSIAH FLINT: I don't know what ter do with that child. In the summer she pulls the wings off flies—

MRS. FLINT: How do yer 'xpect the poor child ter amuse herself on a Sunday afternoon?

JOSIAH FLINT: Wel, I want her ter stop that or I'll make her.

MRS. FLINT: Make her, indeed! I gess I have say over my own child. (*In honeyed tones to* LOLA) Lola, darling, be nice and quiet now—that's a good girl—and when your Paw goes out you can play with the canary some more.

(*The front door opens and* MYRA *comes in. She is a girl about twenty-two, although she seems older. She has a curious charm which grows the more one sees her. She seems quiet but underneath an apparent indifference one should feel a burning passionate nature which is her real self. She removes her coat and hat.*)

JOSIAH FLINT: Oh, there yer are, Myra. Where have yer ben?

MYRA: (MYRA *looks quickly from one to the other.*) Eh—why—ter see Aunt Amy.

JOSIAH FLINT: I hope that's true.

MYRA: (*Sharply*) Why shouldn't it be?

JOSIAH FLINT: There hain't no reason why it shouldn't be. I don't suspect yer of lyin' but I jest want ter tell yer for the benefit of those that might lie (*He looks at* SAMUEL JONES.) that when yer say yer have been to see yer ant I believe yer. If I caught yer lyin' and yer *were* out with that Jew there hain't nothing too strong I wouldn't do, ter punish yer. I am only sayin' this as a warnin'. I ask Jacob ter this here house because it's a matter of business—outside of business he has nothin' whatsoever ter do here—nor in this town neither. We've held out agin Jews for many a long year and we're not goin' ter begin gittin' them in now.

MYRA: Yer brought him here yourself.

JOSIAH FLINT: That's true and I'm regrettin' it now.

THEOPHILUS BRENT: Wel, it don't matter. All things can be remedied if they are taken in time. I dare say Myra realizes herself what a disgrace it would be ter have anythin' ter do with Slovak—outside of being polite to him. It would go hard for any girl in this town who looked at a Jew. (MYRA *puts wraps on seat by window, then comes to back of table.*)

MRS. FLINT: O, for goodness sake, stop all this talk and come ter supper—who's lookin' at a Jew, that's what I want ter know? (*Below her breath*) So much fussin' 'bout nothin'.

JOSIAH FLINT: All this talkin' about Jacob and I wonder why he hain't here yet?

MRS. FLINT: He's late, so I gess he hain't comin'.

MYRA: O, yes, he is.

JOSIAH FLINT: (*Turning quickly to her*) How do yer know? Yer hain't seen him?

MYRA: Eh—well. I saw him the other day. (SAMUEL JONES *raises an eyebrow and looks at* MYRA.)

MRS. FLINT: Wel, let's have supper anyhow. And Lola, go and see where Kitty is. I sent her for some milk a half hour ago—jest down ter the barn. Them hired girls are more trouble than they are worth. (LOLA *goes out. Everyone draws up and sits down at table except* SAMUEL JONES.)

JOSIAH FLINT: Won't change yer mind, Sam?

SAMUEL JONES: No, thanks.

(LOLA *reappears followed by* KITTY, *a pathetic little hired girl who seems ill at ease. She has dark hair, is small and pale with large sad eyes. She serves the table, going back and forth to kitchen.* LOLA *takes her place at table.*)

MRS. FLINT: It's about time yer come, Kitty.

KITTY: Yes, ma'am.

MRS. FLINT: And don't let that coffee boil over—(*She sniffs the air*) I'll bet it's boiling over now.

KITTY: I'll see, ma'am.

(*She goes out quickly to kitchen. The door opens and* JACOB SLOVAK *comes in. He is a medium sized man with dark hair, worn rather long. His eyes are brown, set deep and wide apart. His face is pale and extremely sensitive. He gives the impression of a dreamer and a poet.)*

MRS. FLINT: Good evenin', Jacob. We were wondering where yer were.

JACOB SLOVAK: *(Looking quickly at* MYRA *before answering. She, however, looks away from him. His voice is low and musical. He speaks rather a deliberate English, choosing carefully his words, which he pronounces with a strong Polish accent.)* I regret to be late. I was delayed.

JOSIAH FLINT: *(*JOSIAH FLINT *looks suspiciously at him.)* That's all right. Come, sit down.

JACOB SLOVAK: *(*JACOB SLOVAK *removes his coat.* KITTY *enters, rushing to help him. To* KITTY *)* I thank you.

MRS. FLINT: *(Indicating chair)* Here, sit here! *(He sits at table, facing audience. Everyone is seated at table except* SAMUEL JONES, *who remains by the stove.* MYRA *and* JACOB SLOVAK *do not look at each other.)*

JOSIAH FLINT: *(All bow their heads except* JACOB SLOVAK*)* Oh, blessed Jesus, bless this food ter our use and us ter Thy lovin' service—in Thy name we ask it.

(An instant before the others raise their heads, MYRA *raises hers.* JACOB *and she look intensely at each other, then as the others look up they quickly look away.)*

LOLA: Why doesn't Mr. Slovak say grace?

MRS. FLINT: Lola, hold your tongue! *(*LOLA *annoyingly puts her tongue out and holds it between her fingers.* MRS. FLINT *slaps her hand.* LOLA *looks angry and defiant.* KITTY *brings two dishes of food to table.)*

JOSIAH FLINT: *(Sighing heavily and cutting bread)* I don't know what we are ever goin' ter make out of that child. Full of sass, she is.

MRS. FLINT: Wel, no one hain't askin' yer ter make anythin' out of her. I gess she's as good as any other child in this here town.

THEOPHILUS BRENT: O, come now, no one means any harm—Lola is really a good girl I'm sure. *(Strokes* LOLA*'s hand, she pushes him away.* KITTY *exits.)*

JOSIAH FLINT: Lola—I promise yer a lickin'!

THEOPHILUS BRENT: *(He leans forward pinching* LOLA*'s cheek. She slaps him away. He pretends not to notice.)* What about that heavy snow yer have ben promisin', Josiah?

JOSIAH FLINT: 'expect it's comin' soon, just the same. How was yer ant, Myra? *(*KITTY *reenters with dishes.)*

MYRA: *(Quickly)* Very well. She sent yer all her love.

JOSIAH FLINT: Wel, she needn't have. She knows there hain't no love lost between her and me.

MRS. FLINT: That hain't no way ter talk 'bout yer wife's only sister, Josiah Flint.

SAMUEL JONES: Yer'll never git that farm if she croaks afore yer.

MRS. FLINT: And he'll stand in the way of my gittin' it, too! *(KITTY serves JACOB coffee.)*

THEOPHILUS BRENT: There hain't much use on countin' on relatives. They always live longer than anyone. Got any folks in America, Slovak?

JACOB SLOVAK: *(The others all have been eating heavily, only MYRA has been eating slightly, and JACOB hardly at all. When his name is spoken, he enters the conversation with a slight start, as though he had not been following it.)* Folks, Mr. Brent? You mean what you call relatives of the blood? Why, no. No, I have no one in America. I am quite alone here.

THEOPHILUS BRENT: Funny yer came ter this country if yer didn't know no one here.

SAMUEL JONES: *(Quickly)* And what beats me is how yer speak such first rate English!

JACOB SLOVAK: In my country—as in all Europe—we have more use for languages—we are nearer to people who speak with different languages.

MRS. FLINT: I'll bet yer speak even more languages than jest English.

JACOB SLOVAK: I do. I was brought up in Germany so I speak German and I speak my own tongue, which is Polish, and I speak Russian besides. *(JOSIAH FLINT gives a long whistle.)*

LOLA: Gee—don't they all git mixed up in yer head?

JACOB SLOVAK: *(Laughing)* No, Lola, I have little fences in my brain that keep them all separate. *(To the others)* In America one is more out of touch with people and, of course, it is different. *(During the conversation KITTY passes food and they all eat.)*

THEOPHILUS BRENT: Funny how all the people that Europe does not want somehow end in America. No offense to you, of course.

JACOB SLOVAK: Perhaps we in Europe believe we will find kindness and justice in America and some kind of hope. That is why *we* land here.

SAMUEL JONES: I suppose you were too young to fight in the war.

JACOB SLOVAK: I was fifteen when the war finished.

SAMUEL JONES: What were you doin' then?

JACOB SLOVAK: I was in Germany playing in an orchestra. Had the

war lasted a few more months, young as I was, I would have gone
to the front.

THEOPHILUS BRENT: *(Triumphantly and at least thinking to have
discovered something wrong with* JACOB*)* You would have fought
for Germany?

JACOB SLOVAK: Certainly. Although my father was a Pole, my
mother was a German. I was born, and as I told you, brought
up in Germany. For what other country would I fight?

JOSIAH FLINT: What brought yer ter Amerikie? *(He looks around
slyly at the others to see if now he will catch* JACOB.*)*

JACOB SLOVAK: Conditions were unpleasant in Germany and I
think perhaps I had a longing for a new world. For something
better, fresher. Somehow Europe seemed—not exactly old—how
do you say? I do not mean old—but like bread that is old—

MYRA: Stale, yer mean.

JACOB SLOVAK: Yes, that's it, stale. I had read so much of your
great Whitman, of the way he had been singing of freedom—
great freedom.

SAMUEL JONES: Whitman? Who was he? I never heard of him.

JACOB SLOVAK: I can believe that, Mr. Jones.

JOSIAH FLINT: He was probably one of them politicians always
makin' fancy speeches about nothin'.

JACOB SLOVAK: He was a great poet, Mr. Flint. If this fact happens
to interest you. Perhaps it would also interest you to know that I
thought his songs of freedom and brotherhood echoed the voice
of the American people. I am beginning to think I was wrong.

THEOPHILUS BRENT: How did you git ter America?

JACOB SLOVAK: With this desire for freedom and a new life, I gathered money enough to buy my passage to New York. I left Europe
then turned my face full of hope and confidence to the new world,
as a believer would have turned to Mecca.

MRS. FLINT: *(Full of excitement)* Did yer come in one of them big
ships?

JACOB SLOVAK: Yes.

MYRA: Why, what happened then?

JACOB SLOVAK: I remember standing on the deck as the great ship,
and I, together came up the river. It was the hour of sundown,
because of which they would not let us on the land that evening.
We had to stay on the ship all night; the glory of New York in that
sundown and after in that night, is something I shall not forget.
Like a mist island it was, waving between the sea and sky, with
tall white buildings like pale, slender poets lifting their faces to the

sky, satisfied only to kiss the stars. I remember I felt like kneeling down and praying.

SAMUEL JONES: Gee, that's a funny picture of New York. I went there oncet but I never saw anythin' like that.

MYRA: The buildings looked like poets?

JACOB SLOVAK: *(As though he had not heard him, gazing before him with a fixed, dream look.)* Yes, tall, slender, white poets, with millions of twinkling eyes. "The eyes of the future," I thought. I stayed out on deck all night and with the rise of the sun I saw the colors over the city changing. Violet and rose, then a glorious blue in the sky. Hundreds of little boats rushed about us and everywhere future . . . future . . . and life . . .

MRS. FLINT: *(Leaning forward, spellbound and tensely)* What happened then?

JACOB SLOVAK: *(His mood suddenly breaks and changes.)* Then—oh then, they took me to Ellis Island and my previous illusion was shattered.

THEOPHILUS BRENT: They took yer ter Ellis Island?

JACOB SLOVAK: Just for a few hours. You see by profession I am a musician—a violinist—but I didn't belong to any Union. I couldn't do anything without joining a Union and they didn't want to let me land.

SAMUEL JONES: There might have been other reasons.

JOSIAH FLINT: What was yer first job?

JACOB SLOVAK: After many dark months of despair and starvation I met a man who said he would let me play in a restaurant in Boston. So I went there. But it was no good, unions there, too. I was then discouraged almost, when back came the same man and asked me if I wanted to be—what you call a clerk in a store. He said it, too, needed imagination, like a musician or a poet. I was nearly starving; I accepted. The "job" was to come here to Josiah Flint.

SAMUEL JONES: Yer—that was soft for yer.

JACOB SLOVAK: I don't know. Contrary to what we first think, America is not such a soft country, but I still believe in it. Look at the opportunities you have so generously given me here. *(JOSIAH moves uneasily. KITTY clears away the things on the table as dinner is finished.)*

JOSIAH FLINT: *(For want of something to say)* All mighty interestin'. *(KITTY rattles the dishes as she goes out.)*

MRS. FLINT: I wish that Kitty would stop bein' so nervous. I don't know what is the matter with her tonight.

SAMUEL JONES: Perhaps she's impressed with Mr. Slovak, as all the ladies are. *(*JACOB SLOVAK *does not answer.)*

THEOPHILUS BRENT: Yer know that Kitty's father was a foreigner, too.

JACOB SLOVAK: Really—

JOSIAH FLINT: Yep—a Portuguese, came here for a while sellin' a ploughin' machine and married Minnie Stone. He left on a trip, so he said, but never came back. When Kitty was born, Minnie died. The child had no relatives, so I took her and sent her a schoolin', now that she's grown up we've got her as the hired girl.

THEOPHILUS BRENT: Mighty kind of yer, too, Josiah Flint.

MRS. FLINT: Lucky for her ter git such a nice home.

THEOPHILUS BRENT: *(*THEOPHILUS BRENT *looks out window. He folds his napkin.)* There goes Hezekiah. I gess he don't know I'm here. *(He goes out.* JOSIAH FLINT *signals to* MRS. FLINT, *then coughs with meaning to* SAM.*)*

JOSIAH FLINT: I gess we'll be goin' down ter the barn—eh, Sam? Myra, is there anythin' yer to do for yer mother in the kitchen?

MYRA: I'll see, Paw. *(The men all go out, except* JACOB, *who lingers behind.)*

MRS. FLINT: Come along, Lola. Yer can help Myra.

JOSIAH FLINT: *(As he goes out)* And yer come, too, Jacob. *(*LOLA *and* MRS. FLINT *go into the kitchen.* MYRA *remains alone with* JACOB.*)*

JACOB SLOVAK: Myra. It seemed endless, talking all that time with all these other people.

MYRA: Yes, I know.

JACOB SLOVAK: I am—am so happy we are alone again. *(A pause)*

MYRA: They'll think it funny yer haven't gone down ter the barn with them.

JACOB SLOVAK: They won't notice, and I'll go in a few minutes.

MYRA: *(Sitting down across the room from him. She throws her head back and closes her eyes.)* I'm tired.

JACOB SLOVAK: See, I'll sit here far away from you and be very good. *(He sits at a distance from her.)* Far, far away from you. Leagues and leagues away from you, Myra. But in reality very close. How beautiful you are, Myra—sitting there like that with your eyes closed. I often think of you with your eyes closed—sleeping. There is something so infinitely touching about someone one loves—sleeping.

MYRA: It's nice ter hear yer voice with my eyes closed—it sounds so near, yet very far away. Like sleigh bells that I used ter hear in bed .

at night when I was a kid. Jest a faint tinkle far, far away. They used ter keep me from gittin' scared in the dark.

JACOB SLOVAK: Do you know, all the evening I have been thinking of the sun on your hair, this afternoon out there amongst the trees in the woods; the sun lighted your hair like sharp swords of fire. And your eyes seemed like dark stars dreaming out through the shadows that the trees cast across your face.

MYRA: Oh, Jacob—yer talk like—like no one I ever heard talk before.

JACOB SLOVAK: It's my love talking, Myra.

MYRA: Yer make me feel hot all over—my blood all hot—racing through me—like when I run through the fields in the spring.

JACOB SLOVAK: Myra, I love you. I love everything about you. I love the line of your throat—like that—when your head's thrown back.

MYRA: *(Moving and smiling)* Yer spoil me—no one ever speaks to me the way yer do.

JACOB SLOVAK: *(Sighing and sadly)* Ah, Myra, if you would only see me more alone I would read such wonderful poetry to you, and I would play for you—Beethoven—Liszt—Chopin!

MYRA: Are they sacred music like you play in the church?

JACOB SLOVAK: Sacred? Yes—sacred music! I would read Dante to you—the part I told you about "Love, who didst lift me with thy light."

MYRA: Yer got so much ter think about, Jacob—so much ter occupy yer—yer can't ever be lonely.

JACOB SLOVAK: I'm always lonely—especially here in that bare room over the store—

MYRA: But yer have a piano and yer books!

JACOB SLOVAK: *(Rising)* I need you—Myra. I won't be lonely when we are married. I can hardly say that without trembling all over.

MYRA: *(Rising)* Yer had better go down ter the barn, Jacob, I know they are waitin' for yer.

JACOB SLOVAK: I'll go, but I wish I could stay here with you. I wish we had time enough to talk and plan and—*(He stops as* HEZEKIAH *enters. He draws back stiffly on seeing* JACOB.*)*

HEZEKIAH: I thought yer were down in the barn.

JACOB SLOVAK: I stayed to talk to Myra, but I was just going now. *(He goes out.)*

MYRA: Hello, Hezekiah. How are yer? *(Goes to table.)* Sit down and take off yer things. *(She gathers knives, forks, dishes, etc., folds napkins.)*

HEZEKIAH: I won't take off my things 'cause I've only come for a word. I might as well come out with it, too.

MYRA: Somethin' special?

HEZEKIAH: Wel, yer know pret' near as well as I do—that our Paws wants us ter git married. I kinda wanted it myself until lately.

MYRA: What changed yer mind?

HEZEKIAH: Hearin' talk that you're sort of sweet on that there Jew.

MYRA: What nonsense—Who told yer that?

HEZEKIAH: I heard.

MYRA: The same kind of foolish gossip that's always goin' round in this town. Folks ought ter mind their own business.

HEZEKIAH: I'm glad ter hear that. All the same, Myra, a feller's got ter be careful and not throw himself away.

MYRA: As yer like, Hezekiah—if wantin' ter marry me is throwin' yerself away—

HEZEKIAH: Oh, no offense, Myra. We will probably be gittin' married one of these days—but the same time I believe in weighin' it. *(He rises.)* I'll come again soon now that I know there's nothin' between yer and the Jew. How'd it be if I came for yer next Sunday? We could drive around for a turn. I might even show yer a farm that I have my eye on.

MYRA: All right, Hezekiah—I'll expect yer.

HEZEKIAH: *(Awkwardly)* Yer hain't sore on me, Myra?

MYRA: Why should I be?

HEZEKIAH: *(Shrugs his shoulders.)* Oh, on account of me thinkin' yer would look at that Jew. I oughta know yer wouldn't have.

MYRA: I know yer didn't mean any harm.

HEZEKIAH: That's good—here's my hand. *(They shake hands just as* LOLA *pokes her head in the doorway.)*

LOLA: *(In an irritating voice)* Here comes Jacob back again. *(She draws her head back as* JACOB *enters.* HEZEKIAH *looks at* JACOB, *then turns angrily to* MYRA.*)*

HEZEKIAH: That drive next Sunday is off. I won't come for yer after all. *(He goes out and slams the door.* MYRA *makes a movement as though to go after him, she looks at* JACOB *and hesitates as though torn between them, then she goes to the door and calls after* HEZEKIAH.*)*

MYRA: Hezekiah! Hezekiah! *(She turns back again)* Yer shouldn't have come back!

JACOB SLOVAK: Why not, Myra?

MYRA: Yer know no one knows we see each other like this—not alone.

JACOB SLOVAK: I can never understand why I cannot come and see you—openly, like anyone else. Like Hezekiah, for instance.

MYRA: That's different. We've known each other since we were
children.

JACOB SLOVAK: Yes—but he seems to resent my even talking to
you—like just now—Why shouldn't I talk to you? Why should you
be like this? You always change the minute any one comes around.

MYRA: *(Nervously and irritatedly)* I can't discuss it now—and I wish
yer'd go—

JACOB SLOVAK: *(He rises.)* Certainly—if that's the way you feel.

MYRA: *(Softening, reaches, takes his hand.)* I'm sorry—

JACOB SLOVAK: *(Takes her hand; softly)* Myra—

MYRA: *(Pulling away as though afraid of her own emotion)* Don't—
*(She turns away from him and goes quickly out the kitchen door,
knocking into* KITTY, *who enters. She pauses and looks after*
MYRA. *There is an awkward silence.)*

KITTY: *(Shyly and nervously)* Mr. Slovak, I wanted ter tell yer somethin'.

JACOB SLOVAK: What is it, Kitty?

KITTY: They don't like yer here. I know. I heard them talkin' about
yer before yer came. I listened on purpose ter hear what they
would say about yer.

JACOB SLOVAK: You should never listen to other people's conversation.

KITTY: They don't like yer—I tell yer that, Mr. Slovak.

JACOB SLOVAK: But I have not done anything to them. Why should
they dislike me?

KITTY: Yer are not their kind. It's not fer what yer really are—it's fer
what yer on the outside—that's what counts with them.

JACOB SLOVAK: You wrong them, Kitty. They are pretty good people.

KITTY: *(Shaking her head)* I heard yer talkin' how hard it was fer yer
ter git work. It's like that here—if yer don't belong ter them, they
won't even take yer in. They jest seem ter take yer in while yer can
do things for them. Look at all the things yer have done for them—
but they won't take yer in. There's no use tryin'.

JACOB SLOVAK: I'm sure you are wrong, Kitty.

KITTY: You know my father—he didn't belong here neither.

JACOB SLOVAK: So I heard.

KITTY: Wel, yer see. I know. I jest know yer don't fit neither. Yer
never will. Yer not like these people. I—I am not like them. I gess
it's my father in me—something queer here. *(She puts her hands
to her heart.)* They don't understand me and I don't understand
them. We're strangers. But with yer I feel different, like—*(Her
voice breaks, she drops her head.)*

JACOB SLOVAK: Well . . .

Kitty: I thought if yer were as lonely here as I am; we might be
some use—I might be some use . . . *(She drops her head pathetically.)*
Jacob Slovak: Poor little lonely child—(Kitty *turns and quickly
runs out through the kitchen door.)*
Curtain

Act 2

SCENE 1

The same night in the room of Jacob Slovak *over the grocery store. The
room is simple and bare. Directly upstage there is a door which leads to
the stairway. The stairway can be seen when the door is open. Slightly to
the left is another door which leads into the bedroom. Directly left a fireplace with coal burning in it. An old stuffed arm chair is drawn before the
fire. To the right there is a window with the green shade pulled down. Next
to it against the wall stands an upright piano with an oil lamp on it which
is lighted, and a stool before the piano. In the middle of the room stands a
table with a chair at it. Another lighted lamp is on it, papers, books, ink,
etc. There is also a vase filled with white narcissus. As the curtain rises,*
Jacob Slovak *is alone on the stage. He is reading. After a minute he
throws the book down and sighs. He gets up and walks nervously about.
He throws a log on the fire, lights a cigarette, then throws it away. He goes
to the piano and reads a sheet of music, then he plays one or two notes. He
finally sinks on a chair before the fire with his head in his hands. He should
give the feeling of loneliness and restlessness. After a few minutes the front
door bell rings downstairs. He raises his head and listens in surprise. It
rings again. He rises and goes down to open the door.*
Hezekiah: *(From downstairs and offstage)* I hope I hain't disturbin'
yer. Ken I come up a minute?
Jacob Slovak: *(Offstage)* Certainly—this way. *(They can be heard
mounting the stairs)*
Hezekiah: It's a cold night. Bitin'. *(They enter)* Gosh, it's nice ter
see a fire.
Jacob Slovak: It's not a bad companion when one lives alone.
Hezekiah: *(Awkwardly, after a silence)* I suppose I should apologize
for comin' here uninvited.
Jacob Slovak: It is rather a surprise.
Hezekiah: I hain't got much of an excuse. I came 'cause—wel,
'cause I wanted ter.
Jacob Slovak: It's as good a reason as any other.
Hezekiah: Most likely. Oh, I suppose I could have sent word that I

wanted ter see yer—that I had somethin' ter say—that is, used somethin' like that as an excuse for comin'.

JACOB SLOVAK: Why should you make excuses? What about?

HEZEKIAH: Wel, I didn't come ter say anythin'—at least, not in a way. It's like this—I wanted ter put yer straight about Myra.

JACOB SLOVAK: *(Drawing up stiffly)* Myra—I can't see why we should talk about her.

HEZEKIAH: Oh, I prepared fer yer ter say that—but that's foolish, I jest want ter state a few facts.

JACOB SLOVAK: Really—

HEZEKIAH: Myra and I have knowed each other since we were children.

JACOB SLOVAK: I'm aware of that.

HEZEKIAH: It's always been taken for granted by both our families that we would git married one day.

JACOB SLOVAK: Families sometimes make mistakes.

HEZEKIAH: Not in this case—that's what I came ter say.

JACOB SLOVAK: Then you did come to say something.

HEZEKIAH: Myra and I are goin' ter git married.

JACOB SLOVAK: *(Sharply)* Has Myra said so?

HEZEKIAH: Not exactly—but—it's understood. Most all the folks understand it.

JACOB SLOVAK: And why have you come to say this to me?

HEZEKIAH: Jest thought it might be a good idea, so yer wouldn't git notions.

JACOB SLOVAK: Notions?

HEZEKIAH: Yep. Think it over—Yer'll see what I mean I guess.

JACOB SLOVAK: When I wish any information about Myra, Mr. Brent, I'll ask her and not take it from you or anyone else.

HEZEKIAH: Oh, if yer want ter take it that way—think it over jest the same—it may save yer—well, some trouble maybe—and perhaps some unpleasantness.

JACOB SLOVAK: *(Sarcastically)* Thank you for your interest, Mr. Brent.

(He goes to the door and opens it. He stands by the door, holding the knob, without speaking. HEZEKIAH *shrugs his shoulders and goes out. His departing footsteps can be heard, then the slamming of the door downstairs.* JACOB *picks up a book, then flings it down again on the table. He goes to the window, pulls up the shade and stands with his hands behind his back and his brow to the window pane. Suddenly he draws back, shades his eyes and peers out of the window. He opens the window and leans out.)*

JACOB SLOVAK: Myra—Myra, is that you?

MYRA: *(From outside)* Let me in, Jacob—quick. The door down here is open—I'll come up. *(He slams down the window and runs toward the door. He opens it and* MYRA *rushes into the room.)*

JACOB SLOVAK: How on earth did you get here?

MYRA: I'll explain.

JACOB SLOVAK: *(He closes the door, leaning against it and looking at* MYRA.*)* Hezekiah was just here.

MYRA: I know. I saw him come in and I have been hidin' until he left. What did he come fer?

JACOB SLOVAK: What did *you* come for?

MYRA: *(Hesitating and trying to find an excuse)* I—I wanted ter go for a walk—then—then I thought I'd walk this way ter see if yer light was on. As I came along I saw Hezekiah come in—he didn't see me—I waited until he left so as ter see what he wanted.

JACOB SLOVAK: It's odd that neither of you have ever come to see me before, and that you should have both picked the same night. *(He moves to the table and fingers a book without looking at* MYRA.*)*

MYRA: I've walked many times past here—I've never quite dared to come in before.

JACOB SLOVAK: *(A silence before* JACOB *speaks. Dropping the book and facing* MYRA*)* You shouldn't have come—

MYRA: *(*MYRA *turns to the fireplace, holding out her hands and warming them before she answers.)* You're not very polite.

JACOB SLOVAK: You came because you were concerned with Hezekiah—

MYRA: *(Turning quickly)* I don't even know what he come for—What did he come for?

JACOB SLOVAK: To tell me that you and he were going to marry—to warn me—

MYRA: Do you believe that?

JACOB SLOVAK: I don't know. If we are five minutes alone, you are always worrying what someone is going to think about it—then in comes Hezekiah and tells me you are going to *marry* him.

MYRA: He had no right ter! He has asked me and has spoken ter me about it—it's always ben understood since we were children.

JACOB SLOVAK: *(Breaking in)* It seems to me I've heard enough of that!

MYRA: I wanted ter tell yer that I was sorry about this afternoon— wantin' yer ter leave and—and pullin' away from yer, when yer touched me. I don't suppose there is much use of tellin' yer anythin' now.

JACOB SLOVAK: I'm sorry if I appear—

MYRA: *(Interrupting)* Rude.

JACOB SLOVAK: I wasn't going to say rude. Inhospitable—

MYRA: *(Breaking in)* They're much the same thing—*(A silence)* I'm sorry I came. *(She moves toward the door.)* It wasn't easy neither. *(She puts her hand on the door knob.)* Comin' here, I mean—but it doesn't matter—

JACOB SLOVAK: *(As* MYRA *starts to open the door)* Myra—*(*MYRA *pauses.)*

MYRA: What?

JACOB SLOVAK: Eh—Don't go—please stay a few minutes—

MYRA: But yer said I shouldn't have come—

JACOB SLOVAK: Wait a minute.

MYRA: Well, what is it?

JACOB SLOVAK: Just talk to me for a while . . . *(Quickly)* I want to show you those snapshots of Poland. I'll get them for you. They are in here somewhere—I think. *(He disappears into the room.* MYRA *goes to the door and looks in.)*

MYRA: Whose picture is that?

JACOB SLOVAK: *(*JACOB *reappears)* My mother's. Did I ever speak to you about her?

MYRA: Yes, once. Once, when I first met yer.

JACOB SLOVAK: Oh, yes, I remember. It was the first day I saw you. You came to the grocer shop. I heard you say "two pounds of tea, please." Your voice—it made me turn, then when I looked at you there was a funny little light jumping in the window which caught your hair. Like the light through the trees today. Then—some strange way I talked to you. I said you looked like my mother. That in itself you must have thought funny.

MYRA: I did in a way, but yer said it in such a strange way—so intense—although it didn't seem as funny then as it might now—tellin' about it.

JACOB SLOVAK: But you did, Myra. You did look like her. Something about you that made you stand out from other women, the way she did. You look like her now. Just a minute ago you reminded me of her—very strongly. Turn your face—like that—in profile. *(*MYRA *turns.)* It's striking—Can you see it yourself?

MYRA: She's beautiful. I can't see that I look like her.

JACOB SLOVAK: You have the quality of beauty she had.

MYRA: Where is she now?

JACOB SLOVAK: Dead. *(He breaks off. There is a silence.)*

MYRA: *(Awkwardly)* Now I *must* go—*(Goes up to door.)*

JACOB SLOVAK: I—I didn't mean to seem inhospitable. *(He walks about restlessly then he turns again.)* Take off your hat and coat— oh—just for ten minutes.

MYRA: *(Taking off her hat only and going toward the fire. She remains standing.)* I'll stay jest a few minutes ter git warm. I got awful cold comin' across the meadow. *(A silence)* You haven't asked me ter sit down—

JACOB SLOVAK: *(Pushing the chair toward the fire)* Do—of course— sit down. *(He walks away from her again across the room.)* You should take your coat off—you'll catch cold when you go out.

MYRA: Perhaps yer're right. *(She takes her coat off, struggling a little to get it off. Jacob does not help her. She rises and places her hat and coat on the piano.)* Yer're *not* really very polite—usually a woman is helped when takin' her coat off—

JACOB SLOVAK: *(Without moving or making an explanation)* I'm sorry—*(A pause)*

MYRA: *(Sitting in chair at fireplace, looking about)* It's funny yer havin' these old rooms. I haven't ben in them since I was a kid. I used ter play up here with some other kids, but I had forgotten what they was like. I had imagined them different. It's funny how things are so often different than we picture them. I wonder if they are always different?

JACOB SLOVAK: Do you find it upsetting when they are? For me it is always upsetting. I imagine the way someone is going to look— just where they are going to sit or stand—what they will say—and then when it turns out differently, I am paralyzed. Mentally suspended in air—I can't get back again where I was.

MYRA: Those things are funny, aren't they? *(Embarrassed and looking about the room)*

JACOB SLOVAK: You see, I live very simply. I'm afraid it's disappointed you. If I had known you would ever come here—I would have had it different.

MYRA: What would yer have done?

JACOB SLOVAK: Many things. I would have picked stars and cut little pieces off the moon—and tacked them, and tacked them all around. Such a funny word "tacked." But you see, I don't really need anything else in my rooms when you come—

MYRA: I hope no one gits wind that I am here.

JACOB SLOVAK: They will have to break down my door to know that!

MYRA: I suppose it was wrong of me ter come here, still—still all my life I have never done anythin' I shouldn't do. I've done it in here. *(She touches her brow.)* In my brain.

JACOB SLOVAK: You can't expect me to consider your visit a crime— That wouldn't be much of a compliment to me.

MYRA: I wish sometimes I could tell yer what and how I really feel about things.

JACOB SLOVAK: Why can't you?

MYRA: It's hard ter put feelin's inter words—they turn out different when they git inter words—Words don't seem ter say what yer actually mean.

JACOB SLOVAK: I KNOW.

MYRA: I don't know if yer do. Yer see, yer're different. Yer've had a chance ter see life—know life—yer have never been closed in. I wish—I wish I could make yer understand that difference between us.

JACOB SLOVAK: I'm beginning to think it's this town that makes the difference between us—that gets you thinking one way—while I think another.

MYRA: Yet yer told me yer couldn't git a job anywhere except this town—Yer shouldn't be ungrateful—

JACOB SLOVAK: Ah—here comes that hideous word again. Job! Job! As though there was nothing else in the world. No love—no beauty—only "jobs," "jobs," and making money. *(Sighing)* This country—

MYRA: Yer came inter this country of yer own accord—

JACOB SLOVAK: Do you regret my coming?

MYRA: I didn't say so.

(Another long silence; MYRA *turns her face away and gazes into the fire.* JACOB *turns and looks at her. She moves uneasily and is conscious of his look although she pretends not to be. There is an intensity and poignant tension in the silence.)*

JACOB SLOVAK: Why did you really come here tonight? I didn't quite believe what you told me.

MYRA: *(Evading)* Did you have any reason not ter?

JACOB SLOVAK: No—

MYRA: *(Still without turning)* Well—I didn't tell yer the truth—*(A silence)*

JACOB SLOVAK: What *is* the truth?

MYRA: *(Emotionally but trying to speak coldly)* I came—ah—because —because I couldn't keep away—I kept hearin' yer voice. *(She tries to speak in matter of fact tone.)* I got thinkin' about yer alone here in yer room—lonely—the way yer said yer was terday—*(A silence.* MYRA *tries to break it by moving and poking the fire.)*

JACOB SLOVAK: You say you came here tonight because you couldn't keep away—how am I to really take that?

MYRA: *(Rising)* Whichever way yer take it, won't make it right, although yer have a way of puttin' things that makes them seem the way yer want them.

JACOB SLOVAK: I wish that were true.

MYRA: Why?

JACOB SLOVAK: Because if it were, I would make everything you say seem—as if you were saying—oh, something nice to me—

MYRA: (MYRA *laughs and goes to the window. She stands with her back to the room and looking out. She speaks hurriedly as though she were trying to control emotion.)* When I am with yer I believe things I hadn't oughter believe or even listen ter. I wouldn't go ter any other man like this, because no other man in this town could make me think the way yer do. With yer I can come here and yer don't think any the less of me. If I went ter any other man they would think I was wicked or somethin'. Bad, like the women the minister preaches against.

JACOB SLOVAK: You bad! Never have you done a wicked thing in all your life, you said that yourself.

MYRA: *(Turning)* That's the difference between us. The things yer think are bad and the things I think are bad. That's where yer mix me up.

JACOB SLOVAK: Why do you think it bad to come here?

MYRA: Oh, it's hard ter explain. Yer see, yer have probably always done everythin' yer wanted ter—nothin' may have seemed wrong. Yer have never gone ter church if yer didn't want ter, never had ter smirk and obey people yer hated; never had ter listen ter the bible every day and hear a long line of things that might offend the Lord. Comin' here and speakin' ter yer like this is the first wrong thing I have ever done. If the minister knew of it he would call me "bad." Maybe I am—I don't know—I don't suppose it really matters what the minister says—but it's somethin' in yer words— they're like things I've thought about at night—that most people probably would think were wrong. Before I met yer I didn't feel cheated—I thought things were as they should be—Now I don't know.

JACOB SLOVAK: Know what?

MYRA: All the things yer say. They may be wrong ter listen ter—

JACOB SLOVAK: Can love ever be wrong?

MYRA: The minister is forever preaching sermons ter beware of a man who speaks beautiful words. He said that a man who spoke ter a woman of love and passion was evil and should be shunned.

JACOB SLOVAK: Do I seem evil?

MYRA: Yer don't think love is wicked?

JACOB SLOVAK: I think there is nothing else that really matters in the world—anyone who says differently is not telling the truth—or else they are deliberately trying to see it differently.

MYRA: Yer don't think love makin' is wicked?

JACOB SLOVAK: Do you think praying is wicked?

MYRA: Of course not!

JACOB SLOVAK: The purest prayer is two people passionately in love with each other.

MYRA: *(Laughingly)* If they heard yer talkin' in the church they would say yer were upsettin' the Ten Commandments.

JACOB SLOVAK: Possibly. *(Sinks on piano stool.)*

MYRA: (MYRA *walks to the bedroom door and looks in. Then she turns. She speaks as though this thought had been in the back of her mind since she first looked into the bedroom, only now she expressed it. Pause. Pensively)* I didn't know father had put that bed in there fer yer—I used ter sleep in that bed.

JACOB SLOVAK: *(In a low voice)* You've slept in *that* bed—

MYRA: *(Awkwardly)* Yes—many—times—

(Goes away from the door to the chair by the fireplace. A long silence. Myra looks down. Jacob moves nervously as though to think of something with which to break the tense feeling that surges between them.)

JACOB SLOVAK: I'll show you the snapshots—they *must* be here. *(He rushes to the drawer of the table. Nervously scatters things about and brings forth some photographs.)* See, this is my old house. You can see it's different from an American one. Look at the roof.

(He holds it out to her then quickly withdraws his hand for fear she will see it trembling. He lays the snapshot on the table. MYRA walks over and looks at it, she speaks as though her mind were not on it.)

MYRA: *(Leaning close, then she realizes it and draws away.)* Lovely— lovely—it's a pretty house.

(She drops the snapshot on the table. From this moment on, until JACOB plays the piano, their voices rise until they are unconsciously almost shouting at each other. The emotional tension becomes so great from the strain of hiding their real feelings, that they give way to anger, in which Jacob finally loses all control in a sweeping outburst and rushes to the piano.)

JACOB SLOVAK: *(Turning on Myra)* You're not very interested in my home—

MYRA: What do yer expect me ter say about it?

JACOB SLOVAK: I at least expect you to pretend to be interested out of politeness.

MYRA: Perhaps I'm tired of bein' polite!

JACOB SLOVAK: Oh, yes—maybe Hezekiah—

MYRA: *Yer* got no room ter talk of politeness considerin' the way yer received me this evenin'—

JACOB SLOVAK: You came of your own accord—

MYRA: Oh, now yer're goin' ter throw *that* in my face!

JACOB SLOVAK: No—I'm not. Why do you force me to say things I don't mean? *(In violent outburst)* Why *did* you come? Just to torment me? Perhaps our ideas of politeness are *not* the same. I never claimed they were. You yourself said I was different than anyone in your town—maybe that's why I don't understand you—nor understand why you *really* came here tonight. It's maybe my lack of understanding of you and your kind and your town, that gives me this terrible loneliness—good God! Without my music, I would have gone out of my mind!

(He turns and sinks upon the piano stool, his head and arms crashing down upon the keys. The sound of the struck notes ring out in discordant tone, then gradually die away. MYRA stands in the middle of the room with her hands clenched and her eyes closed. There is a devastating and overpoweringly passionate silence. Then JACOB raises his head and speaks without turning or looking at MYRA. His voice is suppressed but full of uncontrolled emotion. Sharply)

JACOB SLOVAK: Go home, Myra, I can't stand having you here any longer—you're driving me mad—go home—

(MYRA opens her eyes, then goes slowly toward the piano. As she takes her hat off the piano she brushes against JACOB's shoulder. For an instant he doesn't move, then he suddenly jumps up, seizes MYRA's arms.)

JACOB SLOVAK: Myra—*(MYRA drops her head and closes her eyes again.)* Look at me, Myra—You haven't looked at me all night—I haven't dared look at you—Open your eyes—*(MYRA lifts her head, she opens her eyes for a second. They look at each other, then MYRA closes her eyes again.)*

MYRA: *(So emotionally that it is almost inaudible.)* I can't—

JACOB SLOVAK: *(He seizes her in his arms.)* I love you—say you love me—

MYRA: I do! I do! *(They kiss passionately on the lips.)*

The curtain is lowered.

SCENE 2

Same as before, two hours later, as the curtain rises MYRA *and* JACOB *are sitting before the fire.* JACOB *is holding* MYRA *in his arms. The room is in darkness, except for the flickering flames, which have almost died down. There is a silence before* JACOB *speaks.*

JACOB SLOVAK: I'm so happy that if I weren't holding you close like this I'd think it all a crazy madness of mine—not real. It's so warm and intimate having you here like this—as if we were married.

MYRA: *(Moving away from him)* Will yer light the lamp, Jacob?

JACOB SLOVAK: *(Rising)* Yes. *(He lights the lamp, then returns to* MYRA.) Myra, when will you marry me?

MYRA: I don't know yet—*(The door bell rings downstairs.)* *(Frightened)* Who can that be?

JACOB SLOVAK: I can't imagine. *(The bell rings again.)*

MYRA: *(In a panic)* Don't answer! Don't answer!

JACOB SLOVAK: *(With his finger to his lips)* Don't let them hear two voices, whoever they are.

MYRA: My God, what shall I do?

JACOB SLOVAK: Sh! They may go away. *(The bell rings long and more violently.* JACOB *motions again to* MYRA *to keep quiet, then he goes to the window.* MYRA *stands in a state of agitation and starts fixing her hair.* JACOB *opens the window and looks out.)* *(Calling out)* Who is there? *(REV. EZRA HALE's voice answers.)*

REV. EZRA HALE: It's I, Mr. Slovak. I want to speak to you a minute. *(*MYRA *looks desperately terrified.* JACOB *makes a sign to her to be quiet.)*

JACOB SLOVAK: Oh, Rev. Hale, I make you my apologies. I am in the midst of work. Could I not see you tomorrow?

REV. EZRA HALE: It will only take a minute. I have some other visitors with me, too.

JACOB SLOVAK: I will come down.

REV. EZRA HALE: No—we will come up, I beg, Mr. Slovak. You mustn't light up the store at this hour of night and it's too cold out here.

JACOB SLOVAK: I will come down and open the door. *(He draws his head in and closes window. Still holding his finger to his lips)* Your father is down there, too.

MYRA: *(Frantically)* They know I'm here! They've come fer me.

JACOB SLOVAK: Don't worry. What difference does it make? I'll speak to your father now. I'll tell him we are going to marry.

MYRA: *(Terrified)* No—no—Jacob—promise me—not now. I beg of yer. *(Wringing her hands)* I beg of yer!

JACOB SLOVAK: All right—all right—I promise. Don't lose your head, Myra. Go in there and don't move. I will make rid of them as quickly as I can.

MYRA: Tell them yer can't see them.

JACOB SLOVAK: No—no—they would think it strange. Go quickly! *(He rushes downstairs. Unbolting of the door can be heard. MYRA pauses a second, then as voices can be heard she seizes her hat and coat and rushes into the bedroom, closing the door.)*

EZRA HALE: *(Downstairs)* A mighty cold night, Mr. Slovak.

JACOB SLOVAK: Oh, it's you, Mr. Flint, and you, too, Mr. Brent— This is indeed an honor—

EZRA HALE: I'm sorry to disturb you—but only for a minute. May we go upstairs?

JACOB SLOVAK: Certainly. This way. *(They can all be heard mounting the stairs. JACOB enters. EZRA HALE, JOSIAH FLINT, and THEOPHILUS BRENT follow.)*

EZRA HALE: *(Goes to fire to warm himself.)* Ah, plenty of good cheer here, Mr. Slovak. And a piano—bless me, a piano?

JACOB SLOVAK: Yes, Rev. Hale. I was—eh—just working on some music, that is why I might seem rude and in a hurry. What can I do for you? I trust no one is in trouble.

EZRA HALE: Only slightly, Mr. Slovak. *(He goes to the fire and stands before it. MR. FLINT moves uneasily about. THEOPHILUS BRENT rubs his hands and warms them.)*

JACOB SLOVAK: Something I can do?

EZRA HALE: I hope in my coming here that you will regard me in the light of a friend. I wish that I might speak quite frankly to you.

JACOB SLOVAK: If the matter needs frankness—

JOSIAH FLINT: *(Casting a look at THEOPHILUS BRENT and interrupting)* I think we needn't go inter a lot of explanations, Ezra. It's late and there's no sense wastin' everybody's time.

EZRA HALE: I was going to say men should be judged by the manner in which they receive tidings—be they good or bad.

JACOB SLOVAK: *(Breaking impatiently)* Yes—yes, but what have you to tell me?

EZRA HALE: *(He clears his throat and speaks nervously.)* This is a queer little town, Mr. Slovak. I felt it myself many years ago when I first came here—that is why, I think, I can sympathize so much with your case. If I had not had the calling of the Lord, I would have left long ago. Now, it's this way. In spite of the somewhat— eh—strained—yes, that's the word "strained"—in spite of the somewhat strained affair of the church which we had to face together, I like you, Mr. Slovak, and I trust my advice to you will not be taken amiss.

JACOB SLOVAK: Advice?

EZRA HALE: Precisely. Advice. Why don't you leave this town? You are intelligent—very gifted—why not go some place where you have more scope for your talents? What can there be in a town like this for you? What makes you stay here? What holds you?

JACOB SLOVAK: *(Looking toward the bedroom)* I am still at a loss what this is all about.

THEOPHILUS BRENT: If yer'll allow me, Ezra, I think I might state the facts a little clearer.

JACOB SLOVAK: I am a little bewildered, but waiting, gentlemen.

THEOPHILUS BRENT: There are prejudices in this town yer will never be able ter overcome. Go away from here, Mr. Slovak.

JACOB SLOVAK: Prejudices? What sort of prejudices?

THEOPHILUS BRENT: Well, really, Mr. Slovak—fer a sharp man—

JACOB SLOVAK: Because I'm a Jew! You mean because I'm a Jew?

JOSIAH FLINT: I'm sorry yer force us ter say so.

JACOB SLOVAK: *(As though he had been struck in the face)* That is why there is feeling against me—that is why—*(He suddenly looks toward the bedroom.)*

EZRA HALE: Don't take it deeply. You have everything in your favor to make a career somewhere else—

JACOB SLOVAK: And this from you, Ezra Hale—from what you call a minister of God. A minister of God—who I believe is supposed to preach all men are equal in the eyes of the Lord.

EZRA HALE: In the eyes of the Lord, Mr. Slovak—yes. Unfortunately, we are men—

JACOB SLOVAK: You call yourselves men. And you, Josiah Flint! You have used me to make your money. You didn't mind my being a Jew *then,* and now that I have built up your store and you have no longer need of me—you ask me to leave your town.

THEOPHILUS BRENT: Fer yer own sake—yer can gain nothin' by remainin'.

JOSIAH FLINT: Oh, we hain't sayin' we hain't grateful ter yer fer all yer've done—we prove that by comin' here ter-night—friendly like—we might have sent yer a letter jest sayin' "On yer way, Mr. Slovak."

EZRA HALE: Yes—this way we part friends—just dropped in with a bit of advice—that's all.

JOSIAH FLINT: And I'm sorry ter say—after termorrow these rooms

are rented ter a new clerk—Oh, there's no feelin', Mr. Slovak—he's
an old, old friend of mine. Thought of gittin' him a long time
before I knew yer.

JACOB SLOVAK: Gentlemen—I think there is nothing more to
be said.

THEOPHILUS BRENT: *(A little shamefaced)* Wel, we had better push
on—nothin' really against *yer* personally, Mr. Slovak—yer're a fine
man—it's a pity—

JACOB SLOVAK: *(Breaking in)* That I am a Jew, Mr. Brent.

THEOPHILUS BRENT: Wel—yes—it would be different otherwise—

EZRA HALE: I guess we'll say good night.

THEOPHILUS BRENT: Come on, Josiah. Let's clear out.

EZRA HALE: We can let ourselves out all right—don't come down,
Mr. Slovak. Good night, Mr. Slovak.

(He offers his hand, which JACOB *ignores, he turns and quickly goes out,
followed by* THEOPHILUS BRENT *and* JOSIAH FLINT, *who all file out
silently. Their footsteps die away and the door can be heard closing.* JACOB
stands dazed as MYRA *comes out with her hat and coat on.)*

MYRA: *(Again frantically and in a panic)* I must get home! I must get
home!

JACOB SLOVAK: *(Fiercely)* So that's what they think of me. They can
use me to make music in their church of Christ. Christ! What has
He to do with these kind of Christians? I can administer to them,
build up their libraries, their stores, their town and then—then—
"On your way, Mr. Slovak."

MYRA: It don't matter, Jacob—

JACOB SLOVAK: *(Looking at* MYRA *and softening)* No—it doesn't
matter—I have you. That's all that matters. We'll go away, Myra. I
will make a success for you somewhere else. Will you leave with
me tomorrow, Myra? We can get married somewhere else.

MYRA: Jacob—Jacob—

JACOB SLOVAK: Myra—you do love me?

MYRA: Yer know I do—

JACOB SLOVAK: Then why can't I go to your father and tell him that
I love you—that you love me—it may alter things when he knows
that.

MYRA: *(Terrified)* No, Jacob—Yer mustn't tell him—not that.

JACOB SLOVAK: If your father knows we are going to marry, he will
see it differently. Let me go to him tonight—now. You should have
let me tell him here.

MYRA: Oh, no—Jacob—no!

JACOB SLOVAK: Why not? *(With terror in his voice)* Why not? Myra?

MYRA: Can't yer see after what they told yer that would only make it worse?

JACOB SLOVAK: Then we'll have to run away together somewhere else where they look at things differently. Can't you see that, Myra? Can't you see? Do you think I would have let you give yourself to me? Do you think I would have even touched you if I had not thought we were going to marry? I loved you, Myra, and you said you loved me—didn't you?

MYRA: Yes—yes, I loved yer—I love yer now, Jacob. I will love yer always—always—always—

JACOB SLOVAK: Then why waste time? If I go to your father tonight there will be just that much time saved.

MYRA: *(Despairingly)* Yer make it so hard.

JACOB SLOVAK: Hard?

MYRA: *(Emotionally)* I can't marry you, Jacob.

JACOB SLOVAK: Not marry me—you're mad, Myra!

MYRA: *(Shaking her head and in low voice)* I can't—

JACOB SLOVAK: (JACOB *seizes her wrist.*) You don't know what you are saying—you're talking nonsense—otherwise why should you have given yourself to me? If you weren't going to marry me, what right had you to give yourself to me?

MYRA: Because I loved yer—and—and—because—I gess because I thought so much about these things. I'd like ter explain ter yer— but yer see yer're a man—a man can't understand about a woman —not really, because he doesn't know what she thinks about. I told yer I couldn't help comin' here—it's like that, I couldn't help this neither. Yer see with a woman it's different—she's got ter keep things all in here, *(She touches her brow)* tormentin' and tormentin' her. I tried ter explain ter yer—I'll try now. It started long ago. I used ter lay in bed night after night and think about this—my body hot. The branches of the trees knockin' against the winder— I'd think it's a man—a man knockin' there—tryin' ter git in. It never was a special man. I'd try ter put a face on his body, but no face I knew was right. I'd see him climin' through the winder and comin' toward me—I'd throw the covers off—and, and clutch my pillow and cry. And then yer came, and my man's body got a face—yer face. It got yer face because I loved yer—from the very first time I saw yer. After that I used ter think it was yer voice in the wind callin' me—I used to think it was yer step under my winder in the rustle of the leaves. And then I'd see yer every day— alive—real—and I'd know that what I thought at night was jest made up—my dreams. So somehow I jest had ter have yer—ter make it true. Yer real body against mine. I had ter. I had ter. I knew there'd be no ugliness—because yer're so good. But you couldn't understand, unless I was married ter yer. Marry . . . Don't yer see there couldn't be marriage between yer and me? But I love yer so—I had ter have yer or go crazy—that's all.

JACOB SLOVAK: *(Brokenly)* Myra—

MYRA: Oh, it's awful hard ter explain. It's all so mixed up. Waitin' like that and never seein' anyone I liked and then yer comin'—and lovin' yer—but knowin' we couldn't marry. There's somethin' wrong somewhere.

JACOB SLOVAK: There's nothing wrong, Myra—not really, if you'll just let yourself see straight. What you've said just now proves it. In spite of those longings—of what you felt, you couldn't give yourself to anyone but me—that shows you love me.

MYRA: I said I loved yer.

JACOB SLOVAK: What's wrong is with this town—that's why you must come away with me.

MYRA: But, Jacob, how can I go away with yer? Yer haven't any job— Yer haven't any money.

JACOB SLOVAK: I'll get work—you'll see. Just come with me and you'll see.

MYRA: It wasn't so easy fer yer before—

JACOB SLOVAK: It will be now. Somehow it's *got* to be.

MYRA: It'ud take time.

JACOB SLOVAK: *(Enthusiastically)* Yes, I know. But we will fight together. We will have each other. With you by my side I feel as though I could accomplish anything.

MYRA: Oh, Jacob—

JACOB SLOVAK: I know we will win, Myra! Come away and marry me and you will see. We *will* win. You can't love the way we love and not win!

MYRA: But while yer are lookin' fer a job, what are we goin' ter live on? Neither of us have a cent.

JACOB SLOVAK: *(Downcast)* Why—I hadn't thought of that. We couldn't live on so little at first.

MYRA: Little—yer mean nothin'.

JACOB SLOVAK: All right, Myra. I'll tell you what. You stay here until I can find work—and I will find it and then I'll come back for you. Only promise that you will wait. You will wait, Myra?

MYRA: Oh, Jacob—let's not talk about this any more now—I'm so tired—

JACOB SLOVAK: *(Going to* MYRA*)* Myra—don't go like this. You *can't* go like this.

MYRA: *(Weakening)* We'll talk about it tomorrow.

JACOB SLOVAK: I won't be here tomorrow.

MYRA: Don't beg me any more—not ternight—I'll come in the mornin'. *(She starts to move.)*

JACOB SLOVAK: *(Holding her)* No—

MYRA: I *must* go—

JACOB SLOVAK: Say first you'll marry me—you love me—

MYRA: Let me go!

JACOB SLOVAK: I'll never give you up—never!

MYRA: *(Trying to drag away from him)* I can't stand any more! *(Hysterically)* I *must* go home!

JACOB SLOVAK: *(Still holding her)* Myra—Can you forget tonight?

MYRA: *(Frantically and crying)* Jacob—*(For a second she flings her arms around him and with all the passion of her nature she desperately holds him to her. Then she pushes him violently away.)* Let me go! Let me go! *(She rushes out, her footsteps can be heard running downstairs.)*

JACOB SLOVAK: *(*JACOB *hesitates a second, then he runs after her but stops as he hears the door slamming downstairs. He turns and goes rapidly to the window he opens it and calls)* I'll come back for you— I'll come back! *(He goes into the bedroom and comes out with a suitcase. He begins putting his music into it.)*

Curtain

Act 3

Same as act 1 three months later in the Spring. As the curtain rises KITTY *is sitting near the window with a bowl on her lap and peeling potatoes into it. After a minute* MYRA *comes in from outside. She walks slowly and is reading a letter as she enters. She seems paler, unconsciously projects a different attitude as though life had changed her and she had suddenly grown up. Her face looks more thoughtful, more brooding, although it also looks more beautiful, as though some suffering had crept into it and given her a kind of poignant beauty. She advances and sits at the table with her back to* KITTY, *still reading. During the whole act the front door is left open, showing budding trees and signs of spring outside, until the very last minute of the play.*

KITTY: Myra—

MYRA: *(*MYRA *jumping and then holding her hand to her heart)* Good gracious, Kitty—yer scared me! Never do that again.

KITTY: I didn't mean ter scare yer—I thought yer knew I was here.

MYRA: *(Continuing to read again and absent mindedly)* Nope—*(A silence. KITTY continues to peel potatoes and MYRA to read.)*

KITTY: Yer're nervous—hain't yer, Myra?

MYRA: *(Folding her letter and putting it in the envelope)* Nervous? Maybe—I hadn't thought much about it. *(A pause, then quickly)* But don't go round airin' I'm nervous.

KITTY: I wasn't goin' ter say nothin' about it. I jest noticed it myself— that's all—Kinda jumpy like yer seem—as though yer had somethin' on yer mind.

MYRA: Well—I haven't. Never ben more carefree. *(KITTY looks at her, then goes on peeling. Another silence.)*

KITTY: Is that another letter from Jacob?

MYRA: Why have yer got the idea that I'm gittin' letters from Jacob?

KITTY: I seen them with my own eyes when I've ben down ter the post office ter git the mail.

MYRA: And how would yer know they was from him? Yer've never seen his writin' have yer?

KITTY: No. But I jest knew those letters was from him. I don't know how—I jest kinda knew.

MYRA: Well, this isn't. *(She flings the letter on the table.)* Yer can see yerself. It's from Milly over ter Jerrytown. She's thankin' me fer the quilt I made her. She says it looks somethin' grand on her bed. *(Another silence. MYRA unconsciously puts her hand to her brow as though from spiritual weariness. She sighs.)*

KITTY: *(Rising. She stands a second back of MYRA then timidly and gently touches her on the shoulder.)* Why don't yer talk ter me, Myra? Maybe I could help—jest a little. I can see somethin's wrong.

MYRA: *(Straightening up and stiffening slightly.)* Nothin's wrong.

KITTY: *(Drawing her hand back)* Jacob's ben gone three months. Yer hain't ben the same since he left.

MYRA: *(Fiercely)* It hasn't got nothin' ter do with Jacob!

KITTY: Then there *is* somethin wrong—

MYRA: Nothin'—nothin' wrong, I tell yer!

KITTY: *(Unconvinced)* Myra—why don't yer go away with Jacob?

MYRA: *(Leaping to her feet. She walks impatiently across the room, then turns and faces KITTY.)* Don't talk nonsense. Yer don't know what yer're sayin'.

KITTY: I only know Jacob loves yer and yer loves him. Yer should have ben away with him all these three months past. *(MYRA walks back to the chair and sits down again by the table. She clenches her hand and brings it violently down on the table.)*

MYRA: I refuse ter talk about somethin' that don't exist!

(KITTY *hesitates and then with a childlike movement she drops on her knees before* MYRA. *She puts her arms around* MYRA *and her head against her heart as though this gesture would protect* MYRA *from pain.* MYRA *does not move, still holding herself rigidly. Then gradually she relaxes, her face softens, she opens her clenched hand and slowly she moves it toward* KITTY*'s head until it rests on her hair. She strokes* KITTY*'s hair in silence before she speaks.*)

MYRA: It hain't as easy as yer think—

KITTY: *(Straightening up but still kneeling)* But what kept yer from goin' with him? Jacob's so wonderful!

MYRA: I jest *couldn't* go with him.

KITTY: And yer let him go when he loved yer so.

MYRA: Yer couldn't understand neither—Yer're a wop, that's different than my blood, too.

KITTY: But what has that got ter do with love? What has blood got ter do with love?

MYRA: I don't know. I didn't know it had till the other day. Till the other day I thought I couldn't go away with Jacob because no one here would stand fer it—because it would break Maw and Paw's heart. Then I thought I couldn't go because Jacob didn't have a job and I was afraid of facin' poverty with him. Then all of a sudden like—I knew it wasn't none of those things.

KITTY: What was it?

MYRA: I was up alone in the cemetery—I went there somehow ter find peace. The air was fresh and the smell of the earth was strong and good. I don't know why but I knelt down and put my face and lips to the earth and I felt nice and warm-like, as though I was kissin' and touchin' somethin' that belonged ter me. Then I looked up and I saw I was kneelin' on my great grandfather's grave. Then suddenly I knew that him and the earth were the same thing—there wasn't any difference—there never had been any difference—there never would be any difference. That him and his father and his children had worked and toiled in the earth here, and in the end they had come ter lay themselves down in it and become part of it, too. And I knew it was waitin' fer me and my children. Then all of a sudden I felt some life stirrin' in me—somethin' rushin' through me, and I knew it was my blood. *My* blood. Like the blood of all those people of mine layin' there. And I knew it was blood and soil that counts. And I knew that was why I couldn't go away with Jacob. Because his blood is different than mine and his blood wouldn't go in this soil.

KITTY: But when yer have a chance ter marry someone that loves yer

the way Jacob does—someone wonderful like Jacob—a chance ter
go away and see things—somethin' new—

MYRA: *(Shaking her head)* I read in the paper once about a man who
had ben in prison all his life. When his release came he wanted ter
but he couldn't leave his cell. That's where the tormentin' and suf-
ferin' comes in—day and night, night and day—wantin' ter git
away but jest not bein' able ter, yer own self.

KITTY: But if it's somethin' yer really want ter do.

MYRA: When I was a kid I used ter want ter join the circus.
They used ter come and open up right outside the town, and
whenever I could git away I used ter hang around all day and till
they closed at night. I loved the smell and seein' the acrobats and
the white horses with silver bells and white harness, and I loved
the music. But one day the woman that ran the circus asked me if
I wanted ter go away with them—and I was scared and I ran home
and never went back no more. I dreamed of goin', but I couldn't
'cause they was different than me. Somethin' in their blood, too—
different and strange like Jacob.

KITTY: I can't understand—

MYRA: Jacob don't neither. That's because he's him, and yer're yer,
and like him. Different blood than me. But I'm me and I'm jest
not like neither of yer. *(MRS. FLINT enters from the kitchen.)*

MRS. FLINT: *(To KITTY)* So that's where yer are—No wonder
I've ben waitin' this half hour fer them potatoes. *(KITTY rises
quickly and picks up the bowl of potatoes and goes into the kitchen.)*
Where's that child Lola?

MYRA: Don't know—haven't seen her. *(MRS. FLINT goes to the door
and looks out. MYRA picks up the letter on the table and goes into
the kitchen.)*

MRS. FLINT: *(Calling)* Hey there, Lola. Stop that swingin' so high.
How many times have I got ter speak ter yer about that swing?
(No answer) Hey, Lola!

LOLA: *(Offstage)* Yes—

MRS. Flint: Git down off there and go see if Mr. Brent is comin'
down the road.

LOLA: *(Still offstage)* In a minute, Maw—

MRS. FLINT: Yer hurry—I want ter know when he's comin'. I don't
want my cake ter burn but I got ter fix myself up afore he comes.

LOLA: All right, Maw—soon as this swing stops swingin'. *(HEZE-
KIAH and THEOPHILUS BRENT enter. As they get in doorway)*

LOLA: *(Offstage)* Maw's fixin' up but she'll be there in a minute.

THEOPHILUS BRENT: All right, Lola. *(They enter.)* There's nothin' that'll make me so glad as yer askin' Josiah fer Myra terday. Myra's a swell girl.

HEZEKIAH: I know that.

THEOPHILUS BRENT: If I was yer age I'd wish ter be marryin' her myself.

HEZEKIAH: Yes, but—

THEOPHILUS BRENT: *(Jumping in)* Now, don't begin that Jew business again—Myra's gone and forgotten about him long ago. Good God, she's certainly proved that ter yer. I don't know what yer young men want now-a-days.

HEZEKIAH: Wel, I guess I'm satisfied all right.

THEOPHILUS BRENT: Wel, yer ought ter be. Myra's Paw is the richest farmer round these parts. There hain't another man in this town that can have what Josiah will give ter his son-in-law. He's said it himself.

HEZEKIAH: I'm game all right. But there are jest moments when I feel Myra's still thinkin' of that Slovak and harborin' a grudge 'cause we run him out of the town.

THEOPHILUS BRENT: Wel, yer hain't goin' ter let her grudges and a Jew stand between yer and a match like this—womin are always funny—jest don't pay no attention ter their notions. Besides, this community has got ter stand tergether. It don't matter what happened in the past, whether Myra was stuck on Jacob or not. That is the past and we can't let no Jew upset this here town no more. If yer weren't so damn young yer'd know it pays sometimes to close yer eyes on what yer suspects. Anyway, it's yer duty ter marry Myra now. And yer hain't fer tellin' me that yer hain't stuck on her.

HEZEKIAH: I hain't a-sayin' that I hain't—

MRS. FLINT: *(Offstage)* Lol—Lo—*(She enters.)* Oh, how'dy, Theophilus—how'dy, Hezekiah. I didn't know yer was here. Glad ter see yer both. Told Lola ter let me know the minute yer came—but yer can't trust that child nohow.

THEOPHILUS BRENT: Go outside a bit, Hezekiah. I want a chat with Sarah.

MRS. FLINT: Josiah's down ter the barn—if yer want him.

HEZEKIAH: All right. *(He goes out.)*

MRS. FLINT: It was nice of yer ter come. I felt kinda nervous yer mightn't have got my letter.

THEOPHILUS BRENT: Of course I did and glad ter come. After all, it concerns my child as well as yers.

MRS. FLINT: *(Relieved at his tone)* Ah—I'm glad yer feel that way. Sit down—sit down. (THEOPHILUS BRENT *sits. There is a slight pause.*)

THEOPHILUS BRENT: *(Making conversation)* Kinda warm fer May.

MRS. FLINT: Yep. Warmer than last year this here time. How's yer plantin'?

THEOPHILUS BRENT: Fine. Fine. *(There is another silence, he moves uneasily.)* Wel, I gess yer and me have got ter face this thing and talk about it, open like ter each other.

MRS. FLINT: That's what I want. I jest don't want Josiah ter ever know.

THEOPHILUS BRENT: No fear—no fear. I think yer and me can keep it ter ourselves and it hain't likely that Hezekiah or Myra are goin' ter proclaim it around the town.

MRS. FLINT: It would set Josiah somethin' awful agin Myra ter think she would go and do a thing like that.

THEOPHILUS BRENT: Oh, bein' a sheriff I see a lot of things—it's funny though abut Myra—

MRS. FLINT: Wel, it hain't fer me ter blame another womin, much less my own gal—

THEOPHILUS BRENT: Bein' a sheriff I suppose I'm more a man of the world about these things—I can't git as het up—but then I never had a gal—boys is different.

MRS. FLINT: In a way the pore gal is not ter blame; when she first confessed ter me she cried and took on somethin' awful.

THEOPHILUS BRENT: What did she say?

MRS. FLINT: She told me about Hezekiah aforcin' himself on her.

THEOPHILUS BRENT: *(Indignantly)* That's not what Hezekiah told me! He said jest the opposite. Said it was Myra who played on him and offered herself ter him.

MRS. FLINT: What a thing fer him ter say of my gal!

THEOPHILUS BRENT: Wel, wel, no matter what either of them say, the harm is done. The main thing now is ter git them married as soon as possible so everyone won't be gossipin' and lookin' wise when the baby comes early.

MRS. FLINT: Yep, that's the main thing.

THEOPHILUS BRENT: I've already had a talk with Hezekiah and I think I've made him see his duty. Oh, he's willin' all right. He's always ben stuck on Myra. I left a letter at Rev. Hale's house, askin' him ter come up here. I thought after Hezekiah spoke ter Josiah we might arrange about the weddin'. I already let a few hints drop in the village.

Mrs. Flint: It will be a load off my mind when they're married.

Theophilus Brent: Wel, I guess I'll join Hezekiah and Josiah and don't worry—we must jest push the weddin' as fast as we can and pretend as though we wasn't. We can say we want ter see the children married before the summer. Josiah will never catch on.

Mrs. Flint: The Lord grant he won't.

Theophilus Brent: Wel, better days will come, Sarah. Cheer up. *(He rises to go out. At that moment* Myra *comes in. She looks pale and unhappy, although she conceals it under a sullen manner. On seeing* Theophilus Brent *she pauses. There is an awkward silence.)*

Mrs. Flint: We were havin' a little talk, Myra.

Theophilus Brent: Good day, Myra. Yer Maw and me were talkin' about yer.

Mrs. Flint: Yep—and Theophilus is a kinder man than I thought—understandin' like.

Myra: *(Somewhat defiantly)* It's easy ter be, when yer're not a woman, with a woman's worries.

Mrs. Flint: What—what's that, Myra?

Myra: Nothin'.

Theophilus Brent: Wel, anyway, yer ter be married, Myra. Hezekiah has gone ter ask yer father. Yer can thank yer stars yer've gotten off so easy, with a good boy that's willin' ter marry yer. Few men would.

Myra: Oh. There might be others that would.

Theophilus Brent: Goodness gracious, child. Yer hain't seemin' ter realize the seriousness of yer situation. *(*Myra *sinks on a chair.)*

Mrs. Flint: She's tired terday, that's what. Hain't herself. Yer know. *(She motions to* Theophilus Brent *about* Myra*'s condition.)*

Theophilus Brent: *(Nodding his head)* Wel, I'll join them in the barn. See yer later. *(He goes out.)*

Mrs. Flint: Yer hadn't oughta talk that way afore Theophilus. Yer sound like a bold gal.

Myra: What difference does it make now that it's all fixed?

Mrs. Flint: Myra Flint! I don't understand yer.

Myra: Well—yer got what yer wanted—yer and Paw.

Mrs. Flint: We wanted ter see yer marry Hezekiah, Myra. But not this way.

Myra: Marriage is marriage. There hain't two ways.

Mrs. Flint: The way yer talk!

Myra: Wel, if it hadn't ben this way, it wouldn't have ben any way. Hezekiah wouldn't have married me if I hadn't let him—Yer said yerself he was coolin' off. Besides it was yer naggin' as much as anythin' else that made me go through with what I did.

MRS. FLINT: Yer may call it naggin'—I call it, interest. I know what's ter yer interest. The sooner yer git Hezekiah the better fer yer—as fer what yer done, it don't really matter as long as in the end he marries yer. Naturally, I got ter pretend ter Theophilus that I was no party in it—that's fer yer good, too.

MYRA: *(Wearily but rather bitterly)* It's funny how many things done fer yer good seems ter hurt so. *(She puts her hand to her heart. She speaks softly.)* Or maybe it's jest 'cause it's spring—Somehow, with that soft smell in the air—I seem ter have a longin' ter have everythin' fresh and clean—my heart—like all those white lilac blossoms that nothin' has touched yet.

MRS. FLINT: *(Somewhat sadly)* Yer'll git over those ideas when yer married. *(Pensively)* But what gits me is—I seemed ter notice yer felt sick before that day when yer said yer went ter the barn with Hezekiah.

MYRA: *(Startled and frightened. She looks quickly at her mother then pretends indifference.)* I don't know where yer got that idea and it hain't true.

MRS. FLINT: Wel, maybe not. Yer've been so sour fer so long it's hard ter tell whether yer're sick or jext yer regular nature. *(She busies about fixing table.)* Wel, I'll have ter step lively ter fix things fer the weddin'. Funny idea startin' ter be a grandmother afore there's ben a weddin'. Still, I suppose there's ben stranger things. I'm prepared fer anythin' these days. There's ben trouble in this here town ever since that Jacob came. How can anyone expect luck with a heathen around? And Josiah thinkin' himself so smart ter have brought him here!

MYRA: Well, if it hadn't been for Jacob, I'd like ter know where the store would be and yer money, too!

MRS. FLINT: It seems ter be runnin' all right the last three months without him.

MYRA: Naturally, after he set it straight and fixed it all up.

MRS. FLINT: *(Suspiciously)* Yer're always stickin' up fer him.

MYRA: No one else does.

MRS. FLINT: Wel, he had sense enough ter clear out of here, anyway. *(MRS. FLINT goes on arranging things. MYRA sits without moving. MRS. FLINT looks at her, then pauses; her face softens.)* I understand more than yer think. I hain't gone a womin's way all these years not ter understand somethin'—not ter understand that we womin have got ter stand tergether no matter what—right or

wrong. But we got more the upper hand than the men know—
even if we got ter go on foolin' them and livin' as though we
thought they was grander than us—That's where we're stronger,
'cause we know them but they don't know us.

*(She picks up a dish and goes out into the kitchen. MYRA stares tragically
before her then drops her head in her hands. After a few minutes voices are
heard. MYRA sits up. JOSIAH FLINT, THEOPHILUS BRENT, HEZE-
KIAH, REV. HALE and SAMUEL JONES come in. On seeing MYRA,
JOSIAH FLINT's face beams.)*

JOSIAH FLINT: Wel, wel, Myra—we've heard the good news!
Hezekiah has asked ter marry yer. *(He goes over and embraces
her.)* I'm that tickled ter death, Myra! *(He claps HEZEKIAH on
the back.)* And proud of my son-in-law.

HEZEKIAH: *(Laughing)* Wel, I hope we'll git on, Josiah.

REV. EZRA HALE: I'm glad to give you two children my blessing. *(He shakes HEZEKIAH and MYRA's hands. MRS. FLINT
comes in.)*

MRS. FLINT: Yer all here? And heard the news?

SAMUEL JONES: Yes, indeed. Here's my hand ter yer Hezekiah and
ter yer Myra! *(He shakes hands with them both.)*

MRS. FLINT: And what about me, Hezekiah?

HEZEKIAH: *(Kissing Mrs. Flint loudly)* That fer yer. I was jest sayin' I
hope I git on with Josiah. *(All laugh.)*

MRS. FLINT: Git on! Why, of course. Josiah has always had his eye
on yer fer Myra, ever since yer were Lola's age. *(She looks around.)*
Goodness gracious! Where is that child anyway? Lola!

THEOPHILUS BRENT: I jest saw her out ter the barn chasing
the pigs.

MRS. FLINT: *(MRS. FLINT goes to the doorway, calling.)* Lola!

LOLA'S VOICE: *(Offstage)* I can't come, Maw.

MRS. FLINT: *(Going to kitchen door)* Kitty, go lock up them pigs!
(During this scene the others go on talking.)

THEOPHILUS BRENT: Wel, I gess when our two families combine
it's goin ter cause a stir in this town.

HEZEKIAH: There will be many a one that will be jealous.

*(JOSIAH FLINT sits down, filling and lighting his pipe. THEOPHILUS
BRENT also sits, tipping back on his chair and leaning against the stove.
MRS. FLINT goes in and out of the room, joining the conversation now
and then. HEZEKIAH and SAMUEL JONES also sit. REV. EZRA HALE
stands in the center and joins his hands in an attitude of preaching.)*

REV. EZRA HALE: We must not speak of jealousy. Rather of the
peace of the Lord. We should think of the holy state of marriage,

of the beauty and holiness of a young girl coming in all purity to the brave groom. *(*Mrs. Flint *pauses, looking uneasily at* Myra. Theophilus Brent *coughs nervously.* Samuel Jones *stifles a yawn and prepares himself for a long sermon.* Rev. Ezra Hale *continues.)* The brave groom who will defend her through life. Then we must think, too, of the seriousness of marriage. We must pray that it will be the will of the good Lord our Savior to send children—many happy, rosy children. We must pray also—*(At that moment Theophilus Brent interrupts.)*

Theophilus Brent: Some other time, Ezra! Keep that sermon fer the weddin'. How about all havin' some of that harmless cider of yers, Josiah? *(He laughs and winks.)*

Samuel Jones: *(Springing up)* Now yer're talkin'.

Josiah Flint: Come along everybody.

Mrs. Flint: Bring me a glass when yer come back, Josiah.

*(*Samuel Jones *and* Theophilus *go out talking together.)*

Samuel Jones: I told Pete it would never work—*(His voice dies away.* Rev. Ezra Hale *goes out also.)*

Josiah Flint: Comin', Hezekiah?

Hezekiah: Goin' ter have a little talk with Myra first—I'll join yer later.

Josiah Flint: All right. See yer soon. *(He goes out. No one is left on the stage but* Myra *and* Hezekiah. Hezekiah *crosses over and pulls a chair close to her. He sits.)*

Hezekiah: Wel—no more worry, Myra. It's all fixed up and we're goin' ter git married.

Myra: *(Without looking up)* I know—but somehow or other yer needn't throw it in my face.

Hezekiah: Throw it in your face! Oh, come now, Myra—it hain't reasonable of yer ter git sore at me fer nothin'. Yer know I wanted ter marry yer right straight along.

Myra: Well, yer didn't show much sign of it—till—till this happened.

Hezekiah: That hain't so, Myra. Yer know I always loved yer. Ever since we were kids tergether, I've always told yer about all the hopes and ideas I had fer yer and me tergether—gettin' married and havin' a home—and settin' up everythin' tergether. Yer know that—don't yer, now?

Myra: Yes—I guess so—

Hezekiah: Sure thing, no "guess so" about it. I jest wasn't sure whether yer cared about me. A man's got ter be careful. Now I know of course yer do care. Straight stuff and all that—with the baby comin' and everythin'—I wanted ter marry yer all along, but I was pretendin' I didn't. Had ter be sort of careful, but I've always had honest intentions about yer. (HEZEKIAH *leans back and looks at her. After a pause he continues.*) Wel, anyway—yer a fine lookin' gal. I'm mighty proud of yer—there hain't another one that can measure ter yer. Give us a kiss—I hain't had one fer a long time.

MYRA: *(Rising)* Not now, Hezekiah. I don't feel like it now.

HEZEKIAH: I always feel like a kiss—but gals are funny. Let's go and join the folks.

MYRA: All right.

HEZEKIAH: I've got a surprise fer yer. Somethin' grand fer the house. It ought ter tickle yer ter death. (*As they go out* HEZEKIAH *puts his arms around her and gives her a loud kiss on the cheek. He laughs loudly.*) I got one anyway! Yer see yer can't fool me. (*They disappear. The stage is left empty for a few minutes.* KITTY *appears in door. She has in her hand the key to the pig pen. She stops, looking offstage to right, then quickly enters and pauses as though waiting for someone she has seen approaching.* JACOB *enters.*)

KITTY: Jacob!

JACOB SLOVAK: How are you, Kitty?

KITTY: How and when did yer git here!

JACOB SLOVAK: I came back, Kitty, to see Myra. I've got a wonderful position and I've come to tell her about it.—How is she, Kitty?

KITTY: She's all right.

JACOB SLOVAK: Why do you say it that way? Nothing is wrong, is it? Why hasn't Myra answered my letters?

KITTY: I don't know.

JACOB SLOVAK: I couldn't understand why she didn't answer me.

KITTY: Perhaps yer shouldn't have come back.

JACOB SLOVAK: But, Kitty, I *had* to come back.

KITTY: Oh, Jacob, I don't want it ter hurt yer.

JACOB SLOVAK: You mean my coming here?—my pride—what does anything matter if I can see Myra. Where is she?

KITTY: Jacob—Supposin'—jest supposin' Myra won't see yer?

JACOB SLOVAK: Not see me! Why, today we'll go away together—

KITTY: But if she decides against yer? Oh, Jacob—

JACOB SLOVAK: What are you saying? Kitty—what are you saying? Where is Myra?

KITTY: Outside.

JACOB SLOVAK: Call her, Kitty. I can't wait any longer.

KITTY: I'll try.

JACOB SLOVAK: Try? I must see her.

KITTY: Then wait in there. *(He goes into the other room.* KITTY *goes to the doorway and calls)* Myra! Myra! *(She beckons. In a few seconds* MYRA *comes in.)*

MYRA: What is it, Kitty?

KITTY: Don't git angry, Myra.

MYRA: What about? What's happened?

KITTY: Jacob's inside. He must see yer.

MYRA: *(Terrified)* Jacob! Kitty, I can't see him.

KITTY: Oh, Myra—he loves yer.

MYRA: *(Sinks down on chair. She speaks intensely)* I want ter see him, Kitty—but it will ruin my life. I can't change now.

KITTY: He loves yer. It hain't everyone that loves the way he does. He's breakin' his heart fer yer.

MYRA: Yer can't understand, Kitty—

KITTY: See him, Myra. Jest this once. I'll watch so that no one will come—(KITTY *goes after* JACOB. *Myra stands with her hands clenched to her breasts.* JACOB *enters. He stops and they look at each other.)*

JACOB SLOVAK: Myra! Myra! *(They hesitate, then impulsively* JACOB *rushes to* MYRA. *He takes her in his arms; for one second she surrenders and clings to him then she wrenches herself away.)* God, I knew you cared.

MYRA: Don't, Jacob.

JACOB SLOVAK: I've waited all these weeks—waited and waited for one word, just one word from you—hungered for you.

MYRA: I've hungered fer yer, too.

JACOB SLOVAK: How could you have tortured me this way, not writing me.

MYRA: Yer shouldn't have come back—

JACOB SLOVAK: Everything is different—I can support you. I've got a wonderful job now. I'm playing in an orchestra.

MYRA: An orchestra!

JACOB SLOVAK: I can support you now and take you away from this narrow town—We belong to each other—nothing else matters.

MYRA: Yer don't understand. I can't leave here.

JACOB SLOVAK: Myra—you love me!

MYRA: But, Jacob—it's my home—where I've been brought up. If I go away with yer I'll never see my Maw or Paw again—

JACOB SLOVAK: Can't our love make up for everything else?

MYRA: Oh, yer don't understand.

JACOB SLOVAK: You're afraid to trust yourself to me—

MYRA: It's something else—someone—

JACOB SLOVAK: Not Hezekiah! Not the gossip I heard in the village? Not Hezekiah! *(MYRA lowers her head. JACOB rushes to her and holds her wrists.)* It's not true, Myra—it can't be true—

MYRA: *(Breaking away from him)* Listen, Jacob. Sit down here. *(She motions to a chair.)* I have somethin' I've got ter tell yer and I have ter be quick. We may not have long alone. *(Jacob sits in a dazed fashion.)*

JACOB SLOVAK: *(Hardly audible)* What is it?

MYRA: *(Slowly and with much difficulty. She puts her hand to her brow as though to steady and recollect herself.)* I—I am goin' ter marry Hezekiah. *(JACOB gives a cry of pain. MYRA silences him with her hand.)* It hain't the way yer think, Jacob. I don't love him—I love yer—yer—

JACOB SLOVAK: You love me—

MYRA: *(Weeping)* I can't marry yer, Jacob. I couldn't face it—

JACOB SLOVAK: *(Seizing MYRA's wrists)* Myra—do you care that I'm a Jew?

MYRA: *(Looking down)* Don't, Jacob—yer hurtin' my wrists.

JACOB SLOVAK: Why marry Hezekiah?

MYRA: *(A pause before Myra answers. She twists her handkerchief in her hands, hesitates, then speaks very low.)* Because I am goin' ter have a child.

JACOB SLOVAK: A child!

MYRA: Yer child, Jacob.

JACOB SLOVAK: Myra—my beloved—*(He looks at her suddenly awe-struck, then reverently, tenderly. He goes toward her. Myra holds him away.)*

MYRA: Now yer see why I must git married.

JACOB SLOVAK: *(With determination)* Yes—and now you will marry me. *(Softly)* Our child, Myra!

MYRA: It isn't easy fer me, Jacob—yer will never know what I've been through—don't make it harder now. I can't stand much more.

JACOB SLOVAK: Nothing can prevent us from marrying now.

MYRA: Hezekiah—

JACOB SLOVAK: What of Hezekiah!

MYRA: *(Excitedly)* Listen, Jacob—Listen! After that night with yer and when I found I was goin' ter have a child, I didn't know what ter do. I couldn't marry yer—I was nearly crazy. I knew I would be disgraced unless I was married when the baby was born, so I got Hezekiah ter marry me.

JACOB SLOVAK: *(Incredulously)* You got Hezekiah to marry you? What do you mean?

MYRA: I gave myself ter him. It was the only way left ter me. Don't blame me, Jacob, it was the only way Hezekiah thinks this is his child.

JACOB SLOVAK: God! You did this thing, Myra! Myra! You're not telling me the truth—one of us is mad!

MYRA: *(Hysterically)* I'm goin' ter marry him, Jacob. I've *got* ter marry him.

JACOB SLOVAK: *(Horrified)* I can't believe that I am listening to you, Myra—it can't be you—the you I loved—

MYRA: *(Brokenly)* Oh, Jacob—Jacob—I can't go against everythin'—Yer don't even understand me or else yer would understand this thing in my blood—that makes it impossible fer me ter go away with yer. I've ben taught all my life ter hate yer race. *(Pause)* I don't know what I'm sayin'—what I'm doin'—Oh, God—

JACOB SLOVAK: And do you think a matter of race or creed or what you have been taught is going to make me lose my child? Do you think I'll stand by and allow another man to claim *my* child?

MYRA: I can't undo what I have done now. *(Wearily)* Can't yer see that—it's all useless now—there hain't no turning back—

JACOB SLOVAK: You said you loved me—you have nothing against me except that I am a Jew.

MYRA: But yer are a Jew and nothin' can alter that. (MYRA *drops her head and utters a sob.)*

JACOB SLOVAK: You will be the mother to a Jew. What right have you to refuse to marry me? If you were begging me to marry you—no one would think me much good if I didn't. You may be carrying that child, but it's my child, too. I claim the right to be called its father—lawfully—openly—not for my sake but for the sake of the child.

MYRA: It's no use, Jacob—I can't go against the way I've ben brought up.

JACOB SLOVAK: And are you going to bring my child up the way you've been brought up? Taught lies and hypocrisy. Taught to judge a man by color, race and creed rather than by the fineness in him! *(Brokenly)* I won't allow those prejudices to ruin your life and mine. I'm going to fight for you in spite of yourself, for you and our child.

MYRA: I can't marry yer.

JACOB SLOVAK: Then I'll force you.

MYRA: *(Frightened)* How?

JACOB SLOVAK: By telling the truth.

MYRA: Yer wouldn't do that! Fer God's sake, Jacob, yer wouldn't do that!

JACOB SLOVAK: You've broken my heart, but you won't take my child from me. Make up your mind—yes or no—if it's no, I will call everyone in and tell the truth.

MYRA: Yer wouldn't dare. Yer, who say yer love me—

JACOB SLOVAK: Love—love—*(He laughs hysterically.)* You call them and tell them you have decided to marry me, or I'll call them and tell them the whole truth.

MYRA: Yer wouldn't dare—they wouldn't believe yer!

JACOB SLOVAK: Which is it to be?—Say, Myra.

MYRA: *(Weeping)* Yer wouldn't dare! I *can't* marry yer. If yer call I must defend myself—don't make me hurt yer any more.

JACOB SLOVAK: *(Jacob goes quickly to the door. He calls.)* Mr. Flint! Mrs. Flint! Come here quickly—

MYRA: Fer God's sake, Jacob—No—no—(MR. FLINT *calls offstage,* "What is it? Comin.")

JACOB SLOVAK: *(Still calling)* And you, too, Theophilus Brent! *(At that instant* MR. AND MRS. FLINT *come in, followed by* THEOPHILUS BRENT, THE REV. HALE, SAMUEL JONES *and* HEZEKIAH.)

JOSIAH FLINT: *(Looking from* MYRA *to* JACOB) What's up? What are yer doin' here in my house, Jacob Slovak?

MYRA: *(Hysterically)* He's been annoyin' me—tryin' ter git even with yer fer losin' his job.

JACOB SLOVAK: That's not true.

HEZEKIAH: See here, yer hain't tellin' Myra she's lyin'. Not before me—I'll break every one—

THEOPHILUS BRENT: *(Seizing* HEZEKIAH) Easy here—now wait a minute. What's this man ben doin' ter yer, Myra?

MYRA: I—I was here alone when he came in and began shoutin' at me and sayin' if I didn't git his job back—he'd—he'd fix me.

JOSIAH FLINT: I'll fix *him.*

SAMUEL JONES: And me, too—I've ben waitin' fer a chance like this—

THEOPHILUS BRENT: Jest a moment. How dare yer come here, Jacob Slovak?

JACOB SLOVAK: I came to ask Myra to marry me. *(The following three lines are all shouted together.)*

REV. EZRA HALE: Do Jews marry Gentiles?

HEZEKIAH: Myra's goin' ter marry *me.*

JOSIAH FLINT: Git him out of here before I kick him out. (HEZE-

KIAH *and* SAMUEL JONES *start toward* JACOB, *but his gesture stops them.)*

JACOB SLOVAK: I asked Myra to marry me a long time ago—long before—(MYRA *makes a half supplicating gesture and he stops.)*

JOSIAH FLINT: Before what? (JACOB *hesitates and looks at* MYRA, *who has lowered her head. There is a tense silence before* JOSIAH FLINT *speaks again.)* Wel—

JACOB SLOVAK: Before—before—I left here three months ago. (MRS. FLINT *relaxes.* MYRA *hardly moves.)*

SAMUEL JONES: Wel, he had *some* nerve askin' Myra ter marry him!

JOSIAH FLINT: Yer git out of this town now, or by God we'll run yer out.

THEOPHILUS BRENT: *(Breaking in)* He'll git out of this town all right before night fall.

HEZEKIAH: *(Rushing toward* JACOB *)* He'll git out *now* or I'll know why!

MRS. FLINT: *(Leaping forward and standing before* JACOB *)* Yer keep yer hands off him. I hain't goin' ter have no one maltreated in my house! Yer ought ter be 'shamed of yerself, Josiah Flint, wantin' ter lay hands on a man what worked fer yer and fixed yer store the way it never was afore—and worse than that—it's him that made money fer yer that keeps this roof over yer head. And yer, Theophilus—a fine sheriff yer are standin' fer five men jumpin' on one and not bein' able ter run law and order better than that. As fer yer, Ezra—yer were glad enough ter have Jacob keep yer out of trouble when yer needed an organ player in the church. I notice though yer don't help him much when he needs yer.

JOSIAH FLINT: Yer hadn't oughta talk this way when we're protectin' Myra.

MRS. FLINT: I'll protect her myself, and I gess I can git Jacob out of this town as quick and quicker than any of yer.

THEOPHILUS BRENT: Wel, in that case—

MRS. FLINT: *(Breaking in)* Yer all git out now. I hain't goin' ter be upset no more. In future I'll thank yer all fer not managin' fer my gal.

JOSIAH FLINT: Quit pushin' me out of my own house.

(She succeeds in pushing them out of the house. They move unwillingly but they go. Their voices can be heard until they disappear out of sight, with MRS. FLINT *still after them. All the following lines are heard confused and together.)*

THEOPHILUS BRENT: If he hain't out of town in an hour I'll lock him up.

HEZEKIAH: I'll *beat* him up.

SAMUEL JONES: *Christ,* what nerve!

REV. EZRA HALE: The heathen's mad. *(Their voices can be heard dying away.* JACOB *stands without moving and looks at* MYRA.*)*

MYRA: *(Brokenly and low)* Thanks—fer—not—tellin'—

JACOB SLOVAK: You think this is the end, Myra? It will never be the end. I'll come back over and over again in your child. You think you can turn me out, but you can't. You can never get away from me—never—never. Another man may bring up that child, but it will be my child and my race. My race that will come in here and go on. And if you have a son he'll be out there tilling these fields—but remember, it will be *my* blood working this soil.

*(*MRS. FLINT *re-enters and stands with her hand on the door.)*

MRS. FLINT: *(Softly)* Yer go along now.

*(*JACOB *turns and goes out.* MRS. FLINT *follows him to the door and looks after him as he disappears.* MYRA *hesitates, as though she were agonizing within herself whether to call after* JACOB *or not. Then slowly she sinks on the chair and buries her head in her hands.* MRS. FLINT *comes back into the room and quietly and gently closes the front door, as if by this gesture she were forever excluding the truth from the men.)*

Curtain

The Mother of Christ
A Play in Six Parts

The Characters

MARY, *the Mother of Christ*
Disciples and followers of Christ
JAMES
JOHN
PETER
MARY MAGDELENA
PILATE, *a Roman Governor*
PILATE'S WIFE
A ROMAN GENERAL
A ROMAN OFFICER
A ROMAN SOLDIER
TWO SERVANTS *in the house of Pilate*

Part 1

A room in MARY's *house. It is 9 o'clock at night. The room is extremely simple and in the style used in the poorer homes of Palestine. The walls (which are cracked from age in many places) are made of plaster tinted in blue, which has faded almost to white. The floor is earth. The room is small. A door which leads to the street stands upstage to the left. This door is closed. A small, crudely cut window is placed to the upstage right. Directly to the right of the window there is a door which leads into an adjoining room. This door is partly open. A crude table with one or two earthen pots and a candle upon it stands in the center of the room. The candle is lighted. Two or three small primitive wooden benches are arranged about. A large earthen water jar stands near the door. To the left, a hole is cut into the wall and filled in with stones, upon which can be burnt a fire for cooking.*

As the curtain rises, the stage is empty. Through the window can be heard the frenzied VOICES OF A MOB *a little way off. One can distinguish through their hoarse shouts, cries of* "Barabbas!" "Barabbas!" "Deliver us Barabbas." "Free Barabbas in the place of Jesus of Nazareth." *The door opens from the street;* JAMES *and* JOHN *enter. They are both dressed in flowing costumes of the period.* JAMES *in grey;* JOHN *in brown. They are young men in their thirties. Their faces are tanned and lined from wind and privation. They give the impression at once of naïve simplicity and*

Library of Congress Copyright, April 5, 1924. Registration number 67345.

awkwardness, but one also feels in their personality great courage and an indomitable ardor, with an inward burning fire for the cause in which they believe, and in the Master whom they follow. Great anxiety and terror show in their faces. Throughout the scene, from time to time, the angry VOICES OF THE MOB *continue.*

JAMES: *(Placing his hands to his ears.)* Will they never stop that shouting! *(He sinks onto a bench with his head in his hands.* JOHN *walks nervously up and down, peering from time to time out of the window.)*

JOHN: They have been calling like that outside of Pilate's house since early this evening—ever since he sent Jesus to Annas.

JAMES: Yes, and then back to Caiaphas. As if they weren't both in league, being father and son-in-law. A worthy pair, indeed!

JOHN: Pilate has not the courage to make up his own mind. He must hope for advice and backing from Rome. His great fear is that he will become unpopular with the Jews; he would sell his own wife to avoid that. He admits himself that he can find nothing against Jesus.

JAMES: No, but he will. What he can't find he will invent, aided by the lying tongues of the priests and high priests.

JOHN: *(Cautiously)* Sh! Be careful. It will only make matters worse if we get into trouble, too.

JAMES: *(Springing up and passionately)* I'm sure I don't care! I wish it were I that might die in the place of Jesus.

JOHN: *(Despairingly)* Don't speak of dying, I beg of you. I have every hope that Pilate only pretends that he will kill Jesus in order to pacify the Jews. When this turmoil quiets down, he will release him. He bears no ill to Jesus—he has said so over and over again.

JAMES: *(Unconvinced)* Yes, I know—but I also know he will not sacrifice his own popularity to save Jesus.

JOHN: *(In a low voice)* Well, at any rate, do not speak here of the danger that Jesus is in. *(He looks toward the half-open door.)* I did not notice that door was open.

JAMES: *(Also in a lowered voice. He shows fear at having been overheard.)* Is his mother in there?

JOHN: Yes. I was here a few hours ago to see her. She was worn out, poor thing, from anxiety and worry. She promised me she would try and sleep.

JAMES: *(Softly)* I will close the door so she cannot hear us. *(He tiptoes over to the door. As he is about to close it, he looks quietly into the room, then around at* JOHN. *He speaks in a louder voice again.)* Why, no one is here!

JOHN: *(Impatiently)* Of course Mary is there.

(He goes quickly toward the room. They both pass into it. At that moment MARY *enters from the street. She closes the door behind her and leans against it with her hand to her breast as though spent. She gives the impression of being poor and simple. She is dressed in a soft blue garment which shows signs of age. She seems pathetically bewildered and stunned. In her face is great tragic beauty; the tragedy and sorrow that come to simple people who cannot understand the brutalities of life, nor cope with them.)*

JOHN: *(Offstage)* I can't understand where she can be, she—(JOHN *and* JAMES *reappear. They perceive* MARY. *They both rush toward her as though to support her. She waves them aside and stands alone, coming forward.)* You promised me you would sleep. We have all rested but you, during this terrible night. (MARY *turns, looking at him silently for a full minute before she speaks.)*

MARY: Don't you know that a mother never sleeps when her child needs her?

JOHN: But you can do no good. You cannot even see him.

MARY: *(Sadly)* Yes, that's true. But he can feel me. He *must* feel me. He must feel me watching through the long hours of the night with him. When the dawn comes he must know I see it, too—that only I, out of all the world, watch with him. (JAMES *and* JOHN *lower their heads in shame.)*

JAMES: We could not even remain awake to watch with him one short hour, while he prayed in the garden of Gethsemane.

JOHN: *(Tragically and self-reproachfully)* He might not have been captured had we remained awake.

MARY: *(Bitterly)* Judas had already sold him. They would have captured him sooner or later. *(The* MOB *is heard again outside.* MARY *covers her ears frantically.)* Must they always call for his blood? Cannot they take mine? *(A sudden inspiration comes to her.)* Yes, that is it! I will go to Pilate and offer my life in the place of Jesus. I am older and worthless, but the same blood flows in our veins. If they want *his* blood, why should not *mine* do as well? *(She rushes for the door, but* JOHN *bars her way.)*

JOHN: Do not be reckless, Mary. One false step and things may become worse. You may place Jesus in the light of a coward to even allow you to make such an offer.

MARY: He would not know of it. Let me pass!

JOHN: I cannot. For his sake as much as yours.

MARY: *(Angrily)* Let me pass, I say! If I cannot speak to Pilate, I will speak to the people. Ingrates all of them! I will tell them how much it pays for Jesus to try and raise their dead; solace their suffering; give sight to their blind eyes! They are ready enough to take these things from him; accept them; profit by his healing hands—now they want his life in return. *(She sobs and walks wildly up and down.)* It's the hatred of a mob that cannot understand someone superior to themselves. *(Turning quickly to* JAMES *and* JOHN*)* Because he *is* superior to them, and they know it. But they despise superiority; resent independence and fearlessness; envy the very power which makes leadership possible, and which would be to their loss without it. *(Lamenting)* Woe betide the man who places his confidence in the people!

JOHN: Jesus has never done that. This thing comes as no surprise to him.

MARY: Let me pass, I say! *(*JAMES *closes the window, then gently he takes* MARY*'s hand)*

JAMES: Come, Mary, sit here. It is true what John said; let us not do anything hasty.

(He leads her to a seat next to the table. MARY *sinks down with her head in her hand. There is a long silence.* JOHN *and* JAMES *exchange glances of pity for* MARY *and terror at the situation.* MARY *raises her head slowly. She gazes before her and speaks as though to herself.)*

MARY: And yet I almost feel as though this *had* to be—the way I felt when I was carrying him here. *(She places her hand on her body.)* That *had* to be. In a sense this seems the same reason. *(As though recalling something)* He warned me of this—a—long—time—ago; when he was twelve. I don't know if I ever told you—

JAMES: *(Shaking his hand in the negative)* No, Mary.

MARY: It was at the time when we went up to Jerusalem. After we left the city, we missed Jesus. We sought him everywhere; then I finally turned and went back to the city. After three days I found him in the temple, sitting in the midst of the doctors, both hearing them, and asking them questions. You can imagine how astonished I was, and how angry, that he should have made me suffer so, without telling me where he was. I spoke to him and asked him why he had given me such sorrow. He looked at me curiously, as if we were utter strangers; or as if he were delirious and raving. He said, "Why do you seek me? Don't you know that I must be about my father's business?" It was almost as though he were reproaching me for not understanding something *he could* understand—*(Bewildered)* something I don't yet understand. I remember yet another time, when he was a baby and we were escaping from the massacre into Egypt. I was riding an ass and holding Jesus close to my body. Suddenly, through the darkness of the night I saw a black cross against the sky—then he put his small hands up before my eyes as though to shut out a sight that was too soon for me to see. But I felt then as now—as if something was impending *that had to be.*

JOHN: What are you saying, Mary? *(Laughing a trifle incredulously)* An infant knowing enough to shield your eyes!

MARY: *(Making a gesture as though to dispel her thoughts)* Nothing, John. It's of no importance.

JAMES: *(Tenderly and excusingly)* She's very tired.

MARY: *(Pensively)* It's curious how a mother can bring up a child, after having held him close to her for so many years, and then suddenly realize that she doesn't know that child at all. *(Pleading to be convinced)* But I do know him—don't I? After all, he *is* my son—my child—you both know that.

JAMES: Of course—of course, Mary.

MARY: Then why does he want to do these things? Why does he want to get into trouble like this and leave me? Why does he want to talk about things I can't understand? Why is it that we are mother and son, and yet I can't understand him? Why is it that all mothers receive their great sorrow through their children? *(Weeping)* Why is it, he can't remain always my child—the way it was when he was little and needed me? *(She drops her head.* JAMES *touches her tenderly.)*

JAMES: *(Compassionately)* Don't cry, Mary.

JOHN: *(Suddenly and impatiently)* If we could *only* bring some influence to bear. If we only knew some powerful person in Rome to frighten this timid rat Pilate!

JAMES: If we only did! *(He places his hand to his brow.)* And yet they say Pilate has a tender heart—almost like a woman. I wonder—I wonder—Could we not think of some human appeal with which to touch him?

JOHN: It would have to be very great to surpass the appeal that Jesus himself gives out.

JAMES: Jesus appears almost inhuman by his great courage and silence. It makes them hate him all the more, feeling in him a divine strength they cannot understand—a strength they cannot break down. Something weaker would touch Pilate. *(He suddenly looks at* MARY. *At the same moment,* JOHN *reads his thought.* MARY *also understands; she looks from one to the other.)*

MARY: What weaker and yet as strong as the love of a mother?

JAMES: Yes. That is right. Mary was right after all in wanting to go.

JOHN: No. Not the way she wanted to. Calmly and pleadingly, perhaps. But how can we get her to Pilate? He would not see her.

JAMES: I did a favor for the chief guard there. Do you remember, it was his goats I found on the hills and returned to him?

JOHN: Yes, yes, I remember.

JAMES: He might let us in. He seemed a just man. I will fetch Peter. He speaks with more authority than we. We will take him along, too.

MARY: *(Rising and trembling feverishly)* Let us go! There is not a second to lose. *(She sways.* JAMES *and* JOHN *support her.)*

JAMES: Lean on our arms, Mary, but let us lean on your courage. *(They go out.)*

Curtain

Part 2

A room in PILATE*'s house, the same night. It is large and spacious, in Roman style. Pairs of marble Roman pillars stand directly on the right and left of the stage. An ornate door is between each pair of pillars. Upstage left a marble stairway leads downstairs. To the upstage right is a large window overlooking the street. It opens onto a stone balcony. The floor and walls of the room are marble. The room is lighted by great torches. Left upstage is a large table before which* PILATE *sits in a great chair. Documents of state, scrolls and parchments are strewn upon the table before him. He is a weak man who tries to hide his natural timidity by talking loudly. He is dressed in Roman toga. Seated upon a chair before him, but some distance away from the table, is a* ROMAN GENERAL. *As the curtain rises,* PILATE *flings down a parchment he has just sealed and sighs.*

PILATE: I am glad that mob has at last ceased yelling.

ROMAN GENERAL: They have only ceased for a little while. They are probably tired, but they have not gone away.

PILATE: I have never had two such terrible hours since I have been in office.

ROMAN GENERAL: I have rarely seen a mob so stirred up.

PILATE: *(Rubbing his head)* It is difficult to know what to do. I wish I could send to Rome for advice.

ROMAN GENERAL: You would hardly have time, with the Jews clamoring like this. I fear your decision will have to be tonight or early tomorrow morning.

PILATE: For my part, I would like to free him. I can't see that he does any harm. Simply a fanatic, I should say. Surely a man who preaches that if you are struck on one cheek, to turn the other, can hardly be worth fearing. A man who says to love one's enemies, and that if someone takes your cloak, to give them also your coat! *(He laughs.)* I believe he is simply unbalanced.

ROMAN GENERAL: And yet he has such loyal followers.

PILATE: *(With a shrug of his shoulders)* Oh, only simple people. Mostly fishermen.

ROMAN GENERAL: *(Laughing)* And a courtesan—don't forget her.

PILATE: *(Wearily)* One does not get a chance to forget much about this man. I am tired of hearing about him. If it is not that mob outside, it's my own wife inside.

ROMAN GENERAL: Your own wife? What do you mean? *(Jokingly and with exaggeration)* Surely she is not going to join the notorious Mary Magdelena in discarding all comforts and luxury to follow this great man who promises a kingdom in the clouds! *(He laughs.)*

PILATE: *(With sudden fear)* Do not joke about this. My wife has uncanny powers. She has foretold many things through dreams. Even my appointment here.

ROMAN GENERAL: *(A trifle amused)* And has she dreamed about this—this Jesus?

PILATE: *(Still with fear and very seriously)* Yes. My life has not known a minute's peace since the question arose about capturing this man. Every time she sleeps she dreams of him, and today she claims having had warnings about him while awake.

ROMAN GENERAL: *(Interested)* What do her dreams and warnings say?

PILATE: For me not to listen to the Jews—to have nothing to do with them. She claims that this Jesus is great, and good, and that I will be cursed by all time if I judge him.

ROMAN GENERAL: *(Lightly)* Oh, a woman's fancies!

PILATE: I have forbid her seeing me until this matter is settled. She unbalances me.

ROMAN GENERAL: A wise decision. *(A* SERVANT *enters from door to right. He approaches* PILATE *and bows.)*

SERVANT: A message, your excellency, from your wife.

PILATE: *(Sharply)* Well?

SERVANT: She begs to be allowed to see you.

PILATE: I have told her I will not see her.

SERVANT: Then she begs me to tell you, she has had another dream—more terrible than any before.

PILATE: *(Striking the table with his fist)* I will not listen to her dreams, I tell you! Out of my sight! *(He leaps up angrily. The* SERVANT *retreats; as he reaches the door,* PILATE *changes his mind.)* Wait! Come back! *(The* SERVANT *returns.)* What—what was her dream, you fool? Tell it before I have you flogged!

SERVANT: She said to say that she has received another warning, that unless you free this Jesus of Nazareth—not only you, but your whole house would be cursed forever, and your children, and your children's children.

PILATE: *(Beside himself and hysterically)* Her dreams will drive me mad! *(To the* SERVANT*)* Leave us! Leave us, you gaping fool! *(The* SERVANT *goes out.)*

ROMAN GENERAL: *(Discreetly and coughing in his hand)* A strange woman, your wife. *(A* SOLDIER *comes up the stairs. He also bows to* PILATE.*)*

PILATE: *(Still hysterically)* What do you want?

SOLDIER: Pardon, your Excellency, but there is a woman and three men downstairs who desire to see you upon an important matter concerning the man Jesus.

PILATE: Who allowed them in?

SOLDIER: I do not know, your Excellency, but they are talking with the officer-in-charge. He seems to know them.

ROMAN GENERAL: That's odd. *(With interest)* Can the woman be Mary Magdelena?

SOLDIER: No, General. I know Mary Magdelena by sight.

ROMAN GENERAL: Perhaps another conquest of this Jesus. Let's see her. *(Laughing)* He seems popular.

PILATE: *(To* SOLDIER*)* Show them up. Wait! They are not armed, are they?

SOLDIER: No, your Excellency. They seem like simple folk. Timid and afraid.

PILATE: *(With relief)* Ah! Then show them up. *(He sits.* MARY, *followed by* JAMES *and* JOHN, *comes up the stairs. Upon seeing* PILATE, *they hesitate.)*

PILATE: Come forward! Come forward! *(*MARY *comes forward to the center of stage,* JOHN *and* JAMES *hang back.)*

ROMAN GENERAL: *(A trifle brutally)* You'll find I'm right. Another admirer of this King of the Clouds come to intercede for him! *(*MARY *lowers her eyes, which are filled with tragic sorrow.)*

PILATE: Woman, who are you? *(Slowly* MARY *raises her head. She draws herself up proudly. She speaks simply but with great dignity.)*

MARY: The Mother of Jesus. *(A silence)*

PILATE: *(Uncomfortable, touched by her dignity)* And what—what do you expect me to do for you?

MARY: *(Becoming the mother fighting for her child)* Free him! Free my son who has harmed no one!

PILATE: Your son has created a public disturbance. He has roused the hatred of the Jews—his own people. We Romans have nothing against him.

MARY: He is only a poor man, as I am only a poor, simple woman. You can look at me and see what my son is—why, we are so poor; he was even born in a stable. He is harmless, I tell you—he has no power.

PILATE: *(Surprised)* But it is he, himself, who says he has power. He claims to be a King and own a Kingdom.

MARY: *(Distressed and at a loss to know what to say)* But—but—you know how these things are. If you had ever had a child you would know. They get these ideas—ideas that carry them away from their homes, their mothers. They won't take our advice—and then the result is—this.

PILATE: You mean you don't encourage him in all this—in these ideas?

MARY: *(Sadly and shaking her head)* I love him—I want him to stay home with me where I can take care of him.

PILATE: But these—*(Pointing to* JOHN *and* JAMES*)* these followers of his—

MARY: *(Quickly and raising her hand to silence* JAMES *and* JOHN*)* Children, too! Simple fishermen.

PILATE: *(Wearily)* Well, I have already told you that I have nothing against your Jesus.

MARY: Then free him! It is only in the power of Rome to free him.

PILATE: *(Evadingly)* You are mistaken. The Jewish high priests have been the first to condemn him. You know how powerful they are.

MARY: The Jews hate him because he is one of them, and yet not one of them. Enough one of them to make them resent his superiority; not enough one of them to make them want him to be one of them.

PILATE: It has nothing to do with the issue. As for me, I am tired of the whole question. The Jews must decide these things for themselves.

MARY: That is not so. You know your decision will be the last one.

PILATE: *(Finding himself cornered and not wishing to belittle his own power)* That is, of course, so. *My* power is absolute—but in this matter I may wave it aside, having more important matters on hand.

MARY: *(Despairingly)* What more important matter than the life of a man?

PILATE: Oh, that is not so important. The matter arises often when one is in high power.

MARY: But were you the mother of one of those lives, it would be important. *(Sobbing)* You have not had a child—one of those lives—torn from out your womb. You have not laid long into the hours of the night peering into the darkness, hoping and building for the future of that child. And then suddenly, through one gesture of a man in power, see him taken from you—sentenced to die.

PILATE: *(Touched in spite of himself)* I will think it carefully over. Go now. Go.

MARY: *(Brokenly)* I cannot go without your freeing him.

JAMES: *(Coming forward)* Have mercy on her pleadings. *(For the first time* PILATE *is fully aware of* JAMES *and* JOHN. *He turns to them.)*

PILATE: I thought the soldier told me there were three of you. *(A* SOLDIER *who has just come upstairs comes forward.)*

SOLDIER: There are three, your Excellency. The one called Peter remained downstairs. He has just now denied twice that he knows Jesus.

ROMAN GENERAL: *(Slapping his knee and bursting into laughter)* Wonderful friends, these followers of Jesus! First, one sells him for a few pieces of silver, then another denies him twice. *(With great sarcasm)* Really, these Jews do right to be so afraid of his power.

MARY: *(Ignoring him and to* PILATE *)* Free my son—he has done you no harm. *(A* SERVANT *enters from the right. He seems agitated.)*

SERVANT: Your Excellency, your wife commands me to come to you at once and to tell you that she has seen Jesus of Nazareth. She commanded me to repeat these words: "His face is so beautiful; his regard so all-seeing and sublime, that I fell on my knees before him." She says woe betide you, if you condemn this man.

PILATE: *(Exasperated beyond words, yet fearful)* Do not come here with any more messages. Do you understand? I forbid it.

SERVANT: Very well, your Excellency. *(He withdraws.)*

PILATE: *(Holding his head and walking up and down)* Was ever a man in such a position?—and not a soul to help or advise me.

ROMAN GENERAL: Your wife seems to be doing that. *(At that moment the* CROWD *is heard again outside. Their words are inaudible, but they keep up a constant murmur in angry tones.)*

PILATE: There they begin again! How am I to get any sleep this night?

MARY: Free Jesus, that you may sleep in peace. *(The* CROWD *grows angrier.)*

PILATE: Sleep in peace with those angry dogs outside!

MARY: *(Rushing to the window)* Let me speak to them. Let me plead for his life! *(*PILATE *runs forward, seizing her roughly. He pulls her back into the room again and flings her onto the floor.)*

PILATE: You must be mad! Do you want to ruin me? A nice scandal for me if they knew I was weighing your pleadings against theirs. *(*MARY *remains on the floor with lowered head.* JOHN *and* JAMES *come forward to comfort her, but she waves them back.* PILATE *seems a little ashamed at his treatment of her. More softly!)* You must think of *my* position. *(The* VOICES OF THE CROWD *swell.)* I will plead myself for him.

(He goes to the window and steps out onto the balcony. The CROWD *raise a great shout. He raises his hand, and they stop.* MARY *rises to her knees and kneels. Her hands are clenched as though in prayer; her face tortured and agonized. Through* PILATE*'s scene on the balcony she hardly moves.)*

PILATE: What do you want me to do to him whom you call the King of the Jews?

CROWD: Crucify him! Crucify him!

PILATE: But what accusation do you bring against this man?

A VOICE FROM THE CROWD: If he were not a malefactor, we would not wish his life. *(Cries of agreement from the* CROWD *)*

PILATE: Why, what evil has he done?

CROWD: If you let this man go, you are not Caesar's friend; whoever makes himself a king speaks against Caesar.

PILATE: *(Turning to the room and* MARY *with a gesture as though he can do no more. He speaks to the* CROWD *again.)* What shall I do? I see no harm in this man. What do you want me to do?

CROWD: Crucify him! Crucify him. Free Barabbas in his place. *(*PILATE *rushes frantically into the room. He pours water into a bowl and runs to the balcony with it.)*

PILATE: I have told you this man seems to me a just man. I know no reason why you should want his death.

CROWD: *(Threateningly)* Crucify him! *(Loud cries)*

A VOICE FROM THE CROWD: We want his blood.

ANOTHER VOICE: You are no friend of Caesar's!

PILATE: *(Washing his hands)* See, I wash my hands of this man's blood. I will deliver him to you, but I find no fault in him.

The Mother of Christ

(The CROWD *shouts wildly,* "Long live Pilate!" PILATE *returns into the room and closes the window.* MARY *leaps to her feet and flings herself before him, holding to his gown.)*
MARY: Spare him! Spare him!
*(*PILATE *pushes her roughly aside and goes out of the room, followed by the* ROMAN GENERAL. JOHN *and* JAMES *approach* MARY *and lift her to her feet. They sit her on the chair the* GENERAL *has left.* MARY *closes her eyes. She seems completely broken. At that moment,* PILATE'S WIFE *enters the room hastily. She speaks quickly and frenziedly.)*
PILATE'S WIFE: *(To* JAMES*)* Is this his mother?
JAMES: Yes. Who are you?
PILATE'S WIFE: His wife. *(She gestures toward* PILATE*'s chair.*
    MARY *opens her eyes. The* TWO WOMEN *look at each other.)*
PILATE'S WIFE: *(To* JAMES *and* JOHN*)* Go, station yourselves down-
    stairs so that no one will come up. I have something to say to her.
    *(*JAMES *and* JOHN *hesitate, but* MARY *indicates for them to obey.*
    They go down.) I can help you! I want you to meet me in an hour
    at the third street, after you come up the hill on the left. I will
    have obtained the key to the prison where I know they are going
    to put Jesus—when *(She hesitates and then continues.)* when they
    have scourged him. *(Mary shrinks and covers her eyes.)* The officer
    who guards the prison is in love with me. I will get him to leave
    his post, while you go in and release Jesus. Do you understand?
MARY: *(Faintly)* Yes.
PILATE'S WIFE: Go then, quickly! We must not be seen talking. I
    will give you further directions when we meet.
(She goes rapidly out of the room the way she came. Mary rises slowly as though dazed, then goes down the stairs.)
Curtain

Part 3

A prison, one hour later. The walls and ceiling are stone; the ceiling is low. Upstage left there is a small opening in the wall as though leading into a corridor. Directly to the right of the stage there is a small narrow window high up. Through this window, moonlight streams in to the center of the stage. It is the only light in the prison. In the center of the stage on the ground can be seen the top of an iron trapdoor. A lock hangs from it. Beside it lays a crown of thorns and a purple cloak, stained with blood. A second after the curtain rises, Mary enters. She pauses in the doorway as though to accustom herself to the dark. Then she advances quietly and peers about. On seeing the cloak and crown of thorns she gives a low exclamation of pain. She picks them up; on perceiving the blood upon them, she drops them in horror. She looks about cautiously. On reassuring herself that no one is about, she draws out a key and unlocks the lock of the trapdoor. She raises it slowly, staggering under its weight. She kneels and looks down into the dungeon.

MARY: *(In a low, terrified voice)* Jesus! Jesus!

VOICE OF JESUS: Who calls?

MARY: *(Joyously on hearing his voice)* It is I, my son. I have come to save you. Come out, come out quickly.

VOICE OF JESUS: Your mission is useless, Mother.

MARY: *(Again terrified)* What do you mean? *(Groping with her hands)* Where are the steps? You seem so low down! How can you come out?

VOICE OF JESUS: I cannot come out.

MARY: Yes, yes, you can. I will find a ladder. It must be somewhere. Is it down there? I cannot see in the dark. Make haste! There is only a short while to spare while the guard is gone. It's Pilate's wife that has helped us.

VOICE OF JESUS: I cannot come.

MARY: *(Touching again the cloak and the crown of thorns. She speaks almost sobbingly.)* Is it because they have hurt you so, my son? *(Wringing her hands)* I cannot see your face, but there is blood on this cloak and on this crown of thorns—what have they been doing with this crown of thorns?

VOICE OF JESUS: *(Tenderly)* Do not weep, Mother. It is true that crown of thorns has been pressed upon my brow, and that cloak is stained with my blood—that is not the reason I cannot come.

MARY: *(Frantically)* But I have come to save you, to help you escape!

VOICE OF JESUS: The soul cannot escape by fleeing through a prison door.

MARY: *(Tragically)* You don't understand! We will flee together. I will bind and heal your wounds.

VOICE OF JESUS: It is you who does not understand. They would only be reopened again by the sins of the world.

MARY: *(Completely terrified)* Are you delirious? *(Leaning way down)* Give me your hands. I will help you out. Can't you understand we have only a few minutes? Only a few minutes between you and death. The Jews are going to kill you!

VOICE OF JESUS: *(Quietly and calmly)* There is no death.

MARY: *(Hysterically and pitifully)* Jesus! Oh, my son. Have compassion on your mother's agony. Come out, that I may save you before it is too late.

VOICE OF JESUS: *(Deeply tender)* Don't you know, Mother, that I must first save the world. Seeing your agony is one more cross for me to bear—one more cross before the final crucifixion, yet I cannot come.

MARY: *(Burying her face in her hands)* Will you still persist in making me suffer so? You are the only thing I have in the world; the only one I love—yet you are the only person I do not understand, the only one who wounds me deeply.

VOICE OF JESUS: It is only through those we love that we can really suffer, and perhaps suffering, grow to understand that we must accept each person as they are.

MARY: But you are my child—I brought you into the world—I brought you up—

VOICE OF JESUS: I am my Father's child, who is in Heaven.

MARY: You are tearing my heart into pieces.

VOICE OF JESUS: It must be, Mother. I have my work to accomplish.

MARY: *(Suddenly looking up)* Hark, someone is coming! I hear steps.

VOICE OF JESUS: Leave me, Mother.

MARY: I cannot! I cannot leave you to your death like this. *(Calmly and determinedly)* I will not forsake you.

(A ROMAN SOLDIER enters. On seeing MARY, he stops dead with surprise, then goes quickly forward.)

OFFICER: *(Alarmed)* What is this? Has the prisoner escaped?

MARY: Have no fear, he is still there.

OFFICER: Woman, how did you come here? *(Looking about)* Where is the guard? *(He looks again into the dungeon. On being assured JESUS is there he is about to swing back the trap. MARY flings herself down.)*

MARY: Jesus! Jesus!

VOICE OF JESUS: Do not weep, Mother. *(The OFFICER drops the trap and locks it. MARY kneels with her head in her hands.)*

OFFICER: I came just in time. Who are you, woman?

MARY: His mother.

OFFICER: The guard will pay for this! *(Not unkindly)* But you—you must go along now. I will not report you—I, too, have a mother. *(He lifts MARY to her feet. She makes a gesture toward the dungeon, then drops her hand wearily. She turns and goes out.)*

Curtain

Part 4

The same as part 1. Again a room in MARY's house. As the curtain rises, MARY MAGDELENA is sitting to the right, a trifle off the center of stage. She is beautiful with long flowing hair. JAMES is standing by the window looking out. JOHN *walks about. They all show signs of a terrific strain and are intensely worried and nervous. It is about two o'clock of the same night.*

JOHN: I can't understand why Peter hasn't returned. He knows how worried we are.

JAMES: If he has not found Mary, he is probably staying away on purpose so as not to let us know.

JOHN: But he must understand we know he has not found her, or else he would have returned.

MARY MAGDELENA: If he has not found her, why should he return? There is nothing to tell.

JOHN: *(Impatiently)* You always make excuses for everyone, Mary Magdelena. Peter has been gone more than two hours—it's time he returned to say one thing or another.

JAMES: *(Listening at the window)* I hear a step now. (PETER *enters. He seems a trifle older than* JAMES *and* JOHN. *His manner is rough but kindly. There is a great sadness in his face. He pauses a second before he speaks, looking from one to the other.)*

PETER: *(Sadly)* I do not know where she is. I could not find her. I went back and asked the soldier outside of Pilate's house which way she had gone, but he said he did not remember seeing her.

JAMES: She left there with us. It was afterwards that we missed her.

PETER: *(To* MARY MAGDELENA*)* I went to your house also, but she had not been there.

MARY MAGDELENA: I know that. I left only a short while ago myself.

PETER: Then I tried to find out where they have imprisoned him— but I could not.

JAMES: I feel sure Mary has found out, and that is where she is. Hiding outside in the darkness in the hopes of getting a glimpse of him. *(Peter sinks despondently onto a bench.)*

PETER: One will never get over the horror of a night like this—it will haunt one always.

MARY MAGDELENA: It's unbelievable to think of Jesus captured, scourged, and mocked.

(She drops her face into her hands. The door opens slowly. JOHN *rushes and opens it wide.* MARY *stands there. She enters slowly and exhausted.* MARY MAGDELENA *springs up and guides her to the chair upon which she has been sitting. She kneels beside her. The* MEN *crowd about.)*

MARY: *(Gazing before her as though in a dream)* He would not come with me.

MARY MAGDELENA: *(Caressing her)* Where have you been, Mary? We have been so worried about you.

MARY: *(Looking at her)* Why, with Jesus, of course.

JAMES: Did you see him?

JOHN: Where?

MARY: In the prison.

PETER: How did you get there?

MARY: Pilate's wife gave me the key. He could have fled with me, but he would not.

JOHN: *(Astonished)* You mean he could have escaped and he would not?

PETER: Was the way clear?

MARY: Yes. No one was about.

JOHN: He must be mad! What reason did he give?

MARY: He said: "The soul cannot escape by fleeing through a prison door." *(A light comes to* MARY MAGDELENA*'s face.)*

MARY MAGDELENA: *(Softly, half to herself)* He said that?

PETER: I can't understand him; he should think of us who are depending upon him.

MARY MAGDELENA: *(Passionately)* He promised us a Kingdom. He will not fail us.

JOHN: Sh! It is for that the Jews fear him.

MARY: *(Sadly)* He has worn a crown of thorns.

JAMES: If he could have escaped and would not, he must have had some good reason. We should not question him.

JOHN: But we left our fishing nets to follow him—now if he allows himself to be killed, we can follow him no more.

MARY MAGDELENA: I, too, left much to follow him, but not for all the world would I again be what I was. I will follow him just the same after death—anywhere.

JOHN: They may not kill him after all. We have not heard so definitely.

*(*PETER *moves uncomfortably. He places his hands to his eyes.* MARY *turns slowly as though some unknown force guides her. She looks at him. Rising she goes over and takes his hands from his eyes. He rises quickly and stands before her with his face cast down.)*

MARY: *(Breathing deeply)* You have heard something, Peter—speak the truth.

PETER: *(Trying to evade)* Nothing—nothing.

MARY: *(Commandingly and holding his wrist)* That is not the truth! What is it? *(*PETER *again hesitates.* MARY *draws herself up.)* I am strong enough, Peter. What—is—the—truth?

PETER: *(Hanging his head. There is an intense silence.)* Tomorrow at three—tomorrow at three—*(His voice breaks.)* They are going to crucify him.

(MARY gives out a cry. MARY MAGDELENA leads her tenderly back to her seat and kneels again beside her with her arms about her. The two women rock to and fro in despair. PETER sinks again upon the bench. JAMES and JOHN wring their hands.)

JAMES: That this should be!

PETER: *(Hopelessly and sobbing)* We can do nothing.

MARY: *(Looking far before her as though for a brief instant the realization of her son's power dimly dawns upon her)* He seemed to know this always. *(A long pause)* He said my agony would be another cross to carry. *(Closing her eyes)* I must make it lighter for him.

(There are a few minutes of silence, then JOHN moves restlessly. He finally sinks down upon a bench and stretches himself out, leaning upon his elbow with his head upon his hand. He closes his eyes; gradually his arm relaxes and falls upon the bench with his head upon it. He breathes evenly and soundly in sleep. PETER, who has been weeping, gradually ceases; he wipes his eyes with his hands and then drops his head on his arms upon the table. He remains awake a few minutes longer, his eyes appear heavy and finally close in deep slumber. JAMES remains gazing out of the window; after a while he turns. He views PETER and JOHN and is about to sink onto the floor when he sees the TWO WOMEN are still awake. He hesitates, then as they do not turn or notice him, he slips cautiously to the ground. He struggles for a few brief seconds to remain awake, then his head drops onto his shoulder and his eyes close. Only the TWO WOMEN remain conscious of the long, terrible night. Gradually a wan, pale light appears in the sky at the approach of a day. MARY MAGDELENA shifts her position, then slowly her head begins to drop, her eyelids droop. Little by little her head sinks, until it finally rests upon MARY's knee. She, too, relaxes and sleeps. Upon feeling the weight of MARY MAGDELENA's head, MARY looks down upon her, then tenderly and compassionately she touches her hair, smoothing it back. Only she remains wide-eyed and sleepless, gazing out, tragically and sorrowfully before her. Through the window the light changes from lavender to rose, as the dawn streams in.)
Curtain

Part 5

A hill opposite the hill of Calvary, which is supposed to be offstage to right. It is about two o'clock the following afternoon. The scene should give the feeling of overlooking a valley. When the curtain rises, the stage is empty, then MARY, supported by JAMES and MARY MAGDELENA, comes up from the back, as though they had climbed far. They are followed by PETER *and* JOHN. *They all look thoroughly crushed, discouraged, and heavy at heart.* MARY *seems completely broken. She sinks onto a flat rock in the center of the stage.* MARY MAGDELENA *sits beside her to the right.* JAMES *drops onto the ground to her left.* PETER *also sits on a small rock direct left of the stage.* JOHN *remains upstage looking off into the valley. There is a long silence while one feels their utter dejection.* JAMES, JOHN *and* PETER *should give the feeling of the hopelessness which would come to simple, ignorant men when the hand that has been guiding them is suddenly taken away. There is something pathetically touching about the way in which they seem completely lost.*

PETER: *(Staring tragically before him)* I don't understand—I can't believe this is all really happening. I have been hoping up to the very last minute, that he would do something to save himself.

JAMES: Yes. That is what I felt, too. I was sure he was going to do something great and strong—a miracle of some kind.

MARY: *(With an entirely human angle about her son; discrediting any power the disciples attribute to him. She speaks sadly and a trifle bitterly.)* They have beaten and tortured him too much to think anymore of the dreams you and he used to talk about. He is too tired.

JAMES: They were not dreams, Mary. At least we did not think so. We left the sea to follow him, because he told us he was a king, and had a kingdom to offer us. *(Sadly)* Now that is all gone and we have nothing.

MARY MAGDELENA: *(With exaltation)* We have known Jesus! *That* is something.

PETER: Yes, yes, I know. But it is difficult to forget the army of angels he told us he had at his command, and the riches which would be ours. Now they are leading him, poverty-stricken, to an ignominious death, with not one hand raised to save him.

MARY: *(Making excuses for Jesus)* He was a good son—a good son. You should not have attached so much to what he said. But it is all probably my fault—I should have brought him up differently—then he might not have had these ideas. *(She weeps.)* Don't blame him—it is my fault—not his fault. *(*JAMES *and* MARY MAGDELENA *caress and comfort her.)*

MARY MAGDELENA: Don't cry, Mary. It is not your fault, nor his either. *(Slowly)* There is no fault in Jesus. *(There is another long silence.)*

MARY: *(Suddenly beating her breast)* It doesn't seem *possible* that I can sit here like this, and his death so near. *(She rises.)* I *must* follow him—I *must* know what they are doing to him! *(She starts to move.* JAMES *and* MARY MAGDELENA *detain her.)*

JAMES: Don't go, Mary. Please sit down again. You will need all your strength for the last. John will tell you when they reach the top of the hill. *(*MARY *sways a little.* JAMES *leads her tenderly to the rock again. She sinks down.)*

MARY: *(Brokenly)* John! *(John turns.)*

JOHN: Yes, Mary?

MARY: Tell me what you see, John. *(Closing her eyes and clenching her hands)* I must follow him through it all—his agony must be mine. *(Turning to them and sobbing wildly)* Why won't you let me follow him? I have a right—I'm his mother.

MARY MAGDELENA: You know you could not stand it, and it would be terrible if Jesus saw you.

MARY: He knows I am following him here anyway. *(She places her hand over her heart.)* Even at the other end of the world I would follow him. *(Turning to* JOHN *again)* Tell me what you see, John.

JOHN: *(Distressed and about to move away)* I cannot tell you.

MARY: *(Half rising)* Then I will watch myself. *(Her legs give way. She sinks down again.)*

JAMES: No, no, Mary. *(To* JOHN *)* Tell her, John—we can do no more. *(He makes a gesture as though it were useless to refuse further.)*

JOHN: *(Looking off to right)* They are just at the bottom of the hill. A vast mob is following Jesus. He is carrying on his shoulders a great, heavy cross.

MARY: *(With agony in her voice)* Are they striking him?

JOHN: *(Answering unwillingly)* Yes.

MARY: *(As though torturing herself)* Go on—go on!

(During all of JOHN*'s speech,* MARY *sits very straight with her eyes closed. She hardly moves except for her hands, which open and close convulsively. Her face is ashen and tortured.* MARY MAGDELENA *drops her face in her hands, rocking her body slowly from side to side.* JAMES *shakes his face with his hands.* PETER *kneels and gazes before him as though in prayer.* JOHN *speaks as though the words were being torn from him. A darkness comes over the sky, which grows deeper and deeper through the following scene.)*

JOHN: They are just ascending the hill—the Roman soldiers are running forward with long spears trying to disperse the mob, which seems frenzied and mad. *(A pause)* Jesus seems to have stopped and is swaying under the cross—he has fallen on his knees. They are lashing and beating him to make him rise. *(A pause)* He has risen again and is going on. The mob seems frantic. They must be jeering and mocking him because I see their fists and hands—like an angry surging sea of demons—raised high above their heads, swaying and beating in the air. *(A pause)* I can see Jesus plainly now. He is wearing a soiled purple cloak, and a crown of thorns is upon his head. There is a great, coarse rope tied around his body, which the soldiers are using to drag him on. The blood is pouring down his face, into his eyes and mouth. *(A pause while his voice breaks with agony of the scene. When he speaks again, his voice becomes excited.)* A woman has come out of the crowd—she has stopped Jesus and is wiping his face with a cloth. *(A pause)* He is going on again—he is ascending the steepest part of the hill now. Oh! *(He puts his hands to his eyes for a minute.)*

JAMES: What? What?

JOHN: *(Agonizingly and with his eyes still covered)* He has fallen again. *(A pause. He uncovers his eyes.)* He is going on again now. No— wait. A man has come out of the crowd. He is helping Jesus carry the cross. *(A pause)* He has stopped again. Weeping women are blocking the way. Jesus seems to be speaking to them. The soldiers are pushing the women aside. Jesus is going on again. *(A pause)* He is nearly at the top of the hill. They are whipping him. *(A pause)* He has fallen again!

MARY: *(Leaping up)* I cannot bear it—I cannot bear it! *(She suddenly becomes the wildly enraged mother fighting for her child. This is her greatest human scene, where every impulse in her suddenly bursts forth in anger, hatred, rage. She is like a tortured, cornered animal, fighting her last fight with her back against the wall. This whole scene should be played with an uncontrollable, devastating, passionate, outburst.)*

MARY: Curses on them! Curses on every hand raised against him! A hundred thousand curses on their blood! May they die in torture and disease! May their tombs be rent open and the foulness of their corpses fill the air! *(Wildly)* Let me go to them—I will go to them! *(She starts to rush off. JOHN and JAMES seize her. They all surround her, but she fights them frantically off.)* Let me go to them, I tell you—let me tear their eyes! They can kill me, but I will die beside my Jesus! *(They finally overcome her struggles. She sinks exhausted upon the ground, breathing deeply and shaking convulsively. MARY MAGDELENA supports her head. The others gather about her.)* *(Brokenly)* I—have—not—the—strength.

MARY MAGDELENA: *(Deeply, tenderly)* No—no, of course not. Rest, Mary.

MARY: (*Making a supreme effort to sit forward and pushing* MARY MAGDELENA *aside*) No—no—I—must—go—to—him-

MARY MAGDELENA: Not now.

MARY: Yes—*now*, before it is too late. I gave him birth—my hand shall soothe him at his death. (*She passes her hand over her brow as though to awaken herself from a trance. The sky darkens. There is a faint flicker of lightning and thunder in the distance.*) You can all stay here. My place is in the shadow of his cross. (*She starts to move.*)

MARY MAGDELENA: I will come, too!

JOHN: And I, too! (*It grows darker. Again a flash of lightning*)

JAMES: And I!

(*They all go off to the right, except* PETER. *The* TWO WOMEN *clinging together. There is a terrific crash of thunder.* PETER *sinks to his knees, joining his hands in prayer. The thunder rumbles lower and lower in the distance; the stage grows darker and darker with a strange unnatural light.*)

Curtain

Part 6

Two days later. A sepulcher with the stone rolled back stands to the left of the stage. It is night. In the distance, outlined against the sky, can be seen the three crosses on the hill of Calvary. As the curtain rises, MARY MAGDELENA *rushes onto the stage from the right, followed by* MARY.

MARY MAGDELENA: (*Excitedly*) You see, I told you it was true. His body is not there any longer. He has risen. (*Joyously*) It's a miracle after all! Shall I go and tell the others?

MARY: (*Gazing at the sepulcher as though stunned*) Yes—yes. Go—leave me.

MARY MAGDELENA: You will not be afraid here alone?

MARY: (*Shaking her head in the negative, without taking her eyes from the sepulcher*) Go.

(MARY MAGDELENA *runs off to the right.* MARY *stands a minute without moving, then she passes quickly into the sepulcher. In a few seconds, she reappears again. She seems frantic and casts about as though she has lost something. She sinks on a stone beside the sepulcher. She holds her hands tight to her breast and beats them together; a look of poignant agony upon her face. She is more than at any time the pathetically human mother, robbed of her child.*)

MARY: They have taken the last thing from me—even his body. Not one shred of him to hold to me—not a token—not a garment. (*She sobs.*) When his body was there, I could have at least caressed him.

He was dead, but I could have held his body in my arms—I could touch him—I could kiss his face—his eyes—his feet—*(A pause. Slowly her arms drop to her sides and hang limply, as though everything had gone out of them. Her head sinks, forward, her body stoops.)* Gone . . . everything.

(There is a long pause. She sits without moving, the symbol of all human despair, the human mother of sorrow. Then slowly she moves, she draws her body up until she is sitting very straight. She lifts her arms until they are extended before her; the palms of her hands turned toward her as though suddenly they were filled; as though she were holding something in them. She raises her head, a gradual look of supreme exaltation overspreading her countenance. Her attitude is one of listening, as though she were hearing a voice. Through the whole following speech, she slowly changes from the simple, human mother, to the great divine mother of the world. She seems to grow taller, becomes majestic and filled with supreme dignity. The harassed, perplexed, and agonized look leaves her haunted eyes. The human beauty of her sorrow-stricken face becomes the beauty of everlasting and divine compassion. An exalted light burns in her eyes and illuminates her features.)

MARY: *(As though to some invisible presence)* I understand—I understand it all now. It's opening—before me—like a white dove spreading wide its wings in the rising sun. I understand why he suffered —died. I understand why he did not appear to me before he rose. It is not enough that I should only be the mother of one son—I see that now. He wanted to show me that I must be the mother of all the world—of all the struggling, suffering world. In these two hands I must bear the burden, not only of all children, for all time; but of all mothers, for all time. Not one woman who carries a child within her womb, but I shall stand close to her with this hand upon her tortured heart. It was for this he was born by me— to show that woman should solace always. He wanted to show that all genius is misunderstood, even by others—mostly by mothers; who cannot recognize a child must have its own life to live. That the gift of life we give, should ask no reward, demand no price. And that gift is not enough—life asks more of us. It asks that we should give understanding to the fruit that we have borne—not only blind instinctive understanding, but the understanding of God, who knows each one *must* be himself, with his own destiny to follow. *(She turns and looks toward the Cross.)* And that cross— symbol ever more to be, of suffering and sacrifice—will they know your message? Will they know it lies, not in following one faith, but in finding faith in all things? Or will it take centuries and centuries of distorted and complicated religions and teachings, to show us in the end that your wood was crude and simple, the arms that stretched across it simple, too? Simple, but filled with compassion, tolerance, understanding and forgiveness. *(She turns again, looking out.)* Will they understand these things? Or is it only I who understand them, because I am his mother? *(A glorious, radiant light shines upon her face. She rises slowly to her feet, as the final revelation comes to her.)* Because I am—the—Mother—of—Christ. *(In the distance a great, brilliant star appears over the Cross of Jesus.)* Curtain

World Without End

The Characters

PETER WORTH

GARRICK PEEL

ROMOLA CHARRINGTON

CARLOS DUVAL

FABER FLEECE

FINLEY, *the butler*

DARIUS EYRE

IRIS, PETER'*s niece*

DAVID CROSS

MRS. CROSS

ROBERT CROSS

Act 1

The setting is ROMOLA CHARRINGTON'*s country home in England, a lovely old English house—mellowed by age and tradition. It is placed to the right of stage, with a brick terrace stretching out onto lawn. A huge tree grows in the center of the garden with masses of flowers. Garden chairs are scattered about, and cooling drinks are on a table. To left of stage a box-hedge grows. Upstage stands an old stone wall with an iron gate in the center. Rolling country and clouds are seen beyond. It is about five o'clock of a hot summer's afternoon after a glorious day. Through the act, shades change to twilight and then dark.* PETER WORTH *and* GARRICK PEEL *are lounging back, talking languidly.* PETER WORTH *is a man about 42 —tall and handsome with a strikingly strong face. He has dark hair touched with gray.* GARRICK PEEL *is about seven years his junior. Distinctly the horsey, sporting type. His hair is blond. He seems vivacious and gay and rather a "busybody"—whereas* PETER WORTH *impresses one as serious and reserved. As the curtain rises,* GARRICK PEEL *yawns, stretches, then leans over to table, pouring out whiskey and soda into a glass.*

GARRICK PEEL: Won't you have a drink? It's really been a beastly hot day.

PETER WORTH: No, thanks—I never drink, you know, never seemed to have added that virtue to my many others—I'll have that lemonade, though, if you will just reach it over. (GARRICK PEEL *leans over and passes lemonade.*)

PETER WORTH: It's remarkable how it cools off in the evenings down here after such a hot day—must have been a scorcher in town. Glad I was not there.

GARRICK PEEL: Gad, it was!—I damn near burned up. When I got Mrs. Charrington's wire asking me down, I put on all the reserved strength that had not melted away—jumped into a taxi, flew to the train, and just got the last one out. Lucky, I call myself. Hadn't expected a dream and a snore in the country, much less a drink in such a garden.

PETER WORTH: This little garden really is enchanting at this time of evening, full of poetry and shadow. It's the time of day I like most. I love the view from here. *(Laughs.)* You know I've always maintained this is a fairy garden.

GARRICK PEEL: *(Tilts his chair back, also laughs.)* So I've always understood, or rather not so much about the fairy garden as the fairy princess who lives here.

PETER WORTH: I think one might easily call Romola a fairy princess —the kind one dreamed of as a child. Since her illness she even looks more ethereal and unreal. She really ought not to stay here. She should be on the continent in the mountains—*(Sighs.)* but one can't do anything with her. She's very headstrong.

GARRICK PEEL: I was sorry to hear of her illness, although she does not look as ill as I thought she would. A trifle nervous and keyed up perhaps.

PETER WORTH: She does too much.

GARRICK PEEL: *(After a pause in which he drinks)* It's curious to find oneself in England after having been away so long.

PETER WORTH: Let me see, how long have you been away?

GARRICK PEEL: Ten years. Ten years last May.

PETER WORTH: Is it possible? Heavens, it only seems yesterday when we had that farewell dinner.

GARRICK PEEL: That's the way time goes—at least for those at home. To us, out there in India, it doesn't go quite so quickly. It seems to me forty years instead of ten. One gets so out of touch with things—for instance; I never knew Mrs. Cross *(Corrects his slip.)* Mrs. Charrington, had remarried. Oh, I heard a number of things about her, but never that. When did she remarry?

PETER WORTH: She didn't. After her divorce she merely took back her maiden name of Charrington.

GARRICK PEEL: Oh. So that's it. And the gossip that I heard—was that true?

PETER WORTH: How should I know? I don't know what you heard.

But if it was only gossip, I think it safe on general principle, to say it's untrue. What did you hear?

GARRICK PEEL: *(Embarrassed and hesitatingly)* Oh—you know. The usual things one hears about a beautiful woman, I suppose.

PETER WORTH: *(Quickly)* No, I don't know. Especially not about Romola. I'm a great friend and admirer of hers; in fact, I've asked her many times to marry me.

GARRICK PEEL: *(A trifle surprised)* She could not do better.

PETER WORTH: Thanks. She does not feel that way, however, nor do I. She has had many excellent chances.

GARRICK PEEL: I didn't mean anything against Mrs. Charrington. You know I, too, always admired her from a distance; I barely knew her before. But, frankly, do you think it wise to have your niece living with her? After all you are a man of the world and gossip's—well; gossip.

PETER WORTH: *(Angrily)* Gossip's a damn lie. As for Iris, I consider it an honor for her to have such a wonderful woman as Romola to bring her up. If her own mother had lived, she would have been brought up like most English girls, without a thought in her head except to catch some stupid whippersnapper of a boy, go punting with him, and then marry him. As far as rumors go, Romola has an unconventional nature—perhaps she has made the mistake of living too long alone without any woman companion, but what of it? Of course, many men have been in love with her; to some she has not been kind, more from indifference and weariness I expect than from anything else.

GARRICK PEEL: Probably.

PETER WORTH: Well, these men with not too amiable natures who have suffered from her coldness have, of course, had the pleasure of retaliation in saying or insinuating disagreeable things. And then, too, there has been the usual women's jealousy. Jealous of her looks and, above all, her brains.

GARRICK PEEL: She is clever.

PETER WORTH: She is the most intelligent woman in England—always has brains and power around her, but unfortunately—(or fortunately, as you like) they are usually men.

GARRICK PEEL: Well, you must forgive my taste for gossip; out there one welcomes it—there's not much else to keep one going.

PETER WORTH: *(A trifle bored)* It's a pity some other form of amusement can't be found. *(He rises, looking toward the house.)* Here comes Romola now.

(ROMOLA CHARRINGTON *comes out of the house onto the terrace and down the steps. She has a wonderfully graceful figure, her eyes are large and expressive, her face is pale, distinguished and very beautiful. There is a wistful sadness about it. She looks very delicate and ethereal, but there is something distinctly human and sympathetic about her, with a curiously reckless note. She is dressed in a white soft dress, and garden hat. She wears no jewelry and only a thin scarf is wound around her throat and draped about her shoulders. She is followed by* CARLOS DUVAL *and* FABER FLEECE; DUVAL *carries cushions.* GARRICK PEEL *and* PETER WORTH *draw up chairs.*)

PETER WORTH: Hello—you delinquent ones—we have been waiting for you.

(CARLOS DUVAL *puts a cushion at* ROMOLA*'s back and one at her feet, then he drops down on the ground and gazes up at her.*)

CARLOS DUVAL: I was just telling Mrs. Charrington that if I could paint her in this evening light no one would believe that a truly human person had posed for me. They would think it was a spirit from the woods.

GARRICK PEEL: *(Laughing)* Is that why Mrs. Charrington was laughing? It did not sound as if she believed it.

ROMOLA: I'm too old to believe in flattery—although I must admit it is always very nice. I'm afraid flattery is a little like amber; with age one finds a fly in it.

PETER WORTH: It takes a Frenchman to flatter. *(Flicks his flower at* DUVAL.*)*

CARLOS DUVAL: It is not flattery. God and man both alike love beauty—both create it—or rather man endeavors to do so.

FABER FLEECE: I should say rather man loves what is beautiful, whereas God (if there is one) creates and makes beautiful what he loves.

PETER WORTH: Garrick, my dear fellow, when beauty and art get together it's time we withdrew—I am afraid a poet and a painter will make us look flat.

GARRICK PEEL: Not a bit of it. I refuse to move. Although, of course, beauty always does make me look flat. Won't say that about artists or writers. *(Laughingly)* I think poets always talk rot!

ROMOLA: Occasionally soldiers indulge in it, too. For instance, I seem to have heard much rot from India—even about such an insignificant person as myself. *(With humor at* GARRICK PEEL*'s expense)* It seems, also, much of that rot came from you. I hear you have been worrying about my morals.

GARRICK PEEL: *(Confused)* I don't know where you got that idea.

ROMOLA: *(Carelessly)* Oh, from several people. Shall I tell you about myself so as to confirm or dispel your expectations?

PETER WORTH: *(Trying to stop her and make the situation less embarrassing)* Romola!

ROMOLA: *(Continuing defiantly and recklessly; she laughs.)* Oh, Peter darling, don't look so worried. You make it seem as though I was about to pull some dreadful skeleton out of my closet. After all, I can only tell Captain Peel the truth, which may be disappointing to him. *(Turning to* GARRICK PEEL*)* Did they tell you out there in India that I could not divorce my husband, but that it was he who divorced me?

PETER WORTH: Really, Romola, this is unnecessary. *(*GARRICK PEEL *and the others move uncomfortably.* ROMOLA *continues with forced animation.)*

ROMOLA: No doubt they did not tell you—of course, how could they, since they did not know?—that the evidence was planned against me, so that my husband could keep my boy. They do that sort of thing, you know, even in these civilized days of advanced warfare. *(She coughs.* PETER WORTH *rises and replaces the scarf on her shoulders, which had slipped off.)*

PETER WORTH: Is it getting too damp for you?

ROMOLA: No—no, thanks. *(Draws scarf around her.)*

GARRICK PEEL: I must apologize if you have heard anything unpleasant, I assure—

ROMOLA: *(Interrupting)* Don't apologize—it would be dreadful not to be talked about—wouldn't it, Peter? A sure sign that one was growing plain. I only wanted to set you straight, that's all. *(To the* BUTLER, *who appears with tea things)* Where is Miss Iris, Finley?

FINLEY: I don't know Madame. I saw her last with Mr. Eyre, but I just saw Mr. Eyre come in without Miss Iris.

CARLOS DUVAL: I thought they were playing tennis. *(*FINLEY *arranges the tea things.)*

DARIUS EYRE: Hello, everybody. I'm done up! *(He drops on a chair in an exhausted fashion.)* Phew, that youngster of yours can walk. First she played me three sets of tennis, then after we had changed our clothes and had had a shower and I was just expecting a long sleep for my weary bones, she suggests a walk. Of course, I had to acquiesce. I always do with women. She walked me up hill and down dale and now here I am as finished as my old cab horse.

GARRICK PEEL: *(Sarcastically)* The trouble is with you, Eyre, you are much too unselfish. Now *I* should have refused to have walked.

DARIUS EYRE: Selfishness or unselfishness, my dear chap, I have

discovered is merely a matter of pretense one way or another.
When I was young and really by nature selfish, I spent all my time
pretending I was unselfish, because I was wise enough to realize
that people admire unselfishness in the young. As I grew older, and
met sorrow and suffering, I by nature became gentler, tolerant and
unselfish. But I usually pretend I am just the opposite—extremely
selfish and indifferent—sort of a boor you know. The women always like it better. In either case it's a pose, my dear Garrick—
merely a pose.

CARLOS DUVAL: One should avoid posing.

DARIUS EYRE: Then that in itself becomes a pose. Being natural is
the most difficult thing in the world. One can't help posing.

ROMOLA: *(Pouring tea)* Fiddlesticks! *(To* PETER WORTH*)* How
many?

DARIUS EYRE: *(Wearily and half to himself)* Fiddlesticks or no
fiddlesticks, I know it's so.

PETER WORTH: Two, please. *(*ROMOLA *passes him a cup of tea.)*

ROMOLA: *(To* GARRICK PEEL*)* Strong or weak?

GARRICK PEEL: None thanks. I have whiskey and soda.

ROMOLA: And you, Darius?

DARIUS EYRE: Oh—anyway—*(Sitting up)* That reminds me, there
are no more people coming down here today, are there?

ROMOLA: No. Why? Haven't we enough?

DARIUS EYRE: Yes—but that was not the reason I asked. Iris is bringing home some young man she found on the road.

PETER WORTH: Found on the road! Since when does one find
young men on the roadside, like stray cats?

ROMOLA: *(Laughing)* What do you mean, Darius?

DARIUS EYRE: Just what I said.

GARRICK PEEL: Well, you did not throw much light on your remark.

DARIUS EYRE: I can't tell you much. I only know we were walking
along when we came upon a young boy who had lost his way on
a motorcycle. He was very tired and hot, as he had been traveling
all day. Iris very graciously invited him home. As they seemed
to amuse each other, and as he had to walk slowly pushing his
motorcycle which I forgot to add was broken—I walked on ahead
quickly. That's all I know. If you look out the gate you will probably see them coming. *(*FABER FLEECE *rises and looks out.)*

FABER FLEECE: Yes, here they come. Very modern school, indeed.
Youth and a motorcycle instead of a white charger, as it would
have been in the old days. *(*DUVAL *rises and looks out, too.)*

DUVAL: Ah, but we at least have the sky of flame for the background which gives the real color to the picture, and although invisible, I have an idea Cupid hovers somewhere about.

FABER FLEECE: How glorious and inconsequent youth is.

ROMOLA: *(Laughingly)* I expect poor Iris gets weary of all you old men, and Providence in its kindness casts her down a youth for a few bright minutes. Is he a nice young man, Darius? Not boring, I hope.

DARIUS EYRE: No, indeed, very charming, with such lovely manners. He did not want to come in. He felt shy, I think, but Iris insisted. I believe he is going to some house about 30 miles from here.

DUVAL: Here they come. *(He rushes and opens the gate.* IRIS *runs in ahead. She is about 15, fresh and lovely—her eyes shine excitedly. She throws her arms about* ROMOLA.*)*

IRIS: Aunt Romola, dear, you can't guess—*(She looks at* DARIUS EYRE *in disappointment, her expression falls to one of regret, then annoyance)* Oh, *he's* told you.

DARIUS EYRE: *(Hanging his head and looking guilty)* I *am* sorry.

IRIS: You pig! I never can have a surprise for Aunt.

(She runs back to gate and beckons. A YOUNG MAN *enters. He is slight, dark and very pale. His face is that of a dreamer, very sensitive but weak. He seems about 16 years and looks weary and is covered with dust. He carries a cap in his hand and with the other pushes a motorcycle with a kit bag attached onto the back. He leans the motorcycle against the wall. He advances a trifle uncertainly and timidly toward* MRS. CHARRINGTON.*)*

DAVID: I am afraid I am intruding, but your daughter—I mean your sister, insisted—was kind enough to ask me in.

ROMOLA: *(Extending her hand, which* DAVID *takes, keeping his eyes riveted on her in a fascinated way)* She is my niece and I assure you we are delighted you came. Let me introduce Mr. Worth, Mr. Duval, Mr. Fleece and Captain Peel; you met Mr. Eyre—I think. *(The boy shakes hands with each, then his eyes return to* ROMOLA.*)*

DAVID: It's nice of you to want me. I mean to be so kind. *(Embarrassed and quickly)* This *is* a lovely garden. *(Fans himself with cap.)* It was very warm on the road.

ROMOLA: Where have you come from and won't you have something to drink?

DAVID: If it's not too late, or perhaps I am a bother?

IRIS: No, indeed, we always have tea late because we never dine until nine.

DAVID: Then I'd love some tea, if I may. (IRIS *makes tea.* FLEECE *passes bread and cake.*)

PETER WORTH: *(To* DAVID*)* Where did you come from?

DAVID: From London, sir. *(Drawing his eyes from Romola)* I expect to go on about 20 miles.

IRIS: *(To* DAVID*)* How many lumps?

DAVID: One, please.

IRIS: *(Addressing* DAVID*)* You were joining your mother and father, didn't you tell me?

DAVID: Yes, they have taken a house near here for about a month. I left Italy a fortnight ago, where I have been studying, and was just motoring to join them. I have never been in this part of the country before.

IRIS: *(Passing him the tea)* I hope you will stay, and like it.

DAVID: Thank you—I have not been home since I was a child. I've always been abroad.

PETER WORTH: Have you been studying?

DAVID: Yes, sir.

FABER FLEECE: What—Life?

DAVID: *(Embarrassed)* No, sir, or rather, yes, in a way—music is what I have really been studying.

ROMOLA: How delightful. (DAVID *looks up, pleased.*)

PETER WORTH: Now you see, Garrick, *more* art. I tell you we are in a nest, of hornets. *(Looking at* DAVID *and nodding his head to* FLEECE *and* DUVAL*)* This gentleman is a poet and this one an artist and now you, a musician, arrive upon the scene. I think it's time we poor old war dogs retired.

ROMOLA: Peter, I know you have been trying to leave us ever since we came out, now I'll simply make you go, and Garrick, too, and show this young gentleman the north room where he can clean up *(Turning to* DAVID*)* for, of course, you must stay for dinner. I didn't catch your name.

DAVID: Oh, I beg your pardon—Cross is my name, David Cross. (ROMOLA *and* PETER WORTH *exchange a rapid glance. He steps to her side as though to protect her.)* I should love to stay to dinner. I'll take my bag up. *(He moves toward motorcycle.)*

PETER WORTH: Don't bother. I'll tell Finley to bring it up.

DAVID: Thank you.

(Goes up terrace and into house with GARRICK PEEL. IRIS *also goes in, followed by* FLEECE *and* DUVAL. DARIUS EYRE *stretches and rises. From twilight it grows almost dark.* FINLEY *comes out and lights lantern.)*

DARIUS EYRE: I think I'll rest up a bit before dinner. It's going to be a glorious night. *(He goes in house.* WORTH *and* ROMOLA *look at each other in silence.* WORTH *crosses and sits beside her.)*

ROMOLA: *(In shaking voice)* Peter, is it possible?

PETER WORTH: *(Taking her hand)* My dear, I can't say. After all these years I suppose it is impossible to recognize him. How old would he be?

ROMOLA: *(With emotion)* Just about his age. Sixteen years old.

PETER WORTH: *(Thoughtfully)* It's just possible.

ROMOLA: *(Rises in agitation, walking to and fro. Coughs and presses her hands to her temples)* Oh, Peter, could this be he? Could this be *my* David?

PETER WORTH: It's strange that he should have the same name. But wouldn't he recognize you?

ROMOLA: How could he? He hasn't seen me since he was four.

PETER WORTH: That's true. I had forgotten.

ROMOLA: *(Pausing a minute, intensely thoughtful)* I wonder. I wonder if it could be an answer.

PETER WORTH: To what?

ROMOLA: To my wanting him so much.

PETER WORTH: I have guessed that about you many times, when you seemed far away.

ROMOLA: I have longed for him in bitterness and silence.

PETER WORTH: I have often wished that you would have spoken about him—it would have been an outlet; I never dared approach the subject. *(*ROMOLA *hesitates, then sits beside* PETER WORTH. *She speaks as though unwillingly and forcing herself.)*

ROMOLA: Peter, do you know why I have never spoken about that part of my life to you?

PETER WORTH: It is your own affair.

ROMOLA: That was not the reason. I would tell you most things.

PETER WORTH: What was the reason?

ROMOLA: The same one that prevents me from marrying you. I want to make myself suffer.

PETER WORTH: *(Surprised)* Suffer more than you have! Why?

ROMOLA: To expiate.

PETER WORTH: Expiate? *(Laughing)* Nonsense, what have you ever done to expiate?

ROMOLA: *(Hesitates, then continues)* I will tell you—something I have never told anyone. It will shake your faith in me.

PETER WORTH: Do not tell me anything you will regret.

ROMOLA: I must, because your faith in me deserves the truth. I lied to you before. *(She drops her head in silence.* PETER WORTH *starts; upon seeing her suffering he touches her shoulder tenderly.)*

PETER WORTH: Never mind. Don't go on if it makes you unhappy.

ROMOLA: I want to tell you. *(Looking up)* Oh, not to make excuses for myself, but because I want you to know.

PETER WORTH: Tell me then.

ROMOLA: I made you believe that I have lived an innocent life— but that is not true.

PETER WORTH: That was your past, my dear; do not let it bother you.

ROMOLA: You should know it—mostly because you have been big and kind enough not to have questioned me.

PETER WORTH: *(Shrugs his shoulders.)* Why should I? Your life is your own.

ROMOLA: Listen, Peter. When I married Robert I was absurdly young and ridiculously in love with him. I was very poor, so when he wanted to marry me, with his charm and wealth, I felt as though it was the arrival of a fairy prince. The first year we were married nothing could have been more wonderful. David was born. I was supremely happy. After that Robert began to neglect me. We were living in the country and he was always making excuses to go to town for business. Then vague rumors reached me that he was again seeing a woman who had once been his mistress. I was desperately wounded and too proud to inquire into the truth of the matter. In order to retaliate I began encouraging Robert's best friend, who had plainly shown me on several occasions that he was more than interested in me. When Robert was away, I asked him to the house—first, because I wanted to convince Robert that I, too, could have love in my life, and secondly, because I was genuinely lonely—this man really cared for me and helped me pass the hours I would otherwise have spent in despair. One night when Robert was away, and he had come for dinner, a great storm arose and forced him to stay all night. At the time, I did not think anything of it. The servants were in the house—David and his nurse nearby—and he was Robert's great friend. It all seemed natural. A few days later Robert chanced to find a love letter his friend had written me. The letter was more or less innocent, but it aroused Robert's suspicion. He grew wildly jealous; then he found that his friend had spent the night in the house a few evenings previously. The butler, who it seems bore this man a grudge, testified against me. The accusation was so deplorable to me that I left with David and went up to London. I was so bitterly hurt I felt I could not return without Robert's deepest apologies. But they never came; instead he started divorce proceedings, naming his friend as correspondent. He also stopped all my money. To make a long story short, he won the divorce case on the servant's evidence, which were all lies—paid for, it afterwards turned out, by this woman who wished to marry Robert and who has since done so. Robert was granted the custody of David. As I was left without a cent, I did not fight it further, as I felt I could give him nothing, while Robert had everything to offer him. Through all this, I would have gone mad if it had not been for this man who loved me. I did not love him but because he helped me, and stood by me, and because I felt I was branded anyway, I allowed him to become my lover, but I denied it always. Later, when my aunt died and left me the money on which I now live, I broke off my relation with him. Then I became so ill and went to Switzerland to live. For months I saw no one and nearly died. On my return to England I heard Robert had remarried. A few years ago, when he was old enough to understand them, I wrote David several letters; none of which he answered. I thought he was ashamed of me, so I wrote him no more; then, too, I felt losing him was my punishment—that I should accept my suffering.

PETER WORTH: My dear, you should have told me all this a long time ago. I would have made you forgive yourself.

ROMOLA: There is no one that can forgive me but David. I have waited for his forgiveness all these years. Peter, do you think this is David?

PETER WORTH: If it is, I would not tell him the truth. Stick to your original story. There is little understanding in youth.

ROMOLA: Oh, Peter, how I want him; the madness that is going through me for my boy—and yet, I can't pretend it is all because of a maternal feeling.

PETER WORTH: *(Surprised)* What do you mean?

ROMOLA: *(Hesitatingly)* I mean—somewhere—something in me, still loves Robert—or perhaps it is something in me still clinging to the only real love of my life. I want my son because he is my son, but I think I want him mostly because he's Robert's son, too.

PETER WORTH: How strange women are!

ROMOLA: I never even wanted to face the truth myself until tonight. For years I have been evading it, filling my life recklessly with other things. But now I see it differently. I suppose all of us are trying to forget something.

PETER WORTH: Don't worry about these things.

ROMOLA: But it's true; I'm always trying to forget. For women it's more difficult than for men. I suppose there are thousands of women all over the world in just such a position as I am in—unable to forget.

PETER WORTH: Don't talk this way; you will only make yourself ill. Come in the house. *(He rises.)* It is growing chilly.

ROMOLA: No, send the boy out here. I want to speak to him.

PETER WORTH: All right, my dear.

(He bows his head and goes into the house. ROMOLA walks over and picks a flower; she stands lost in thought with her back to the house, pulling the leaves from the flower. A few minutes elapse; DAVID descends the steps.)

DAVID: *(Coughing slightly and embarrassed)* I beg your pardon—but did you send for me? (ROMOLA *starts, turns, pulls herself together and impulsively extends her hand, but instantly pulls it back again.)*

ROMOLA: Why, yes—It's so delicious here this time of evening in the garden, and as you could not change for dinner, I thought it would be nice to talk a bit. *(There is a silence and both are obviously embarrassed.)*

DAVID: That, that was very kind of you. Can't I get you a wrap?

ROMOLA: No, thanks, come and sit down. *(She goes over and sits down on a garden bench. DAVID sits on a chair.)* That is not very comfortable, come and sit here. *(She motions with her hand for him to come and sit beside her. He crosses over and timidly sits down next to her.)* Tell me a little about yourself.

DAVID: *(Gazes at his feet, because ROMOLA stares at him so intensely.)* There is very little to tell about my life, and besides, it would probably seem very dull to you.

ROMOLA: *(With conviction)* No, indeed, it would not. If you only knew how much I would love—*(Corrects herself.)* How much I love to hear about young people. Somehow I feel we could be very great friends.

DAVID: *(Looking up pleased, and seeming a little reassured)* You don't know how wonderful that would be. I have very few friends, and I don't think many people like me.

ROMOLA: I am sure that is not so. I liked you at once.

DAVID: Oh, I am so glad—because, do you know I have never met anyone like you before—I mean, someone so kind and—and so lovely—and then, someone to notice me. I shall think about you on my way home tonight.

ROMOLA: *(Quickly and with terror in her voice)* I mean, it will be too far to go in the dark. You must spend the night here.

DAVID: You are awfully kind, but I must go on, they will have expected me before this.

ROMOLA: Who will have? *(Closing her eyes and in low voice)* Your mother?

DAVID: My father and his wife—or I suppose I should say, my stepmother. I have no real mother.

ROMOLA: Is—is your mother dead?

DAVID: *(Hesitating and looking away, then feebly)* Yes.

ROMOLA: It must be lonely without her—or don't you miss her?

DAVID: *(Rising and twisting his fingers uncomfortably and nervously)* Oh—ah—it's hard to explain. I do miss her horribly; although I can't even remember her, and I seem to miss her more every day. I suppose it's because I don't get on with my stepmother and I don't seem to understand my father.

ROMOLA: Isn't your stepmother kind to you?

DAVID: Oh, it isn't that. It's the small things. I expect young boys are rather trying. I get so on her nerves. Somehow I always seem to whistle at the wrong time, or tap my feet when I shouldn't, or be in the house when I should be out. It's lucky I'm seldom home. But do you know there are times when my mother seems very close to me.

ROMOLA: Perhaps because she is thinking of you.

DAVID: *(Bitterly)* I doubt it.

ROMOLA: You mean, you doubt the dead can think about us?

DAVID: It isn't that—oh, you can't understand.

ROMOLA: Perhaps I could. In a manner we are a little bit alike. I once lost a boy.

DAVID: I'm so sorry.

ROMOLA: Tell me—*(In low voice)* Would you rather go on tonight than stop here?

DAVID: *(A trifle at sea, but unconsciously beginning to feel her emotion)* You know I would rather stay here. *(There is a tense awkward silence. His voice shaking)* You are trembling, Mrs. Charrington, I knew you would be cold. Let me fetch your wrap.

ROMOLA: No, no, I am not cold. You will stay the night though, won't you?

DAVID: Yes, since you really wish it.

ROMOLA: *(Casting a look about and shivering slightly)* It's become so dark. I can't see you. Would you mind getting the lantern on the gate?

*(*DAVID *goes over and takes down a small lantern off the gate.* ROMOLA

stands with her hands clasped as though praying. DAVID *returns and is about to put the lantern on the table, when she takes it from him and impulsively holds it up to his face. She gazes intensely and longingly at him. He drops his eyes and breathes hard. Suddenly she casts the lantern aside— seizes him in her arms and kisses him.)*

DAVID: *(Shaking with emotion)* Mrs. Charrington!

ROMOLA: *(Realizing that without meaning to she has played on his passion, she makes a visible effort to pull herself together and calm her own inner turmoil.)* Forgive me—*(At that moment, and before she has time to continue,* IRIS *opens a window upstairs and looks out.)*

IRIS: Why, Aunt Romola, you have not yet dressed for dinner; you will be very late.

ROMOLA: *(With an effort)* I'm coming now.

*(*IRIS *withdraws and closes window.* ROMOLA *goes quickly into the house with her head slightly bowed.* DAVID *remains as though spellbound with a half-perplexed, half-exalted expression on his face, looking wonderingly at the lantern.)*

Curtain

Act 2

Morning room inside of ROMOLA'*s house. It is 10 in the morning. Large French windows open out onto a brick terrace where sun streams in.* IRIS *and* DAVID *are finishing breakfast at a little table on the terrace. Inside, the room is a simple Queen Anne style with quaint little mantel to right of stage and an old portrait hanging over it. A door leads out to left showing a winding stairway in the hall. Upstage left a small grand piano is open, with a stiff needlework lounge in front of it. Two easy chairs face each other before the mantel, with a small table and telephone beside one of them. The walls are painted a soft green; vases of tea roses are on the piano, table and mantel. A photograph of* ROMOLA *is also on the mantel. From the room one can see out into the garden where flowers in various colors grow abundantly.*

(After a pause)

IRIS: What are you thinking about?

DAVID: *(Looking up quickly)* Thinking? Oh—nothing.

IRIS: *(Laughing)* But you must be thinking about *something*. Never mind if you won't tell me. *(She drops her napkin, which* DAVID *picks up and hands to her.)* Thanks.

DAVID: Oh—it isn't of much importance—what I was thinking, I mean.

IRIS: Then you *were* thinking. You see I knew it!

DAVID: I was thinking it was curious, the way Mrs. Charrington insisted upon my spending the night.

IRIS: She was afraid you would lose your way in the dark, had you left.

DAVID: It was very sweet of her, of course, and I was awfully pleased to have stopped on—only it did strike me rather off. The way she asked me, I mean. *(Quickly, in fear he has hurt her feelings)* I'm not criticizing her—she's been wonderfully kind and I think she is the most beautiful woman I have ever met. (IRIS *appears a trifle annoyed.)*

IRIS: You must not mind my aunt's ways—she is very often queer, but everyone is used to it. You know, she is not my *real* aunt.

DAVID: No, I did not know that.

IRIS: I am an orphan. My only relative is Colonel Worth. Some years ago he asked Aunt Romola to adopt me. I love her just like a mother.

DAVID: *(Reflectively)* Fancy you not having a mother, either.

IRIS: Why, I thought you said you had one.

DAVID: No, not a real one, not even a lovely substitute like yours. I have a stepmother and—and—oh, well, I might as well say so—I dislike her intensely. In fact, I *hate* her.

IRIS: Oh, how awful to have to live with someone you feel like that about.

DAVID: I haven't lived at home for a number of years. I don't think I ever shall. *(Sadly)* I doubt if I ever will have a home.

IRIS: Oh, don't say that.

DAVID: It's funny I should speak to you, too. Do you know I have never, never spoken about my home life to anyone, and until last night, for years I have never allowed anyone to mention my mother's name in my presence. *(Points to piano.)* Music has been my mother and friends together. I don't know why, but I feel so depressed today, and last night, too. Do you ever feel sad?

IRIS: *(Lightly and without understanding)* Yes, sometimes. (DAVID *looks at her and then looks away.)* Now, what are you thinking about?

DAVID: Only that young people never seem to understand.

IRIS: *(Angrily)* Understand what, I pray?

DAVID: *(Timidly)* It's hard to explain.

IRIS: Well, since I don't understand, and since you seem to cherish the illusion that you are so much older than I am, I will leave you, *old* Mr. Cross. *(Jumps up from table and drops him a bow and proceeds to leave room.* DAVID *springs up and bars her way.)*

DAVID: *(Entreatingly)* Please don't go. Don't be angry. I really did not mean to offend you. You see, I am not quite used to people, especially women. I am so sorry, it is all *my* fault, I know. It's something here. *(Places his hand to his heart.)* Something I can't explain—a dull ache like loneliness, an empty feeling as one might feel if all the world had turned against one, or a cold hollow sensation as one would have standing in the shadow after having been in the sun—although I can't really say that because I somehow feel *my* heart has never felt the sun.

IRIS: How strangely you talk. *(Hesitates to leave.)*

DAVID: Come, don't leave, and please forgive me.

IRIS: I'll forgive you this time.

DAVID: And I'll try not to speak strangely, although I know I feel it. More so today than usual because last night—because last night— *(He hesitates.)*

IRIS: *(At once curious. Coaxingly)* Oh, do tell me—what about last night?

DAVID: *(Hesitating)* I never do tell people things and, perhaps, I shouldn't tell you this.

IRIS: *Please* do. Especially if you never tell anyone else. It would be so nice to be the only person. *(She runs to lounge and sits down. Beckons him to sit beside her, which he does. Excitedly)* Go on, go on—because last night, what?

DAVID: Well, just before dinner Mrs. Charrington sent for me out in the garden, and—and—well, she asked me if I would stay for the night, or if I would rather go on. Then we had a peculiar, rather disconnected conversation, and finally she held a lantern to my face, and looked at me very queerly, for what seemed to me a long time. I was rather embarrassed—I do not remember what I said, but suddenly—well, before I knew it, she put her arms around me and—*(He fidgets and blushes.)* and—and kissed me.

IRIS: Kissed you!

DAVID: *(Dropping his eyes)* Yes, it's the first kiss I have ever had from a woman since my mother left. I don't know if I should have told you this, but it was strange.

IRIS: Fancy Aunt Romola kissing you. That *was* off. What do you mean by saying ever since your mother left? Isn't she dead?

DAVID: *(Sadly)* No.

IRIS: *(Tenderly but still curiously)* Won't you tell me about her? I never tell secrets and I should so love to know this one.

DAVID: There is not much to tell. You see, my mother and father

were divorced when I was very little. I remember my mother
vaguely. I know she was beautiful although I can't recall her face.
What exactly did happen has always been a mystery to me, but
I know she did something—*(Looks away and drops his eyes.)* I
mean—she—acted badly with some man. Oh, how I *hate* to say it,
and—well, she had to give me up. After that she went abroad to
live and I have never seen her since.

IRIS: Oh, how sad.

DAVID: My father married again and as I was very unhappy at home
they sent me to school, first in France, and finally Italy. I have
never had anyone who really loved me, except my father in a half-
hearted way. I think he became very bitter after my mother left
and I always feel he has never really loved anyone else except her. I
think my stepmother did everything in her power to marry him.
And since then she has always done everything to poison him
against my mother.

IRIS: It must have been so lonely abroad for you. Weren't you afraid
all alone in foreign schools?

DAVID: *(Smiling)* No. It's been pretty lonely, of course, but I have
not minded so much because I had my music, and then I have
had my daydreams about my mother; I usually dream about her
at night, too.

IRIS: Have you never heard anything about her?

DAVID: No, never. I never speak about her. You know, I suppose it's
silly, but I always pray to her and I always love to sleep out under
the sky because there I feel somehow she is closer to me. The stars
and I are great friends always.

IRIS: *(Laughingly)* How can one be friends with the stars? You *are* a
queer boy.

DAVID: *(Shrinking)* Oh, don't say that. That's what they used to say
in school and it hurt my feelings.

IRIS: I'm so sorry. But why don't you look for your mother?

DAVID: Because I am afraid.

IRIS: Afraid of what?

DAVID: Afraid of the truth. You see, in my heart I have never really
believed the things that they have implied and said against her, but
I have thought about it so much that when I meet my mother I
shall ask her if they are true. If they are not, all my life I shall beg
her forgiveness. But if they are true, *(His face grows tense.)* I shall
go away and never, never want to see her again. *(He turns slowly to*
IRIS *and gazes at her.)* Do you ever feel afraid of the truth, or, I

wonder, if it is only I who trembles before it? One hears so much about the beauty of truth and yet I think there is nothing that one feels so much fear about.

IRIS: But your mother, she might not tell you the truth—she might deceive you.

DAVID: She could not deceive me. I shall know.

IRIS: Well, maybe. You are an awfully clever boy; I liked you the minute I saw you yesterday on the road.

DAVID: *(Somewhat embarrassed)* That was very nice of you.

IRIS: *(Wistfully)* I wish you could stay on a bit. It would be nice to have you.

DAVID: It would be nice to stay.

IRIS: You could teach me to ride your motorcycle. Do you know, before I came here with Aunt Romola I used to live with an old lady in London and sometimes during the spring and summer, I used to get up at four o'clock in the morning and ride my bicycle on the street?

DAVID: Why did you do that?

IRIS: Oh, just for fun. That's why Uncle Peter decided to bring me down here so Aunt Romola could be sort of a mother to me. He said I didn't have any bringing-up.

DAVID: Did you want to come?

IRIS: Yes, rather. They promised me lots of long white kid gloves. I used to be mad to wear long white kid gloves like all the ladies in Court photographs. I used to think that when I grew up I would have hundreds and hundreds of very long ones, and wear them *all* the time.

DAVID: *(Laughing)* You don't think that now, do you?

IRIS: *(Laughing, too)* No, not now. *(There is a silence.)*

DAVID: What are *you* thinking about?

IRIS: Only that I hope—I hope you are going to like me.

DAVID: Why, I do like you immensely already.

IRIS: *(Brightening up)* More than anyone else? More than Aunt Romola?

DAVID: Why—why, differently, of course.

IRIS: *(Discouraged)* Oh, dear, everyone likes her better. I think it's simply because she is older—I wish I were older.

DAVID: Older people wish they were younger.

IRIS: I don't believe it. *(PETER WORTH enters.)*

PETER WORTH: Good morning!

IRIS: Hello!

DAVID: Good morning, sir.

PETER WORTH: What are you two young people chatting about so earnestly at this hour of the day? As I came along I never heard such tense voices.

IRIS: Oh, David has been helping me arrange the flowers. *(To* DAVID*)* I may call you "David," mayn't I?

DAVID: Of course.

IRIS: We were just going into the garden to get some more flowers.

PETER WORTH: Have you had your breakfast?

IRIS: Of course, silly, it's nearly eleven. Come on, David, I am going to make you work.

(She picks up a flower basket and they go out. WORTH *looks at his watch, then sits down. He starts to read paper, sighs and puts it down. Rises and rings bells.* FINLEY *enters.)*

FINLEY: What is it, sir?

PETER WORTH: Oh, Finley, is Captain Peel up yet?

FINLEY: I don't think so, sir.

PETER WORTH: And where are the other gentlemen?

FINLEY: Mr. Eyre has gone out riding, sir. Mr. Fleece and Mr. Duval are in the garden.

PETER WORTH: That's all, thank you. *(*FINLEY *retires.) (Calling)* Oh, Finley!

FINLEY: *(Reentering)* Yes, sir?

PETER WORTH: That reminds me. Get me London on the wire and Doctor Welling's wire. Tell him Colonel Worth wishes to speak to him for Mrs. Charrington.

FINLEY: Yes, sir.

PETER WORTH: Let me know when you get it and connect me here.

*(*FINLEY *goes out.* WORTH *walks about, then sits and reads paper. Phone rings on table, he jumps up and takes receiver off.)*

PETER WORTH: Yes, yes, that's right, Finley. Go ahead. Is this Doctor Welling's office? Oh, how do you do, doctor. *(Pause)* Yes, I am speaking for Mrs. Charrington. *(Pause)* Yes, I am down here at her place and I wanted to ask you to fill that prescription for her again. *(Pause)* In rather a bad way, I am afraid. *(Pause)* I fear so. *(Pause)* I think so, too—I have been trying to get her back to Switzerland, but you know how difficult she is to manage. It did her so much good the last time, but she has some ridiculous idea about the next time she goes she will never come back. *(Pause)* Of course, I know that, but I can't convince her. *(Pause)* I'll try, but I don't think she will. *(Pause)* I am very well, thanks. Been hot in town, hasn't it?

(Pause) Thanks awfully. I'll do my best. Good-bye. *(He puts receiver down and settles in chair, picks up paper again. He just starts to read when* FINLEY *comes in.)*

FINLEY: Beg pardon, sir. But I wonder if Mrs. Charrington could see a lady who is asking outside for her?

PETER WORTH: A lady asking for Mrs. Charrington?

FINLEY: Yes, sir.

PETER WORTH: What sort of a lady?

FINLEY: She didn't say, sir—just insisted on seeing Madame. Said she had to and would not go away until she did.

PETER WORTH: As urgent as that?

FINLEY: Yes, sir.

PETER WORTH: Wouldn't give her name?

FINLEY: No, sir.

PETER WORTH: *(Goes to window and looks out.)* Very odd. Is that she, Finley? I suppose so, seeing that ladies do not drop off the trees here.

FINLEY: No, sir.

PETER WORTH: Well, you had better ask her in and tell Mrs. Charrington. No, wait. I will tell her myself. I am sure she is up. Bring the mysterious lady in.

FINLEY: Very well, sir.

(They both go out opposite doors. FINLEY *reenters with the* WOMAN. *He withdraws.* WOMAN *raises her veil and looks about, then walks over and takes* ROMOLA*'s photo in her hand. She gazes at it intently. While she is doing so,* ROMOLA *enters noiselessly. She is in a gray morning gown and looks tired and ill. She coughs—*WOMAN *starts—and turns around.)*

WOMAN: Oh—ah, I beg your pardon. I am so sorry to have come so early. I—ah—hope I am not disturbing you.

ROMOLA: Not at all. To whom have I the pleasure of speaking?

WOMAN: *(Shifting uneasily)* Eh—don't you know me?

ROMOLA: *(Scrutinizes her carefully, then kindly shakes her head and smiles.)* I am afraid you will have to forgive me. If I have seen you before I can't remember it.

WOMAN: I'm Mrs. Cross. *(*ROMOLA *starts, then slowly gazes at the other woman.)*

ROMOLA: No, I have never seen you before. Not even your photograph, as I notice you have mine. *(Makes a gesture to photograph Mrs. Cross still holds in her hand, which she confusedly replaces on the mantel.)* Now that I do see you, why have you come?

MRS. CROSS: *(Visibly nervous and embarrassed)* I—I almost wish I had not come. It's—it's rather difficult you must admit.

ROMOLA: I am sorry if it is difficult for you. If you would tell me
what you came for, perhaps we would be able to finish quickly,
this obviously is a painful interview for us both.

MRS. CROSS: *(Visibly excited and beside herself)* Oh, it's only this.
I am so unhappy. There is no one in the world I can come to
except you.

ROMOLA: *(Icily)* Indeed.

MRS. CROSS: *(In an unnatural and strained voice)* Eh, I wanted to
come and see you before—I—eh—hoped you would not mind.
(Looking around nervously) Do you mind if I smoke?

ROMOLA: *(Stiffly but with dignity)* No.

(MRS. CROSS *takes out a cigarette case, offers one to* ROMOLA, *who
refuses it—then nervously starts to light one herself. She changes her mind
however, blows out match and puts cigarette back in case.)*

MRS. CROSS: You might ask me to sit down. *(Laughing nervously)*

ROMOLA: Certainly, if you wish. *(They sit.)*

MRS. CROSS: You don't seem—you don't seem exactly pleased by
my visit, Mrs. Charrington.

ROMOLA: I have never been accused of hypocrisy. If you have come
for any real reason I should like you to tell it to me. It is rather
useless, I think, our trying to prolong what seems to be a rather
unnecessary conversation.

MRS. CROSS: I know it is queer, but it can't be helped. Oh, if you
only knew how I have suffered in trying to make up my mind to
come here. *(Continuing helplessly)* You see, you see, it's this way.
Robert has never, never forgotten you.

ROMOLA: *(Straightening and raising her head)* I think you had better
leave my husband out of this, if you please.

MRS. CROSS: You mean, *my* husband, if it comes to that. *(Then
more weakly)* Oh, well, it does not matter *whose* husband, that's
not the point. *(Floundering around)* Well, I mean it does matter,
but not just that way. You see, you see, it's this. Can't you do something to make Robert stop caring for you?

ROMOLA: *(Growing rigid)* I fail to understand you.

MRS. CROSS: *(Becoming distracted)* Oh, dear, oh, dear, it's this way,
you see—he has never ceased to love you. I knew he still loved you
when I married him, but I was foolish and thought I could make
him care for me. I loved him so. *(Cries.)* For years and years he has
never spoken your name and if I ever did he would fly into a rage.
I was never good enough to speak your name.

ROMOLA: *(Growing more calm as other woman becomes more excited)*
I can't see how I can help you.

MRS. CROSS: Only in this way. A few weeks ago Robert was offered a big and influential position in South America, on the condition he would remain there for seven years. I pushed the offer myself as I longed to take him away—I feel if I could get him there I could have him closer. Now for some reason or other he won't decide before he sees you. He said he wanted to come to this part of the country and take a house for a rest; I never dreamed about you, so we came and took a house near here. Only ten days ago I discovered through my chauffeur, who knew yours, that you were near us. Of course, I knew then why my husband wished to come. He tried hard enough to leave me in London.

ROMOLA: And now, what do you expect me to do?

MRS. CROSS: Help me!

ROMOLA: Do you mean to say you were planning to take David to South America for seven years?

MRS. CROSS: No. He never will live with us and so he was going back to Italy to study music. He was coming here yesterday but never reached us.

ROMOLA: Really—Mrs. Cross, I'm afraid I can't help you!

MRS. CROSS: You can if you want to. If my husband comes to see you, send him away. Refuse to have anything to do with him. Tell him you hate him. Tell him he must promise to go to South America with me. Advise him, and make him see it is his duty, but above all, never mention my coming here. If he knew or even suspected, it would finish me.

ROMOLA: If Robert should come here, as you say—which I very much doubt—I would not see him, so I could not advise him one way or another. *(She rises.)* I think that is all we can say to each other.

MRS. CROSS: No, no, there is something more. If you will help me, I will tell you the truth about something—

ROMOLA: *(Turning toward the bell, about to ring)* I'm sorry—

MRS. CROSS: It's about David. (ROMOLA *does not ring. Pauses a minute, and then turns.)*

ROMOLA: David?

MRS. CROSS: Yes.

ROMOLA: What do you mean?

MRS. CROSS: I mean—he never received the letters you wrote him.

ROMOLA: What are you saying?

MRS. CROSS: I will tell you, so you will see I mean well. I took the letters and never gave them to David.

ROMOLA: *(Half-incredulously)* You did that?

MRS. CROSS: Yes. I wanted to turn him against you—thinking if I kept him I would have had more of a hold on Robert—I did not realize the boy was a link between you and that he would become a detriment to my life. *(She weeps.* ROMOLA *stands horrified.* MRS. CROSS *grows uneasy under her gaze.)* So you see how I have suffered.

ROMOLA: You took my letters! You dare to come here and tell me that?

MRS. CROSS: *(Looking up surprised)* I told you as a favor. *(*ROMOLA *rings the bell.)*

ROMOLA: The butler will show you out. *(At that moment* DAVID *comes in followed by* PETER WORTH *and* IRIS. *He stops dead as he feels the tension between the two women.)*

DAVID: *(To* MRS. CROSS*)* How did you get here? I saw our car outside. *(Looking at* ROMOLA *and then again at* MRS. CROSS*)* I did not know you knew each other.

MRS. CROSS: So it's here where you were last night instead of coming home—rather a joke on Robert. He was expecting you. *(She laughs.* DAVID *looks at* ROMOLA, *a light of comprehension overspreading his face.* FINLEY *appears.)*

ROMOLA: *(Without taking her eyes from* DAVID*)* Please show Mrs. Cross to her motor, Finley. *(They exit;* DAVID *and* ROMOLA *still gaze at each other.* PETER WORTH *takes* IRIS*'s arm and they, too, go out.)*

ROMOLA: *(Weakly)* David—do you know me?

DAVID: *(Without moving and as though in a dream)* Mother! *(*ROMOLA *sinks on a chair.)* Why didn't you tell me last night?

ROMOLA: *(Hardly audible)* I couldn't—it was too much— *(Terrifiedly)* Oh, David, will you love me?

DAVID: *(Slowly and thickly)* Are the things they said about you true?

ROMOLA: *(Sadly)* Does it mean so much to you that I should be perfect in anything except my love for you?

DAVID: Are the things they said about you true? *(*PETER WORTH *reenters the room.)*

PETER WORTH: Don't ask your mother that question. Ask it rather of me.

DAVID: *(In hard tones and still looking at his mother)* You love her and stand against me. I stand alone as I have stood all my life—utterly alone. You would lie for her. *(Hoarsely)* I *must* have the truth. *(*ROMOLA *pushes* WORTH *aside.)*

ROMOLA: I will have no one answer for me—no one protect me. No one between my son and myself. It's been too long, too long that way. He must look into my eyes and see the answer himself.
(She sinks down on chair and drags DAVID *on his knees before her. For a brief instant she hesitates, then seizes his shoulders and looks into his eyes. There is a tense moment, then he cries out.)*
DAVID: Mother, Mother, forgive me! *(He throws himself at her feet. She lifts him and gathers him in her arms.)*
ROMOLA: Oh, my darling, my darling, you have come back. You must never, never, leave me again. *(Sobs in his arms.)*
DAVID: Oh, Mother, how can you forgive me?
ROMOLA: Forgive you, David? What have *I* to forgive? Rather how shall you forgive me?
DAVID: I have longed for you so, and although I fought against it, I always knew in my heart the things that were said about you were not true.
ROMOLA: *(Fearfully)* Don't let us say anything more about that!
DAVID: No—never again. That is finished forever. From now on we must never fail each other. (ROMOLA *puts her arms around him.)*
ROMOLA: *(In tones of exaltation)* My David. *(Tenderly and pathetically)* My boy.
DAVID: I will never leave you now—*(Radiantly)* Mother!
Curtain

Act 3

It is night in ROMOLA's *sitting room. The room is decidedly simple but in excellent taste. The walls are paneled in cream color. To the extreme left upstage there is a door leading out. Next to it is a lovely old fireplace. A soft lounge is drawn before the fire. Upstage, French windows open out onto a balcony. They are drawn closed and curtains hang from them. To the extreme right upstage there is a door leading into the bedroom as well as a door leading out, which is closed. An old desk in center of stage with two candles burning on it. Books and chairs scattered about. The room is lighted by the candles on desk and mantel and a little lamp on a small table. The chairs and curtains are soft blue; a deep tan rug is spread on the floor. A telephone stands on the desk. As the curtain rises,* ROMOLA *is seated on a lounge before the fire. She is dressed in black evening gown. In the candlelight the paleness of her face stands out and shows the strain of illness. She leans her head back and closes her eyes.* DAVID, *in dinner coat, stands by desk a minute fingering a pen, then he goes over and sits at his mother's feet.*
DAVID: I hate going out when you feel so wretchedly.

ROMOLA: *(Coughs, then smiles, opening her eyes.)* I can never feel wretchedly again now that I have you—when I can reach and touch your hair. *(She puts her hand out and strokes his hair. He takes her fingers and kisses them.)*

DAVID: That's just why I feel such a beast, leaving you to go to this old party. But Iris is so anxious to go, and I hate refusing to take her.

ROMOLA: Of course, dear, I understand. Besides, I want you to see young people and enjoy yourself. *(Her face saddens.)* You have had so few happy times. *(Brightening)* I shall slip into my wrapper and curl up on the lounge and read a while, then in the morning you shall tell me all about the party; who was the prettiest girl and all that. *(She laughs, in which he does not join.)*

DAVID: *(Reflectively)* Mother, sometimes I can't believe all this is true. I am so frightfully happy that I feel it must all be a dream—that something horrible and cruel will happen to awaken me.

ROMOLA: Don't say that, it—it frightens me when you talk that way. We have waited so long for this happiness; it has been so long coming, that now we must hold to it for all we are worth.

DAVID: I know I shall hold to you. *(He kneels beside her, putting his arms about her)* You wonderful, wonderful mother! I'm so happy these days that I feel as if I were walking on the rim of a cloud. I don't believe anybody in the whole world could ever have been as happy as I. *(Drawing back a little and looking at her)* How could they have been? Because no one in all time has ever found anyone as beautiful as you!

ROMOLA: *(Laughing)* David, you spoil me. You should be careful or you will find yourself with an old and very egotistical mother on your hands.

DAVID: *(Laughing also)* I'll take a chance. *(Seriously)* No, but truly Mother, I wonder if you realize how much this all means to me? Finding you, I mean, and having a home.

ROMOLA: I think I do, darling, if it means as much to you as it does to me. *(He kisses her shoulder, her arm and her hand.)*

DAVID: *(Happily)* I must keep kissing you to make sure you are really here and that someone is not going to pinch me and wake me up.

ROMOLA: *(Laughing)* Oh, then your kisses are not as flattering as I thought. *(DAVID laughs, too, then suddenly grows serious.)*

DAVID: I want to tell you something. Something I have wanted to say since that first day when—when—we found each other.

ROMOLA: What is it, David?

DAVID: *(Straightening up and kneeling erectly beside her. He takes both her hands, speaking reverently and fervently.)* I want to tell you that I always believed in you. Always. Long before I met you even. I used to pretend that I might doubt you—but down deep in here *(He places his hand and her hand to his heart.)* I knew I didn't. Then when I met you—when I found you that day—some devilish thing in me made me ask you that question. *(He lowers his head.)* I have felt so ashamed since. So contemptible that I should have even seemed to have doubted you.

ROMOLA: *(Lowering her head, too, and looking away)* It doesn't matter, David. You were right to ask. I understand.

DAVID: That's only because you're so wonderful. So good. *(ROMOLA makes a gesture of denial.)* Yes, yes, that's it—so good. Oh, not good in the stupid sense, but in the big sense. Good in the sense of everything fine, in all truth and beauty. I'm so proud of you, Mother—so afraid for myself that I may not be big enough for *you*.

ROMOLA: David, you mustn't talk this way. Let us not judge each other by anything we do or—or have done. But only by the love we have for each other. That—that must be the test.

DAVID: Yes, I think so.

ROMOLA: *(Pensively)* David, would you always love me now, no matter what happened?

DAVID: I shall always love you—nothing *is* going to happen; we must take good care of that.

ROMOLA: *(Half to herself)* Yes—we must take care of that.

DAVID: What, dear?

ROMOLA: Nothing—nothing. *(Laughing)* Away these gloomy thoughts!

DAVID: Do you know what I spend most of my time thinking about?

ROMOLA: No—what?

DAVID: Our future. The wonderful, wonderful times we are going to have together. How I am going to become a great musician and rich and famous for you. You'll see; you will be proud of me yet!

ROMOLA: I am already. The proudest mother in all the land!

(DAVID takes out his watch and looks at it.)

DAVID: Heavens, it is late—nearly 10:30. If Iris doesn't come soon I shall go to bed instead of dancing. *(He stretches.)* I'm tired. *(IRIS enters. She is dressed for a party and looks very charming.)*

IRIS: Oh, here you are, David. I'm ready, are you?

DAVID: *(Laughing)* Ready? *I've* been ready for hours.

IRIS: Do you like my dress? *(Turning to David)*

DAVID: I should say so. She looks lovely, doesn't she, Mother?

ROMOLA: She always does.

IRIS: *(Obviously pleased)* I'm so glad you like it.

DAVID: *(Laughingly)* I suppose you expect to dance every second?

IRIS: Certainly I do—and with you—I expect you not to leave me a second.

DAVID: Don't count on me, for goodness sake—I can't dance at all.

IRIS: We can always sit out. I think I would rather like it better.

DAVID: I may come home early.

IRIS: I think that is horrid. I thought you would ask me for supper.

DAVID: I wish I could ask Mother for supper. *(IRIS pouts.)*

ROMOLA: *(Laughing)* Now, David, don't be foolish.

DAVID: When I say nice things to you, you always accuse me of being foolish—Well, we'd better go! *(He jumps up.)*

IRIS: Then come on. *(She bends over and kisses Romola.)* Good night, Aunt. I do wish you were coming. Darius and Captain Peel just decided to come with us, so I shall be well escorted. I'm very excited. *(ROMOLA smiles and returns kiss.)*

ROMOLA: Enjoy yourselves. *(Coughs and then continues.)* And don't stay out *too* late or dance too much.

IRIS: We won't. Good night. I'll just run and get my wrap.

DAVID: I hope you won't cough much tonight, Mother; perhaps I'll be able to slip back early—before the others—and come in and say good night again.

ROMOLA: All right, dear, but don't hurry back too soon and spoil your fun.

DAVID: I won't. *(He walks to window, opens it and looks out.)* It's getting very cold. Be sure and wrap up in bed and don't open the window too much, will you darling?

ROMOLA: *(Laughing)* No, I shan't.

DAVID: *(Closing window and stepping back into room. He speaks rather tragically.)* Our friends, the stars, are not out tonight. I hate it when they are not out—they always seem to bring you closer to me.

ROMOLA: *(Laughing)* You funny boy—run along now. They will be waiting.

DAVID: Good night, or rather au revoir. I'll try and come back soon. *(He kisses her again and goes out.)*

(Her eyes follow him as he leaves. She sighs and rises, walks slowly to window, throws it open and looks out for a brief space, then closes it and stands with her back to it, facing room. A pensive smile is on her face as though she were recalling DAVID. Slowly, and still smiling, she blows out candles on mantel and desk. The room is left in darkness except for fire and small

light on table. She goes into the bedroom. There is a silence and stage is left empty. Suddenly a soft tapping is heard on the window, then it is pushed softly open and a man's hand appears, then the window is opened wider and a MAN *enters. He is dressed in dark clothes and wears a soft hat pulled down over his eyes. He comes upstage cautiously and looks about room. Hearing a noise from the bedroom, he slips back against a wall into the darkness.* ROMOLA *enters again in a soft negligee. She moves a little lamp from the table beside the bed to a table near the lounge. She is about to pick up a book off the desk when she turns and sees* ROBERT CROSS. *She utters a low cry and drops back.* ROBERT CROSS *steps forward with extended gesture.)*

ROBERT CROSS: *(In voice filled with emotion)* Romola!

ROMOLA: *(Faintly)* Robert!

ROBERT CROSS: *(Coming nearer and with shaking voice)* Romola, forgive me for coming this way. Forgive me for frightening you.

ROMOLA: *(Interrupting and in low voice)* What do you want here?

ROBERT CROSS: I wanted to see you. I've longed so to see you. I'm desperate.

ROMOLA: Why did you come that way? *(Pointing to window)*

ROBERT CROSS: I knew you would not see me if I came any other way. I've been out there in the darkness so many times hoping to see you, and tonight—tonight when I saw you at the window in here, I came straight to you.

ROMOLA: *(In terrified voice and on the defensive)* You have not come to take David away?

ROBERT CROSS: Were it that, I would have come before. I've come to ask your forgiveness.

ROMOLA: Forgiveness?

ROBERT CROSS: Yes. I have never been able to get away from the wrong I did you.

ROMOLA: You seem to come a little late. You might have thought of this when you first decided to divorce me.

ROBERT CROSS: Oh, I was mad then. Insanely jealous because I thought you had betrayed me—then, too, I was pushed into it— well—you know by whom.

ROMOLA: If this is all you have come about, I must ask you to leave. Everyone is in bed.

ROBERT CROSS: *(Not heeding her)* The servant who testified against you, died a few months ago. He sent for me first and told me he had been paid to testify against you.

ROMOLA: Did you only learn that now?

ROBERT CROSS: Of course. Do you think I knew it before?

ROMOLA: It really does not interest me. This is all ancient history—something I have buried and which I wish to forget.

ROBERT CROSS: Romola! *(Entreatingly)* Don't send me away. I've longed so to see you.

ROMOLA: Between us there is a wall so high that the mere scaling of that balcony *(Points to window.)* could never get you over it. I ask you to leave me.

ROBERT CROSS: Don't be cruel. *(His voice breaks.)* I want you to help me. I need your help. *(He draws closer to her. For an instant she almost softens, then she pulls herself together and moves away from him.)* I don't know what has been the matter with me, but since I divorced you I have not had a minute's peace—lately I can't go on without you. I need your help so desperately.

ROMOLA: *(In hard tones)* Help? You didn't help me much.

ROBERT CROSS: I know. I don't blame you for hating me. I only ask a little mercy—just to see and talk to you a few minutes—to straighten things in my mind. Oh, I know you won't believe me—but I—I love you—I always have loved you. *(He drops on chair and buries his face in his hands.)*

ROMOLA: We can't discuss or argue this here now. We are strangers—utter strangers. I can't be found in my room at this hour of the night with any man.

ROBERT CROSS: Strangers!

ROMOLA: You forget I did not force this visit. I did not ask you to come, nor are you welcome now that you are here. I ask you for the last time to leave me.

ROBERT CROSS: *(Springing up)* Since you despise me so, I will go. It may seem odd or untrue, but all these years I have carried a picture of you in my heart—a picture of you as you were—when—when you cared. *(Drops his voice.* ROMOLA *raises her hand as though shielding herself from a blow.)* I think during all the years that we've been parted I have been merely waiting to see you again. A passionate, frenzied longing to see you again. Picturing you as I knew you, and in my loneliness, it gave me courage to come here tonight, and ask your advice—but I won't bother you after all. *(Drops his arms in weariness.)* Somehow I had not counted on your hatred. *(He walks slowly to table; about to pick up his hat.)*

ROMOLA: Robert, I am very ill—my days are nearly at an end.

ROBERT CROSS: *(Pausing and looking up)* Don't say that.

ROMOLA: It's true. I know it better than anyone.

ROBERT CROSS: I love you.

ROMOLA: It must only be forgiveness that can play a part between us—love has ceased to be. *(A long pause)* Before you came, I felt that having David back was all that mattered—now, just this second, I see differently. I see there is still something else for me to do before I die. . . . I must cast out of my heart all bitterness.

ROBERT CROSS: *(With emotion)* How stupid people are! How blindly they throw away the best things of life—recognizing it too late. Romola, I do love you—is there nothing in you—nothing of what used to be—not even a spark?

ROMOLA: *(Sadly)* Sparks can't continue smoldering when the fire has been quenched.

ROBERT CROSS: I would give my life to have even your forgiveness— I have never loved anyone but you. (ROMOLA *moves to desk and stands with her head bowed. He steps forward and takes her hand. His voice quivering with emotion and excitement)* Romola, I have had a wonderful opportunity offered me. One I have long dreamed of. It's in South America but I must *promise* to stay there for seven years. A man is waiting now in London for my answer; they must know before tomorrow morning. What I came to ask you is—shall I accept it, and—and will you come with me? (ROMOLA *draws her hand away and looks at him as though he had gone mad.)* I know it sounds insane, but Romola, Romola, I want you. I cannot go on without you. We could go there and start fresh. A new continent and a new life!

ROMOLA: *(Hoarsely and incredulously)* Are you trying to make me do the very thing you accused me of with another man?

ROBERT CROSS: I—I don't understand.

ROMOLA: Perhaps not, when it was *you* who took my child from me because *I* was not capable of taking care of him! *(Sarcasm) You* who cast a shadow over my name. *You* who pretended to think I had gone away with another man. And then you divorced me unjustly for what you are now asking me to do with you.

ROBERT CROSS: I know I was mistaken and God knows I have repented, but this is different. You *are* married to me.

ROMOLA: Nonsense. No tie of any sort exists between us.

ROBERT CROSS: Yes, yes, we are married. We have never ceased to be married. You, yourself, used to say that nothing could ever dissolve our marriage. Do you remember how you said we were as one and would be for all eternity? *(Frantically and passionately)* Do you remember the first night we were married and you told me that?

ROMOLA: *(In broken voice)* That was long ago—when I was foolish enough to believe in love—but it was you—you who killed that belief—

ROBERT CROSS: What can I do to make up for it?

ROMOLA: Go to that telephone—call the man in London and say you will go to South America—then go home and tell your wife to get ready to leave with you.

ROBERT CROSS: Romola—

ROMOLA: That is my answer to your question. *(He turns wearily and phones.)*

ROBERT CROSS: Strand 1471. *(There is a pause while he waits for an answer.* ROMOLA *remains immovable.)* Hello—hello, yes, it is I, Robert Cross. Is Mr. Hill there? Yes, give him my name. *(Pause)* Mr. Hill? Yes, yes, I got it—very well, thanks. *(Pause)* Yes, that's what I called for. *(Pause)* Yes, I will go on Saturday. *(Pause)* I'll be in tomorrow. Goodbye. *(He drops the receiver, then rises. In listless tones)* This is forever, Romola.

ROMOLA: *(Staring ahead)* Thank you for phoning. *(There is a silence.* ROBERT CROSS *picks up his hat.)*

ROMOLA: If this is forever—now that you are going—I will tell you that I have never cared about anyone else either—(ROBERT CROSS *looks up as though disbelieving, then a radiant look overspreads his face.* ROMOLA *holds out her hand.)* Good bye, Robert— every success to you.

ROBERT CROSS: *(Passionately)* Romola, if you love me I will not go!

ROMOLA: *(Startled)* You gave your word.

ROBERT CROSS: For South America, yes—but not for tonight— we're here alone tonight—we love each other—

ROMOLA: *(A trifle weakly)* Leave me, Robert.

ROBERT CROSS: Let me stay—we have only this night—this night out of all our wrecked past—out of all our lonely future.

ROMOLA: *(Backing away as though fearful of being convinced herself)* No—no—protect me—for David's sake.

ROBERT CROSS: David would understand—he is the child of our love—Romola—(*He seizes her in his arms; with an effort she pushes him away.)*

ROMOLA: I have transcended all this—I must transcend it into something higher—something worthy of David. *(Weeping)* I have so much to make up for.

ROBERT CROSS: *(Bitterly)* You cannot really love me. *(A door suddenly bangs downstairs.)*

ROMOLA: What was that? *(They both listen—steps are heard.)*

ROBERT CROSS: Someone is coming.

ROMOLA: *(In terrified voice)* Go—go!

ROBERT CROSS: No—no—not yet.

ROMOLA: For God's sake—

ROBERT CROSS: No—Romola—

ROMOLA: Then, in here!

(She pushes him in her bedroom, throws his hat in after him and locks the door. She rushes to lounge and picks up book, pretending to read. She is just in time as DAVID *enters.)*

DAVID: *(Happily)* I managed to get away. I couldn't bear to think of you here alone and our wasting these minutes not being together. *(He goes over and puts his arms around* ROMOLA *and then pauses.)* Why, what's the matter, Mother? You look so disturbed.

ROMOLA: *(Feebly)* Matter—why—why nothing, dear.

DAVID: *(Anxiously)* You haven't been ill or anything?

ROMOLA: Why, no, David. *(Avoiding his eyes)* I have been sitting here ever since you left and was just going to bed. How was the party, dear?

DAVID: Oh, not much fun. I wanted to come back to you. I was worried about you. Then, too, I suppose I am not used to dances and feel rather strange. *(He walks about room and stops before the desk.)* Whose glove is this? *(He picks up* ROBERT CROSS*'s glove.)*

ROMOLA: *(Nervously)* Why, it must be yours, David.

DAVID: No, it isn't. *(He dismisses it from his mind and sits on the lounge beside his mother.* ROMOLA *puts her arms about him.)*

ROMOLA: You ought to go to bed, David. I'm tired, too.

DAVID: Oh, not yet. After coming home early just to see you. I'll read to you a while. What shall we read? *(He looks at the book* ROMOLA *has on the lounge beside her.)* Not that. I'll read some poetry. *(He rises. Looks at the window.)* Why did you open the window? You know you shouldn't sit reading with the window open on your back at night—and you promised me you wouldn't. *(He rises and walks toward the window to close it—looks up at sky.)* On the way to the party the stars came out. It made me much happier.

ROMOLA: Are they out now?

DAVID: *(Peering out)* No, and there are dark terrible clouds coming up in the sky.

ROMOLA: *(A trifle frightened as though by an evil foreboding)* Oh, no, David—

DAVID: Yes, the sky is quite black. *(Turns to her.)* But you see it does not matter—the stars are gone but I have you. *(He leaves the window and enters room.)* What were we saying before? Oh, yes—a book. I'll get one in your room. *(Before* ROMOLA *has time to stop him, he goes quickly to her bedroom door.)*

ROMOLA: *(Unable to control herself)* No—no, David. *(He tries the door; on finding it locked he turns.)*

DAVID: *(Surprised)* The door is locked!

ROMOLA: *(At a loss to know what to say)* It—it doesn't matter—read something else.

DAVID: *(Alarmed)* Why is the door locked?

ROMOLA: Why—eh—I didn't know it was.

DAVID: *(Trying the door again and turning. He sees his mother's agitation.)* You did know it was locked. Why are you lying to me? *(He pauses a moment, walks quickly to the desk and picks up the glove. He speaks sternly.)* Who is in there?

ROMOLA: David, David, don't question me like this.

DAVID: *(Growing white)* Where is the key to that room? Why have you lied to me?

ROMOLA: *(Springing up)* David!

DAVID: Yes—lied. While I was dancing you have had someone here— the owner of that glove—I see I came home too soon.

ROMOLA: *(Rushing to him)* Let me explain.

DAVID: Don't touch me . . . I don't understand you.

ROMOLA: David, for God's sake, listen. *(She throws her arms around him, he pushes her away.)*

DAVID: Keep your arms for your lovers—everything you denied—is true. *(His voice breaks. At that moment banging is heard on the bedroom door.)*

ROMOLA: Take this key, David. *(She hands him the key. He rushes and unlocks the door.* ROBERT CROSS *comes out.)*

DAVID: Father!

ROBERT CROSS: How dare you speak to your mother that way?

ROMOLA: Leave it between David and me, Robert.

ROBERT CROSS: I will not. How dare he speak to you like that— apologize to your mother at once, and take back every word you said.

ROMOLA: *(Entreatingly)* Don't ask that.

ROBERT CROSS: I will not move from here until he does.

DAVID: Mother—I'm, I'm ashamed.

ROMOLA: It doesn't matter, David.

DAVID: Forgive me, Mother—it's because, because I love you so. But you—*(Turning on* ROBERT CROSS*)* I would like you to explain why you are here and why, all these years, you have taught me to believe lies of my mother—of such a wonderful mother—

ROMOLA: *(Brokenly)* Oh, David, oh, David, don't talk to him this way—I don't deserve it. *(She sinks at the desk and buries her head in her hands.)*

DAVID: *(Huskily)* I don't—understand—You don't deserve it?

ROMOLA: *(Standing up with a gesture of despair)* No, I don't deserve it, and even to keep your love, and, oh, my God, how I want it,—I can't go on lying.

ROBERT CROSS: Lying?

ROMOLA: *(Pitifully)* Yes—my life has been different—

DAVID: You *have* lied?

ROBERT CROSS: Romola, what are you talking about?

ROMOLA: The truth.

ROBERT CROSS: But I believe you innocent.

ROMOLA: It has nothing to do with you—and yet everything—I *was* innocent until after my divorce—*(Turning to DAVID)* David, help me now.

DAVID: *(Pressing his hand to his temple)* Help you, help you. Oh, my God, I don't understand—Mother, Mother—*(Dazed but tenderly he takes a step toward her then suddenly wheels around to ROBERT CROSS.)* And you, what are you here for now?

ROBERT CROSS: I came to ask Romola to go to South America with me.

DAVID: *(Incredulously)* You—came—to—ask her that when you are married to another woman?

ROBERT CROSS: Yes, because we love each other—because we have lived for each other all along.

DAVID: It is not true. Mother has lived for me—*(Wheels around in a frenzy)* and yet, that is probably a lie, too—perhaps she has been living for you. Yes, that's it, she has been living for you or probably some other man, too. *(Laughs hysterically then brokenly goes on.)* And now she was planning to go down to South America with you, to help you throw over your wife and abandon me again! *(Laughs wildly.)*

ROMOLA: David, in God's name, that is not true. *(Throws her arms around him.)* Listen to me.

ROBERT CROSS: *(Emphatically)* Listen to your mother!

DAVID: *(Insanely)* Is it true that you care for him in spite of the many times you told me that I was your whole life? *(Points to ROBERT CROSS.)*

ROMOLA: David, spare me.

DAVID: *(Frantically)* Do you love him? Did you tell him so tonight?

ROMOLA: *(Weakly)* Yes—but not the way you think.

DAVID: *(With his hand to his temple and as though speaking to himself)* So that's it—and you have had a lover before. And I—I have wanted it so to be beautiful.

ROBERT CROSS: *(Angrily)* Don't talk that way.

ROMOLA: You have been everything to me, David. Once long ago—after you were taken from me—when I was so lonely—I did have a lover—but not since then—since then I have lived for you.

DAVID: *(Brokenly)* I understand, Mother—I—I—didn't mean to say those terrible things—forgive me—I do love you—I just want a little time to think things over—it's life that's difficult—*(He goes blindly out through the door to extreme right.)*

ROMOLA: I love him so.

ROBERT CROSS: He's hot-headed, as I was in my youth. But he'll get over it and calm down. *(A pause)*

ROMOLA: You must leave now, Robert.

ROBERT CROSS: *(Wearily)* I suppose so. Where is my hat?

(Suddenly a shot is heard. Terror comes over both their faces. There is an instant of hesitation, then ROBERT CROSS rushes into the other room. ROMOLA stands, hardly breathing. There is a dead silence, then ROBERT CROSS reappears from the room again. His face is grey and ashen. He puts his hand out to ROMOLA as though to give her support. In a voice unlike his own)

ROBERT CROSS: He's shot himself.

(ROMOLA rushes into the adjoining room. ROBERT CROSS follows her. She utters a low cry. In a minute they reappear.)

ROMOLA: *(With unnatural strength)* Go—leave me.

ROBERT CROSS: I can't leave now—he's my son, too.

ROMOLA: You have had him alive all these years—let me—have—him—dead—

(She goes into other room again. Knocking is heard on the door to the left. ROBERT CROSS pauses, then jumps out of the window as PETER WORTH speaks outside.)

PETER WORTH: *(Outside the door)* Romola, are you awake and did you hear a shot? *(Pause and then he knocks again.)* Romola, let me in. *(He bangs on the door, then opens it and dashes in. In terrified voice at not seeing her)* Romola, where are you? *(He rushes into adjoining room.)* My God!

(There is another silence and a few minutes elapse. Then PETER WORTH enters supporting ROMOLA in his arms. Her hair is disheveled and her eyes wild. He places her on a chair, where she sits gazing directly in front of her. He goes to table and with shaking hand pours out water in glass for her. He hands it to her but she ignores it.)

ROMOLA: *(In dead voice; without moving, and as though to herself)* The dream is ended—but life will go on the same—world without end.

PETER WORTH: *(Brokenly)* My dear, my dear, it kills me to see you look this way.

(He drops on his knees and buries his face in her lap. Sobs shake his frame. ROMOLA places her hand on his head and stares vacantly before her.)

ROMOLA: You can take me to Switzerland, Peter. I am through with England now.

Curtain

The Dark Light

The Characters

SVANHILD STRANDENES

IVAR STRANDENES, *Svanhild's twin brother*

SOPHIA MUNK

DOCTOR ERLING KJELLAND

TURID HOLMBOE

OLAF HALVORSEN

SANDVIK

The play is laid near Stavern on the west coast of Norway. The time is the present.

Part 1

Early in September of the present time. The living room in the house of SVANHILD STRANDENES *in a remote spot on the west coast of Norway. The room is comfortable and in taste. The walls are paneled a soft green. On the floor there is a deep brown rug. To the right there is a fireplace with a lounge drawn up before it. To the left there is a large table with a soft easy chair near it. There are two or three more comfortable chairs in the room and a small table. On the tables there are lamps and vases filled with flowers. There is a wide French window in the up center of the room, which opens out into a garden. On either side of the window there are bookcases filled with books, which reach to the ceiling. There are also many books and magazines strewn about the room. Bright chintz is used on the furniture. There is a door upstage right, which leads out into the entrance hall of the house, and another door upstage left. The room looks much lived in.*

It is ten o'clock in the morning. The sun streams in. The window is open, and beyond the garden one can perceive the sea. The breaking of the waves against the rocks can be heard faintly.

As the curtain rises, SANDVIK, *an old gardener, enters from the garden with the morning newspaper in his hands. His hair is white and he is slightly bent with age. There is something gruff but lovable about him. He places the newspaper on the table and goes out again into the garden.* DOCTOR ERLING KJELLAND *comes in from the hallway. He is a man about sixty years of age with an alert and kindly face. He is dressed in rough country clothes. He walks out into the garden a moment, then re-*

Library of Congress Copyright, February 6, 1926. Registration number 74466.

enters, opens the newspaper, settles himself comfortably in a chair and begins to read. OLAF HALVORSEN *enters from left doorway. He is tall, good-looking, about thirty years of age. He does not at once see* DOCTOR KJELLAND. *He takes a cigarette from the table, lights it and starts to hurry out. He suddenly sees* DOCTOR KJELLAND, *stops, and appears embarrassed.*

DOCTOR KJELLAND: *(Without putting down the newspaper)* I'm afraid you won't find her. She went up the beach as early as five—I saw her from my window—then I dozed sweetly and comfortably to sleep again and never opened an eye until eight o'clock.

OLAF HALVORSEN: I'm ashamed to say I only just got up. *(He looks at his wristwatch.)* Good heavens, it's after ten! I'm afraid I'm keeping up with my city hours. I did mean to try and wake up earlier in the country.

DOCTOR KJELLAND: I expect it's the strong sea air here. It always makes one sleepy—especially at first.

OLAF HALVORSEN: Still it was stupid of me. I should have made an effort and gone out early with Svanhild.

DOCTOR KJELLAND: *(Looking up)* I don't agree with you.

OLAF HALVORSEN: Perhaps you're right; five o'clock *is* a bit stiff!

DOCTOR KJELLAND: I wasn't thinking of the hour; I was just thinking that probably nothing would have annoyed Svanhild more than to have had you get up and go out with her.

OLAF HALVORSEN: *(Good-naturedly)* Thanks.

DOCTOR KJELLAND: Oh, not because it's you any more than anyone else. She doesn't like anyone to go out with her—that's why she always goes out early when there is no one about. She likes to collect feathers by herself.

OLAF HALVORSEN: Collect feathers?

DOCTOR KJELLAND: *(Laughing)* Now don't pretend that you have been visiting in this house without knowing about Svanhild's collection of feathers. Haven't you seen them?

OLAF HALVORSEN: Really—I don't know a thing about them.

DOCTOR KJELLAND: A great number of them are on the wall in her lighthouse. You've been up there, haven't you?

OLAF HALVORSEN: Yes—She took me up there the day I arrived. A strange idea having a lighthouse built onto a house like this.

DOCTOR KJELLAND: It caused enough difficulty with the coast officials getting them to allow it. They finally agreed, on condition that they could count on the light always being kept burning. Svanhild has to see to that. That's her responsibility and she brought it upon herself through such a hobby.

OLAF HALVORSEN: I know she told me about it—she told me of some notion that if it ever went out it would mean her death. I didn't notice the feathers though nor hear anything about them.

DOCTOR KJELLAND: They fall along the beach from the flying birds. I've never yet discovered any real reason for collecting them—just an idea of hers, like so many others. Ask her yourself about them—I believe she has more than a thousand. But tell me about yourself. Do you know, I rather like you. More than most of the young men that come here. Where did you meet Svanhild?

OLAF HALVORSEN: At a party in Oslo. I liked her at once—she seemed to stand out from everyone else there. I saw her once again two days afterwards, then I asked if I might come and see her here. I'm afraid I rather besieged her with letters and wires.

DOCTOR KJELLAND: Um—do you mean to continue besieging her and hanging about?

OLAF HALVORSEN: *(Embarrassed)* I don't know that I can exactly help myself.

DOCTOR KJELLAND: You mean because you're in love with her?

OLAF HALVORSEN: Yes, I suppose that's what I do mean, and I suppose I will go on hanging about for as long as she lets me—at least until I get courage enough to ask her to marry me.

DOCTOR KJELLAND: Afraid to ask her?

OLAF HALVORSEN: I haven't much hope. You see, to begin with, I don't understand her. She seems like something very different from me—there is something so direct about her—something sharp—wild—

DOCTOR KJELLAND: *(Laughing)* Now you are talking about the way she talks about her feathers.

OLAF HALVORSEN: Perhaps, but it's true—I don't understand her. Even her poetry mystifies me, although I pretend to understand it. Then this—this terrible hatred she has for her brother—her own twin brother. How can she be like that? Why last night she seemed almost inhuman when Miss Munk received that letter saying her brother was arriving today with his fiancée. I frankly admit I don't understand a nature like hers, and the curious part is, I don't understand myself for loving her. I love her in spite of herself and in spite of myself.

DOCTOR KJELLAND: *(Smiling)* Love seems to have a way of playing such tricks.

OLAF HALVORSEN: It isn't as if I were a school boy with a first infatuation either. You've known her and her brother for a long time, haven't you?

DOCTOR KJELLAND: Before they were born. I brought them into the world, as a matter of fact.

OLAF HALVORSEN: I didn't know that.

DOCTOR KJELLAND: And I knew their mother and Sophia Munk, who was their mother's best friend, years before that in Oslo. Right here in this very room, as a young man, I felt as you now feel. I was in love with Sophia. *(Sighing)* But she would have none of me. When these children's father died and later their mother— although she was no relation she undertook to bring them up. They always call her "aunt." I've hung around her since those early years; now I'm an old man and it's too late to mend my ways. But it's not too late for you. Don't begin the same thing with Svanhild.

OLAF HALVORSEN: *(Laughing)* I'll try not to make it as long and drawn out. How long since Ivar has been home?

DOCTOR KJELLAND: Let me see—I don't quite remember. Nearly two years I should say—if not more. At least two since he has been in this house. He has seen his aunt in Oslo. I don't think he has been up here since Svanhild's last book of poems came out. The one with which she had such a great success.

OLAF HALVORSEN: It's strange—isn't it—that they should both be poets and that her poems should be so good and his so bad?

DOCTOR KJELLAND: I wouldn't say his were bad. Svanhild has achieved fame and Ivar hasn't. But that doesn't always matter. Then, of course, I can't judge these things very well, I'm not much of a poet. I suppose from a worldly point of view she has been successful in everything where he has failed.

OLAF HALVORSEN: That is just why I can't see why she should dislike him so much.

DOCTOR KJELLAND: You mean she has nothing of which to be jealous?

OLAF HALVORSEN: I suppose that's what I mean. Svanhild doesn't have to fear competition from Ivar.

DOCTOR KJELLAND: Yes—you're right. But I don't think that has anything to do with this—this feeling between them. Svanhild is not like that. She is very generous about other people's work. Being ahead of Ivar in everything hasn't been her fault. She just couldn't help it. Although they are twins, even when they were children she was always ahead of him in everything—she was always stronger—wilder—more daring than he. She has always been fearless about everything—her own life—life itself—her reputation—anything at all. She could ride the wildest horses— drive the fastest cars—swim out in the roughest seas. Why, twice she saved Ivar from drowning. I always felt that increased the feeling between them; he seemed to resent owing his life to her. In a way I understand it, too. Then they began writing poetry at the same time. She at once had her poems accepted in newspapers; he never could. Then she had her book published, which made her leap into fame. He ran rather wild after that—got in with the bad crowd, began drinking—got frightfully in debt. Svanhild had to help him out; he gave her his share on the house for paying his debts. I must say she didn't want to take it, but he insisted—that's when he said he wouldn't come here anymore because it was no longer his house. Then she said she wouldn't live here either and went around the world with some girl, but she came back without her after six months. She has lived here ever since, winter and summer. When her aunt goes to Oslo in the winter, she lives here entirely by herself, except for Sandvik. She spends her time writing.

OLAF HALVORSEN: And collecting feathers—

DOCTOR KJELLAND: Yes, probably. I fancy we all have some strange pastime that comes under the title of pleasure.

OLAF HALVORSEN: Nevertheless, I noticed she did seem rather pleased last night at the beginning of the letter about Ivar coming home. It was only when he mentioned his being engaged and bringing his fiancée here that she lost her temper and wouldn't allow her aunt to continue reading.

DOCTOR KJELLAND: Did you notice that?

OLAF HALVORSEN: Didn't you?

DOCTOR KJELLAND: (*Folding his newspaper and placing it on the table. He rises and speaks in a way in which to dismiss the subject.*) I don't think I was listening very attentively.

(SANDVIK *comes in from the garden with his arms full of flowers.*)

DOCTOR KJELLAND: Ah, Sandvik! Good morning.

SANDVIK: Good morning, sir. Miss Sophia has been out in the hot house cuttin' these flowers—wants the house pretty for Master Ivar.

DOCTOR KJELLAND: So that's where she is! I wondered where she had disappeared.

(SANDVIK *places the flowers on the table and touches them tenderly. Then he peers at the flowers that are already in the vases and feels the water, measuring how high it is.*)

SANDVIK: No wonder they die—cut and squeezed in like this. Why can't they let them live their lives out in the greenhouse or in the garden? Under the sun and stars—that's the natural place for them.

OLAF HALVORSEN: You won't find most people agreeing with you— especially florists or people who live in the city.

SANDVIK: Miss Svanhild agrees with me. After all, their lives are short. Yer make friends with a flower in the morning, then yer come back in the evening and she's dead. *(Tragically)* I've seen more deaths than most people could guess about. They say it makes yer cheery and gay like, ter work among flowers, but I don't know—it's kind of sad, too, ter see them drop their heads, then fade and die. Yer ought ter know, doctor. I guess yer know how it is. Yer must have seen a lot of people die, too.

DOCTOR KJELLAND: I have, indeed. *(SANDVIK starts to go out, then he turns, hesitating a moment, to speak.)* Well—Sandvik?

SANDVIK: Eh—yer not thinkin' there will be any trouble with Master Ivar comin' home and bringin' a young woman with him—a strange young woman?

DOCTOR KJELLAND: He's going to marry her—it's quite natural he should bring her home to see his aunt and sister.

SANDVIK: Yes—but yer know how Miss Svanhild feels and bein' this is her house—I don't want no trouble for her, I don't. Must take care of her.

DOCTOR KJELLAND: Don't worry your head, Sandvik—things will straighten out somehow. They always do.

SANDVIK: I hope so, sir. Thank yer, sir—thank yer. *(He goes out.)*

DOCTOR KJELLAND: Sandvik has been in the family more than fifty years. He can never believe that Svanhild and Ivar are grown up. *(He walks out into the garden and speaks from there, looking to the right.)* I hear the heavy footfall of an approaching angel.

(SOPHIA MUNK appears. They enter the room together. She is a woman of fifty years, although she seems younger. She is not at all beautiful but there is something very sympathetic about her. Her hair is pulled straight back in a small knot showing her brow and very kind grey eyes. She is frail, aristocratic, and very Scandinavian looking. She is dressed simply but with care. One would know at once that she liked clothes. She is carrying a large scissors and a basket full of flowers. As she enters, she laughs.)

SOPHIA MUNK: My heavy footfall as you call it is a matter of many years training. I learned long ago that before entering a room one should in some way announce one's approach. Many times it saves much embarrassment. A cough answers the purpose, but that seems to me rather—too obvious. Then, too, one can trip and fall, but that needs skill or else it's clumsy. Really, the heavy footfall is the best! *(She takes faded flowers out of the vases and begins arranging fresh ones.)*

DOCTOR KJELLAND: Surely you don't flatter yourself that we were talking about *you.* You might have spared the soles of your shoes and come in quite noiselessly. Our conversation has been entirely about Svanhild.

SOPHIA MUNK: *(With a smile and looking at Olaf)* You surprise me. *(Seriously)* I do hope Ivar finds everything the way he wants it. I'm so nervous about meeting this—this girl. It seems almost silly to use the word "fiancée." I can't think of Ivar engaged. It's strange, but it never occurred to me that he ever would be, although I suppose I should have expected it sooner or later.

DOCTOR KJELLAND: I don't understand why, when he took her away from her home, he didn't marry her at once.

SOPHIA MUNK: It seems quite natural to me, that when her family opposed their marriage, that he should bring her to his own family.

DOCTOR KJELLAND: Well, in my day I would have been romantic enough to have wanted to marry a girl immediately, if I had arrived as far as eloping with her. He could have brought her up here as his wife, instead of his fiancée.

SOPHIA MUNK: He probably wanted Svanhild and me to look her over.

DOCTOR KJELLAND: I don't know what good that is going to do. I hope he intends to marry her no matter what your "looking-over" verdict may be—now that he has taken her away from her home— burnt her bridges and all that.

OLAF HALVORSEN: It's easier for a woman to bring a man into a family than for a man to bring a woman. Especially where there is a sister.

DOCTOR KJELLAND: *(Laughing)* You said it! Especially where there is a Svanhild!

OLAF HALVORSEN: Sisters are always critical. I have one and I know.

SOPHIA MUNK: I do hope Svanhild is going to behave properly. At least, I hope she won't be too much of a savage. After all, Ivar hasn't been here for such a long time, and in a way this is just as much his home as hers. I want him to be happy here, and certainly wherever I am *is* his home. I should like him always to feel that. It has been a very curious thing to me the way Svanhild and Ivar have always seemed to be constantly at war—even when they were children it was the same thing. And yet the strange part is, I always feel that one is not quite complete without the other. I often think that it is that incomplete thing in Svanhild that makes her so strange and wild—so difficult to deal with. And Ivar, too— incomplete in a different way—poor Ivar—

DOCTOR KJELLAND: Ivar has always been your weak spot, Sophia.

You and he had always much in common, although he may have changed now since he has been away from your influence.

SOPHIA MUNK: You flatter me. I never had any influence on either of those two children. If I had ever had any—or had any now—Svanhild would not be the way she is. She wouldn't have all these ideas of hers—a lighthouse flashing over our heads all night with the light going in and out my room and keeping me awake. I can sleep in total darkness or in light—one or the other. But this constant flash, flash, darkness—light—light—darkness—drives me quite mad.

OLAF HALVORSEN: Why not try a heavy green shade for your window?

SOPHIA MUNK: I would know that revolving flash was going on outside just the same—the mere idea of it would make me nervous and keep me awake. Then, too, there would surely be a crack somewhere in the shade. I find these kind of protective things in life always have a crack in them—haven't you noticed that?

OLAF HALVORSEN: *(Laughing)* You are a pessimist!

DOCTOR KJELLAND: The truth is she has a great mania for always facing everything squarely in the face. "Never hide behind anything," is her motto. *(To* SOPHIA*)* You'd spare yourself much if you didn't have that obsession.

SOPHIA MUNK: Well, it's better than going through life blindfolded and always thinking that you are one day going to get what you want—when you *aren't!* (She laughs; throws a flower at him, which he catches and puts in his buttonhole.)

DOCTOR KJELLAND: Blindfolds are very comforting. It's like constantly playing a game. "Blind man's bluff," I think it is called, if I can remember far enough back into my nursery. I seem to remember one always stretched out and caught something—in spite of the blindfolds!

SOPHIA MUNK: Yes, a bang in the nose!

DOCTOR KJELLAND: Well, my dear, in the relative scheme of the universe that's something.

SOPHIA MUNK: *(Sighing somewhat sadly)* If I had had any influence, I wouldn't have allowed Ivar to leave home. It's been lonely without him.

(As SOPHIA MUNK *speaks these words,* SVANHILD *appears in the doorway of the garden. Until she speaks, no one perceives her. She is curiously startling looking. Not so much because of her physical appearance but because of an undefined quality which she projects. She is medium height and slender although she gives an impression of great physical strength.*

She seems very boyish without actually being masculine. There is something untamed and wild about her, as though she were in some way connected with the elements and already a part of them. Her hair is so burnt by the sun that it glitters and seems bright gold. It is straight, and seems untamed. It stands out and back from her forehead like wings. Her eyes are set deep and wide apart under a beautiful brow; they are an unfathomable blue with a strange look of eternity in them. Her face is not beautiful but sensitive, alert and arresting. Her mouth is a trifle too large but strong—at moments it betrays a certain tenderness she would like to conceal. Her skin is clear and radiant. She is dressed carelessly and somewhat untidily, although she wears her clothes with style. She has on a bright blue jumper such as a sailor might wear; she wears it over a pair of dark trousers. A scarlet scarf is thrown around her throat. In her hands— strong, vital hands—she carries many bird feathers. With her entrance she brings in the feeling of wind; of white foam-spray tossed up from great giant waves; of the sting of clear, whirling gold sand and carried along by a gale.)

SVANHILD: Influence seems to me such a secondhand thing. It's accepting a point of view which doesn't come through one's self.

OLAF HALVORSEN: *(Jumping to his feet and speaking happily)* Svanhild, I'm so glad you've come—I thought you never were coming!

DOCTOR KJELLAND: And he was advised by a very wise man not to go after you. *(As he is speaking, SVANHILD advances carefully and lovingly placing the feathers on the table. She picks up a rather large white one and examines it.)*

SOPHIA MUNK: Yet I always felt you had a very strong influence on Ivar had you chosen to use it constructively. It's that light, careless thing in you that made you—

SVANHILD: *(Holding up the feather and interrupting.)* That light thing like this feather. Light and useless to most people except to those who understand it and love it. To you it's probably only the feather of a sea gull, to me it's a white arrow. Look—look, it *is* a white arrow! A white arrow that has sped far in high places—that has penetrated the clouds and then come down with a message to me.

OLAF HALVORSEN: What message?

SVANHILD: The futility of so-called useful things and people.

OLAF HALVORSEN: I think we could dispute that—

DOCTOR KJELLAND: I shouldn't bother. I am sure Svanhild has a long string of ideas by which she can convince you.

SOPHIA MUNK: We were talking of Ivar. I hope you are going to be nice to him. It will be hard for him at first after not having been here for so long, and you know how nervous and excitable he becomes.

SVANHILD: Hysterical, you mean.

SOPHIA MUNK: Now *please* don't say that. You know it was always your calling him hysterical that made him hysterical. Do try and help him out, especially now that he wants to marry.

SVANHILD: *(Sharply)* Why should he bring that girl here? She has no place in my house.

SOPHIA MUNK: *(Angrily)* You don't even know the girl and if this is the attitude you are going to take toward your brother, I will have nothing more to say to you one way or the other.

DOCTOR KJELLAND: Oh come, I don't think Svanhild is going to be inhospitable to anyone in her own house. *(SOPHIA gathers up her scissors and basket and leaves the room.)* Don't bother Sophia that way, Svanhild—now I shall have to go after her and calm her down. *(He exits.)*

OLAF HALVORSEN: *(After a pause and on perceiving a dark and far-away look on SVANHILD's face)* I shouldn't get bothered and all that sort of thing.

SVANHILD: *(Suddenly breaking the mood and tossing back her head)* Bothered—I? Great heavens, I don't get bothered!

OLAF HALVORSEN: I don't think that's true. You pretend to be stronger than you really are.

SVANHILD: I don't pretend anything. I simply am what I am. If people can't see what that is and dress me up in false and glorified lights—that's their stupidity, not mine.

OLAF HALVORSEN: I think you are really softer and gentler than you want people to know. I wish you would tell me about these feathers. For what actual reason do you collect them?

SVANHILD: *(Her face softening as she touches the feathers)* You wouldn't understand.

OLAF HALVORSEN: I might.

SVANHILD: I don't collect them for reason—at least not reason the way you mean it. I collect them because I love them. *(Passionately)* Because they have flown in high places; because they have beaten against wind and gale; because they have been nearer the stars and sky than I have ever been; because in moonlight they have been swift flying wisps of silver and at sunset they have been wings of flame. Because they have flown low over the sea, barely touching its breast with the lightness of their caress. They are more beautiful than trees—rocks—flowers, because they know freedom and are not bound to roots and earth. Because they are swift—light— exquisitely delicate, yet strong—strong—defiant in wind and storm. *(Softly)* Lonely when they drop to earth like this and can fly no more in high spaces. But they *will* fly again, once more they will fly, because I have found them and I understand their desire to fly.

OLAF HALVORSEN: *(Shaking his head in bewilderment)* I can understand collecting books or paintings or porcelains—all those things have value, after all, they are investments, but collecting *feathers*—

SVANHILD: They are like collecting dreams. Each one of them is a dream—

OLAF HALVORSEN: But what do you mean saying they will fly again, that they will fly once more?

SVANHILD: *(Excitedly)* When I have collected clouds and clouds of them, I shall take them up to a great height on a mountaintop. I shall take them up when a gale is blowing; then I shall let them all go and they will be carried far and wide by the wind. I think that will be so wonderful, as though I had created and made each one a bird.

OLAF HALVORSEN: After all this collecting you will let them go like that? But I thought you loved them so—better than anything—that you want to keep them.

SVANHILD: *(Intensely)* One must always let go the thing one loves most. It is better to free it with your own hands than to have it tear itself away from you. *(With suffering)* Then the wound isn't so deep—the pain so great.

OLAF HALVORSEN: *(Sighing hopelessly)* Well, I don't understand you. Will you collect something else then?

SVANHILD: *(Changing her mood to one of lightness and gaiety)* Oh, yes—Probably.

OLAF HALVORSEN: I hope something with more—more value. Do you know what?

SVANHILD: Yes. I've made up my mind already. I'm going to collect pieces that fall from meteors—pieces of stars. I'll have to go all around the world to do that.

OLAF HALVORSEN: *(Resignedly)* You're a strange girl. I want to ask you something.

SVANHILD: What is it?

OLAF HALVORSEN: *(Nervously)* You must have an idea. You know I love you.

SVANHILD: No, I hadn't thought about it.

OLAF HALVORSEN: I'm sorry. I thought you had. I want to ask you if you'll marry me.

SVANHILD: *(Kindly)* Oh, I'm so sorry, Olaf. I didn't think you'd ask me that. But you see now that you have—it really would be quite impossible. You see yourself we wouldn't understand one another.

OLAF HALVORSEN: I don't think that matters. I admit I don't understand you, but I love you and I'd accept—your collecting or any of those other fads. Writing poetry and all that sort of thing.

SVANHILD: *(Looking up a trifle amused)* Fad? Fads? Olaf—is it a fad that you breathe?

OLAF HALVORSEN: *(Smiling)* No, naturally not. What has *that* got to do with it?

SVANHILD: Nothing—nothing—

OLAF HALVORSEN: *(Laughing)* Just another idea—like feathers and stars. But seriously, Svanhild, if you only would—

SVANHILD: *(Breaking in)* There isn't any use, Olaf. I'm not going to marry now. I have my life already as it is. Do you realize I live up here even all winter absolutely by myself? With no one but Sandvik and my books and my writings and my lighthouse and glorious, glorious wind and storms. Do you think I could give that up?

OLAF HALVORSEN: But you must get lonely for someone with whom to talk.

SVANHILD: You have heard people say the sea talks to them—well, it does. The pounding of the sea talks to me and the shrill cries of the sea gulls. Why, when I'm here alone in winter, they come right up before the house and let me feed them from my own hands.

OLAF HALVORSEN: Will you think a little bit about it? I can't help loving you.

SVANHILD: Thanks. But I'm afraid it won't be much use.

OLAF HALVORSEN: You're not in love with anyone else? *(SVANHILD hesitates before she answers, then her answer is unconvincing.)*

SVANHILD: No—no—of course not. *(At that moment SANDVIK comes running in. He is in a state of excitement.)*

SANDVIK: Excuse me, Miss, but Master Ivar is just arriving. *(He runs out again.)*

OLAF HALVORSEN: *(On seeing that Svanhild does not move)* Aren't you going to meet your brother?

SVANHILD: No, I'd rather stay here. You go. I'll wait for Ivar here. Really—I'd rather.

(OLAF *hesitates a moment, then he crosses and takes* SVANHILD*'s hand. He bends and kisses it, then he goes quickly out.* SVANHILD *rises and stands by the table, absently making patterns with the feathers. Her mind is not on them; suddenly she puts a finger of each hand to her temples as though to hold them tightly and stop them from beating. She stands tense and for these few moments seems a tragic figure. Her hands drop at her side, she lights a cigarette nervously and walks about. She seems to be wrestling with herself to face some deep emotion. In a few seconds voices are heard approaching.* SOPHIA, DOCTOR KJELLAND, OLAF, IVAR *and* TURID HOLMBOE *enter.* IVAR *is slender and very delicate looking. His features are beautiful and poetic but almost too sensitive. He seems far too highly strung, as though something would snap in him at any moment. One would know at once that he was neurotic and detect a condition of hysteria. He is everything the contrary to* SVANHILD. *Where she is daring and fearless, he seems timid and fearful. Where she suggests strength and force, he seems weak and unforceful. Where she suggests the masculine, he suggests the feminine. His brow and hair somewhat suggest hers, but otherwise there is no resemblance between them. In his face there is great beauty and charm—that irresistible charm that weak people often have. There is also something very sad about him—an elusive melancholy note—a quality of indecision and almost childish fretfulness that makes him appear even weaker than he might really be. His hands are white, slender, and nervous, rarely quiet and often fluttering like caged or wounded birds.* TURID *is small with dark hair. She is beautiful, with large frightened eyes set into a small, childishly wistful face. She is unsophisticated and timid. Her clothes are simple and lack style. She hangs back behind* SOPHIA, *who, as they enter, is holding her hand and endeavoring to make her feel at home.* OLAF *is carrying two bags, which he places by the door. As they enter,* SVANHILD *in the far corner of the room turns and faces them. She betrays no sign of any emotion except a slight tightening of her hands.*)

SOPHIA MUNK: (*Dragging* TURID *forward*) Svanhild, this is Turid— or rather, I suppose I should say, Miss Holmboe.

SVANHILD: (*Advancing and extending her hand*) I hope you will let me call you Turid—it was nice of you to come to us. (DOCTOR KJELLAND *and* SOPHIA *exchange relieved glances.*)

TURID: (*Taking* SVANHILD*'s hand timidly*) I—I think it was nice of you—so nice of you to let me come. I was so afraid that Ivar was wrong in bringing me. (*At the mention of* IVAR*'s name,* SVANHILD *turns toward him. They face each other for an awkward moment.* SVANHILD *is the first to speak.*)

SVANHILD: *(Without moving)* Of course it was right of you to bring her, Ivar. Naturally, Sophia is very glad.

SOPHIA MUNK: *(Quickly and with forced gaiety in order to be convincing)* We're all glad. Why even Sandvik has been so excited to meet Turid I didn't know what we would do with him.

IVAR: *(Awkwardly, looking away from* SVANHILD *and gazing about)* Pretty much the same—nothing changed.

SVANHILD: Oh, a few things.

DOCTOR KJELLAND: More grey hairs in my head. But tell us about you—you see we all know about ourselves, but we don't know about you. Have a cigarette?

(He offers TURID *a cigarette, who refuses one, then* IVAR *who takes one.* IVAR *fumbles nervously with a matchbox and tries three times to light the cigarette.* SVANHILD *strikes a match and holds it out to him.)*

IVAR: *(After lighting his cigarette)* Thanks. You always had a way of making a match strike right straight off.

OLAF HALVORSEN: *(Laughing)* People like Svanhild don't help the match business. Her hands are too firm—her strikes too accurate!

SOPHIA MUNK: Sit down a minute—won't you? I don't know why we are all standing so formally. Or would you rather go upstairs and wash up right away, Ivar dear? Lunch will be ready soon.

DOCTOR KJELLAND: Oh, sit down a minute. Do. *(They all sit except* SVANHILD, *who remains standing by the table.)*

SOPHIA MUNK: Tell us the exciting piece of news that you spoke of in your letter, Ivar.

IVAR: It doesn't seem so exciting now.

TURID: It's *wonderfully* exciting. Let me tell them, Ivar!

IVAR: No—no, not now.

SOPHIA MUNK: Please do. Don't be silly, Ivar. What is it, Turid?

TURID: *(Unable to control herself)* It's about his book of poems!

SVANHILD: Book of poems? Have you completed a book of poems?

TURID: Yes, indeed, and he has had them accepted to be published.

SOPHIA MUNK: How lovely!

IVAR: *(Jumping up)* It's of no importance at all—I wish you wouldn't tell these things, Turid.

TURID: But we spoke about it. You said yourself you would read them aloud your first night home.

DOCTOR KJELLAND: And that's quite right. It will make this evening something very interesting to look forward to.

TURID: *(With flashing eyes)* They are such beautiful poems. The most exciting part is they belong all to me. There is only one copy of each in Ivar's own handwriting. They are really mine and no one else has them. I keep them in that bag. That's why I won't let it out of my sight. It's a glorious and great responsibility. I'm going to type a copy of each to send to the publisher. They accepted them by just hearing Ivar read them.

DOCTOR KJELLAND: *(Kindly)* Well, well, that is very exciting.

SOPHIA MUNK: I should think so. You will surely read them tonight, Ivar, won't you?

IVAR: I don't know.

TURID: Of course he will. *(To* SVANHILD *)* You will ask him to—won't you?

SVANHILD: I ask him now. You will read them, won't you, Ivar? *(They suddenly look at each other.)*

IVAR: Oh, you know it is useless for me to read my poems to you. You wouldn't think they could ever touch yours.

SVANHILD: Thank you for making me seem so charmingly modest!

SOPHIA MUNK: *(Quickly and jumping up)* Come, Turid. I will show you your room. You must want to brush up a bit.

SVANHILD: Oh, by the way. I've decided to give Ivar my room in the lighthouse. It's nicer than the guest room on this floor—and I'm going to sleep in the wing next to Turid so she won't be lonely in a strange house.

TURID: Oh, thank you so much—I hope it won't put you out.

SOPHIA MUNK: That's sweet of you, Svanhild. Come, Turid. Lunch ought to be ready very soon. I'm sure you and Ivar are starved. *(She takes* TURID *'s hand, and they go out.)*

OLAF HALVORSEN: I'll carry the bags upstairs. *(He takes up the bags.)*

DOCTOR KJELLAND: I'll help you. Exercise is good for an old man. *(He takes one bag from* OLAF, *and they both go out.* IVAR *starts to follow.* SVANHILD *looks after him. He pauses as though she had called him and turns. There is an awkward pause, neither of them speak.* IVAR *betrays his embarrassment by looking down at his hands and twisting his fingers.)*

IVAR: *(Nervously and finally looking up)* You—you haven't changed at all—

SVANHILD: I think you have—a little.

IVAR: It's more than two years.

SVANHILD: I expect living in the open keeps one unchanged—at least under a weather-beaten face it's difficult to know whether one changes or not. Nature's cosmetics!

IVAR: I suppose you want to ask who is publishing my poems?

SVANHILD: No—I hadn't thought of it. Is it a good house?

IVAR: *(Bitterly)* No—small and unknown.

SVANHILD: It's foolish to let that make you unhappy. If the poems are really good they will come through anyway, no matter who publishes them.

IVAR: It's easy enough for you to say—you've always had luck in everything.

SVANHILD: And haven't you had some, too? You wrote you loved Turid and you have won her—haven't you?

IVAR: *(Sinking on a chair with his head in his hands)* Oh, Turid, yes. She has been wonderful to me—sweet and all that. Even left her family. They wouldn't have any of me and cut her off. Called me an erratic, mad poet.

SVANHILD: Well, then—I was right. You *have* her and that is luck— you should be happy.

IVAR: *(Springing to his feet)* Oh, yes, I know all *that.* But there are other things—

SVANHILD: What?

IVAR: Oh, nothing. Nothing you would understand. Madness. *(He laughs almost hysterically.)* Madness. *You* wouldn't understand. You with your strength, your balance, your indifference—your hatred of me. You couldn't understand pain—such pain that has made it impossible for me to build up anything in my life.

SVANHILD: The strong build on their pain—the weak sink under it.

IVAR: Those poems—they are my pain. So much cries of me, that I'm ashamed—ashamed—

SVANHILD: *(Tensely)* They are love poems to Turid. She said they belonged to her.

IVAR: To Turid?

SVANHILD: Yes. They are love poems, aren't they? *(*IVAR *nods his head in the affirmative.)* Then—then they are to Turid, of course.

IVAR: *(Evadingly)* Oh, Turid's wonderful—wonderful—I know I don't deserve her—

SVANHILD: Oh, that's foolishness—it's silly to undervalue yourself. That's always been a bad habit of yours—it's time you outgrew it. *(*TURID *enters. She has taken her hat off. She pauses timidly in the doorway before entering.)*

TURID: May I come in, Ivar? Miss Munk asked me to come and tell you to get ready for lunch.

IVAR: Yes, of course, come in. I'll get ready now—we mustn't be late for lunch.

SVANHILD: Now don't begin upsetting this house with punctuality. Anything I hate is this idea one must always eat at certain hours, or do this at certain hours or that. Habit and routine—there is nothing more boring.

IVAR: Well, God knows no one has ever accused me of such things. I naturally thought Auntie wanted her meals on time, she always did.

SVANHILD: Well, she doesn't now. I've reformed her.

TURID: *(Worriedly)* I'm sorry I said anything—

SVANHILD: It doesn't matter—you'll get used to these family squabbles. I'll talk to Turid while you're brushing up, Ivar.

TURID: *(Timidly)* I should love to talk to you.

IVAR: I won't be long. *(He goes out.)*

SVANHILD: *(Sitting down on the sofa)* Sit here beside me, Turid. *(*TURID *advances slowly and sits beside her.)* There, that's better. We must be friends, you know.

TURID: *(Genuinely)* Oh, I hope so!

SVANHILD: It's curious your wanting to marry Ivar. I can't exactly see him in the light of a husband. And you seem so dependent. I would have thought that a more forceful, stronger man would appeal to you.

TURID: It's just that childlike, weak thing in Ivar that I love. I wanted to take care of him the minute I saw him. Most of the time he seems like a little boy with so many imaginary hurts and pains.

SVANHILD: You are more observing and older than I thought. You seemed yourself, at first, so afraid and very young.

TURID: *(Laughing)* I *was* afraid of you—I think I am even yet—a little.

SVANHILD: Afraid of me?

TURID: It's just—just that you are so different from anyone I have ever known. I've thought a lot about you since I've known Ivar—

SVANHILD: *(Breaking in)* Because he talked about me? Told you things about me?

TURID: He only spoke of you once. No, twice. The first time he had been drinking too much. It wasn't his fault. He had several glasses of brandy. I think the brandy was stronger than he realized—anyway, he wasn't quite himself.

SVANHILD: So then he talked about me!

TURID: Yes. He said wonderful things about you. I never before or since heard him talk this way about anyone. He said you were beautiful and when he spoke your name he looked the way he sometimes does after he has written a poem. It was this time that he spoke about you that started me wondering about you.

SVANHILD: You wondered about me?

TURID: Yes. Ivar never talked about you after that except once. But I felt him so often thinking about you. I somehow knew he was often thinking about you. I was thinking about you, too. The strange part was, when I knew he was thinking about you I would say, "What are you thinking about, Ivar?" he would always answer, "Nothing," or else change the subject. And many times when I was thinking about you, he would ask me of what I was thinking. For some unexplainable reason I, too, would answer "Nothing."

SVANHILD: And when, then, did he again speak about me. What did he say?

TURID: Oh, well—nothing—it doesn't matter—

SVANHILD: *(Leaning forward with interest)* What did he say? Why shouldn't you tell me? *(TURID moves awkwardly and still does not answer.)* Tell me—please.

TURID: *(Embarrassed)* He seemed to forget what he first told me about you—This time he just told me that—that you hated one another and that he didn't want me to ever really know you. *(Svanhild throws her head back and laughs.)*

SVANHILD: So he said that! That we hated one another! Tell me how he looked when he said it. *(Still laughing)* I should like to picture him saying it.

TURID: I don't see how you can laugh at such a thing. It seems terrible to me. As a matter of fact, Ivar looked miserable when he said it, he—

SVANHILD: *(Breaking in with mockery)* He looked miserable when he declared his hatred, did he? That's like Ivar. No vitality. *(With passion)* When I speak of hatred, I speak with fire and vengeance!

TURID: I don't believe he hates you. I don't understand either of you. I had hoped to bring you together.

SVANHILD: Perhaps you will, Turid. Who knows?

TURID: Now you are making fun of me.

SVANHILD: No—I'm not. But you see I start with a handicap—several in fact. You say you're afraid of me, I doubt if you even like me; then even if you did grow to be fond of me you would always love Ivar more than you could ever love me. And then you say he doesn't want you to know me—so, of course, what chance have I against that?

TURID: *(Distressed)* You mustn't think I don't like you—and—and I'm only afraid of you because—because I think you are so strange. You see, I had read your poems and then—then when I saw you—

SVANHILD: You were disappointed in the author? *(TURID shakes her head in the negative and looks down at her hands.)* I suppose you never could like me—at least not as much as Ivar?

TURID: It's different.

SVANHILD: Why?

TURID: I don't know—I suppose because Ivar's a man.

SVANHILD: Love is love. What difference can it make whether it's for a man or woman?

TURID: I hadn't thought about it quite like that—perhaps you're right. But I love Ivar so much—why, he seems more like my child. Do you know how I met him?

SVANHILD: No.

TURID: Well, you see, as you perhaps know, I came from a small town in Sweden. One day I was invited to a tea where there was going to be a poet whom they said might read his verse. Of course, we were all terribly excited. All the other girls dressed up, but I didn't bother much because I never thought he would look at me. When I got to the tea, there was Ivar looking so beautiful. Then, I don't know how—I never have known—out of all the room he came and talked to me. It was like a miracle, then instead of leaving that day he stayed on and on—and we loved each other. Ivar asked to marry me but my father was furious. He said Ivar should be in business and that poets were useless. He forbade my marrying Ivar and said if I saw him again he would disinherit me. So I ran away with Ivar to Stockholm. So you see, he is everything to me now. I have no friends and I can't go home. If Ivar didn't marry me now, and ever stopped loving me—I don't know what I'd do—I think I'd—*(She breaks off)*

SVANHILD: What would you do?

TURID: Oh, I suppose it sounds silly—but I think—I think I would kill myself in despair.

SVANHILD: You should never kill yourself in despair. That is letting life get the better of you. Kill yourself when you're happy; when you have in your hands the thing you have wanted the most. Go out of life triumphantly—laughing—on a high note, like this— *(She makes a sharp line going up in the air with her finger.)*

TURID: *(Sadly)* Without Ivar I could feel nothing but despair.

SVANHILD: Will you let me read his poems before he reads them aloud tonight? I hate being read to.

TURID: Oh, I wouldn't dare. He would never forgive me.

SVANHILD: You don't love him as much as you say.

TURID: How can you say that!

SVANHILD: Because if I read them quietly to myself I could perhaps help him with them—in the end I am sure he would be glad I had read them.

TURID: But you *will* hear them tonight.

SVANHILD: That is no good. I must study them and go over them—one by one, every line.

TURID: If they were only typed I shouldn't mind giving them to you—but like this—there are no other copies. It was a sentimental idea of Ivar's not to have them typed—to have only one copy in his handwriting. I have promised not to let them out of my care until they are typed.

SVANHILD: Nothing can happen to them here in this house. I shan't let them out of my hands. Give them to me before tonight and I will give them back to you. If they are as beautiful as you think—he need never even know that I have read them. If they seem to be wrong I can tell you and you can make suggestions as though they had come from you.

TURID: *(Surprised)* You want to help Ivar?

SVANHILD: Why, of course. You said you wanted to bring us together—here's a chance.

TURID: *(Helplessly and worried)* I don't know what to do.

SVANHILD: *(Taking her hand and pleadingly)* Let me see them.

TURID: You will surely give them back before tonight?

SVANHILD: Give them to me after lunch and before dinner meet me here and I will give them to you while everyone else is dressing.

TURID: Oh, I would like to!

SVANHILD: Then you will?

TURID: Yes—yes, I will. It's generous of you to want to help Ivar.

SVANHILD: Then we understand each other? *(Ivar enters on the last line.)*

IVAR: *(Quickly)* What about? What do you understand each other about? *(TURID jumps to her feet.)*

SVANHILD: Many things, and why not?

TURID: *(Nervously)* We have had a lovely talk, Ivar.

IVAR: That's good—and lunch is ready.

SVANHILD: *(Rising)* Well, come, Turid. I suppose you are hungry and one must eat sometime or other.

(IVAR extends his arm to TURID. At the same instant, SVANHILD holds out her hand to her; TURID hesitates between them, then she takes SVAN-HILD's hand.)

SVANHILD: *(With emphasis)* Come, Turid. Follow me. I'll lead the way.

(She goes out to right, still holding TURID*'s hand.* IVAR *stands a minute helplessly—he pauses as though struggling with himself, then he slowly follows.)*
Curtain

Part 2

Same as part 1. One hour before dinner the evening of the same day. The lamps are lighted and there is a fire burning in the fireplace. The windows leading out into the garden are closed as there is a terrible storm raging outside. Through the entire scene the rain can be heard beating on the windows and the wind circling and howling around the house. One can also hear the distant boom of the sea as the waves break furiously upon the beach and rocks. As the curtain rises SANDVIK, *from the outside, struggles to open one of the windows. He has difficulty doing so on account of the wind and rain, but he finally succeeds and enters the room. The door bangs and closes behind him. He is dressed in an oilskin coat and hat which are glistening and wet with rain. He takes from underneath his coat a small plant. He gazes about for just the right place for it, then he places it tenderly upon the table and bends over it, straightening the leaves.*

SANDVIK: It's well I thought of yer, darlin'—yer never could have stood this wind. Yer see what it is ter have someone who loves yer. It's a great help in life—that's what I always say.

(While he is speaking TURID *enters. She is dressed for dinner and upon entering the room she starts when she sees the bending form of* SANDVIK.*)*

TURID: Oh, you frightened me! You look as though you had come out of the sea, all wet and gleaming. Do you always come into the house all wet like this?

SANDVIK: Miss Svanhild and I don't care about wet nor storm. In the winter we leave the doors open so the rain and sun and we ourselves, can come in whenever, or however we like. It's only when Miss Sophia is here that I'm more careful.

TURID: *(Looking at the plant)* What have you got there?

SANDVIK: One of Miss Svanhild's favorites. I brought it in to save it from the storm because of her. I know she loves it.

TURID: Would she care if anything happened to it?

SANDVIK: Her? Why she would feel somethin' awful. Once I saw a flower pulled out of its bed by its roots—a nasty little village boy did it. When Miss Svanhild found it she took it in her hands and bent over it and—and there were tears in her eyes.

TURID: Svanhild! Why, I can't imagine her crying!

SANDVIK: Yer wrong there. She like ter pretend to be hard and strong outside—inside she's kind and warm and sometimes weak. Sandvik knows. We don't stay here all winter with only ourselves not ter know each other.

TURID: *(Warmly)* You are making me see her differently. I wanted to see her the way you see her. You love her, don't you?

SANDVIK: Love her—why there's no one like her. *(Tenderly)* You should see us in winter, sometimes when she's tired. She won't say she's tired but I know. When she's in bed I bring her up a cup of tea—when she's finished it I know she wants me ter tuck her in. She wouldn't ask, but I know. So, I tuck her in and sometimes— *(He hesitates as though he should not say.)*

TURID: Sometimes what?

SANDVIK: I—I sing ter her until she falls asleep.

TURID: *(Touched)* You *do* love her!

SANDVIK: No one could help it who really knows her—brave and strong she is, but lonely—sometimes like a little lost bird. She's lonely—wantin' somethin' when no one sees, she's weak and gentle, too—all mixed up with everything else—wonderful, that's what she is.

TURID: I think you are right. I felt so from the first moment I saw her.

SANDVIK: I know I'm right.

TURID: I wish this storm would stop, it frightens me.

SANDVIK: It's the worst in years. Nothin' can stand against it.

TURID: I don't see how Svanhild can bear this place in winter.

SANDVIK: It's the wildness in her soul that loves wild places. She likes it best in winter and sits up in her lighthouse through all the worst storms.

TURID: *(Warming her hands by the fire and laughing)* People have strange tastes.

SANDVIK: There yer are right, Miss. There yer are right.

(He gives the plant a parting caress, then goes out to the left. TURID *stands nervously clasping and unclasping her hands. After a minute* SVANHILD *enters. She is dressed in a brilliant flame-colored dress, cut simply like a Greek tunic. She looks very striking and alive. She carries a manuscript envelope in her hands.)*

SVANHILD: I'm sorry. Did I keep you waiting? Everyone seems to be dressing for dinner so we can be alone for a while. *(She holds up the envelope.)* You see, I've brought you back your precious poems.

TURID: *(Joyously taking the envelope)* Oh, thanks—I'm so glad. *(Anxiously)* What did you think of them?

SVANHILD: Well—that's what we must talk about. I'm afraid it's going to be a little difficult.

TURID: You didn't like them!

SVANHILD: You mustn't get upset about it. Let's sit down and talk them over quietly.

TURID: But—but you *didn't* like them?

SVANHILD: No, I didn't. And apart from the value of the poems themselves, it is naturally very difficult for me to tell you that I don't like them—I mean, as I suppose they are all love poems to you.

TURID: *(Crushed)* Why—why don't you like them?

SVANHILD: For a number of reasons—principally because the poems in themselves are not good. I'm sorry they have been accepted for publication. I think it will be a great mistake if he publishes them—it will surely hurt him very much.

TURID: *(Sinking down into a chair)* You see, I don't know much about poetry. I thought they were beautiful.

SVANHILD: No doubt Ivar read them to you. I know he reads beautifully, but you mustn't be taken in that way. When poets read aloud their own poems, I find they either ruin them or make them sound more beautiful than they are.

TURID: Why should it hurt him to publish them? They may not be perfect but surely they have some beauty—some value. Why did the publisher take them? *(Suddenly)* You don't think because of your name—because he's your brother?

SVANHILD: The thought never occurred to me. I have no idea why they took them. But I think he should wait until he has something worthwhile to give. Oh, don't be discouraged, I know he will one day—he is just not ready yet. I, of course, can't say all these things to him, but I think you should.

TURID: He wouldn't listen to me—he'd laugh at me. He knows I don't know anything about poetry.

SVANHILD: Then we will have to think of something else. If you really love him as you claim you do, you must save him from publishing these poems. In the end he will thank you.

TURID: But what can I do? I have no influence with him—at least not concerning his work.

SVANHILD: But as he loves you so much he'll listen to you. I'm sure you could influence him in his work—at least indirectly, without his knowing it.

TURID: I doubt that. I sometimes wonder if deep down I have any influence with him at all—on any subject.

SVANHILD: Nonsense—of course you have. Otherwise I'm sure he wouldn't trust you with his poems.

TURID: *(Brightening)* That's true! I hadn't thought of that. It's such a wonderful precious trust, too. *(Cast down again)* Perhaps I've misused it—been unfair to his trust.

SVANHILD: Just because you showed the poems to me? If I had liked them, you wouldn't feel this way. It is only because I don't like them that you are worrying.

TURID: You mustn't think I'm ungrateful to you for having taken the trouble and been kind enough to read them. I'm fearfully grateful to you for my sake as well as Ivar's. You see, I've always wanted so much to be able to help him with his work—to be capable of helping him. I'm really not ungrateful—please don't think I am—only—

SVANHILD: *(Breaking in impatiently)* I don't want gratitude. Why should I? It is such a tiresome word anyway. At least when it is used where there isn't anything to be grateful about. It's like the word "duty"—it makes one think of chains and being held drearily down. But what did you mean by only? Only what?

TURID: I was going to say—only I wish you had thought the poems beautiful.

SVANHILD: I do, too. It would have been much easier—especially for me. But these things can't be helped, and one must just face them. Besides, after all—it's only my opinion—which may be quite wrong.

TURID: I don't think so. You are too fine a poet, I'm sure, not to recognize the worth in someone else's work. Oh! If only we knew what to do! It seems heartbreaking—terrible—that they are not as beautiful as I thought them.

SVANHILD: These are the only copies of the poems in existence—aren't they?

TURID: Yes.

SVANHILD: You are sure Ivar has no others?

TURID: I'm sure.

SVANHILD: And in a way they really belong to you—as much, I mean, as they belong to anyone.

TURID: Ivar gave them to me—I think perhaps he will dedicate them to me, although he hasn't said so. I like to believe they are mine—somehow they seem a part of Ivar.

SVANHILD: It's always so difficult, of course, to advise anyone else. I am trying to think what I would do if I were in your place.

TURID: What would you do?

SVANHILD: *(Thoughtfully)* I think—with my own hands I would

destroy these poems. I would take it upon my own shoulders to
save him. They ought never to be published.

TURID: *(Horrified)* Destroy them! Wipe them out entirely?

SVANHILD: *(Walking furiously about)* Ah, there we have it! You talk
about love, but you don't know what love is. You and all the other
people that talk about love, but who are not willing or courageous
enough to make one daring gesture for its sake!

TURID: *(Trembling)* He would never forgive me.

SVANHILD: If it is that, that you are fearing, it is a matter of thinking of yourself—not of Ivar.

TURID: *(Crying)* I'm not thinking of myself. I'm not!

SVANHILD: *(Softening)* Don't cry. Look at it instead as a test—a test,
say—to try the strength of your love.

TURID: But it may be trying too much the strength of Ivar's love for
me. He may never forgive me.

SVANHILD: You don't love him.

TURID: I do—I do. You don't know how much or you couldn't
say that.

SVANHILD: You are only concerned with his forgiveness, not for
making his reputation as a poet. Really only concerned for yourself, not for him.

TURID: It isn't fair for you to say that. I would do anything for Ivar—
but this—this seems so terrible.

SVANHILD: He will understand afterwards and write something so
much more beautiful that you can really be proud of.

TURID: *(More hopefully)* Do you think so? Do you really believe that?

SVANHILD: Yes, I do. I am sure of it. But he must begin over again.
With these—these poems behind him.

TURID: *(With admiration)* When I listen to you I feel everything
will be all right. That everything *must* come out for the best. As
though I must do always as you say.

SVANHILD: *(Laughing)* You mustn't feel that!

TURID: But I do. As terrible as this seems to me, I somehow feel it is
so right to do as you say. As though you know everything—there
is something curious about you which makes me feel that way.

SVANHILD: Oh, but you must feel that way about Ivar, too.

TURID: Not entirely—and if I do it is because I love him—with you,
it's because you seem so strong.

SVANHILD: Well, I have only told you what *I* would do in a position
like this. You must, of course, judge and act for yourself. In the
end one must always do that.

TURID: Your judgment is better than mine. *(Terribly troubled)* He is going to read the poems after dinner, you know.

SVANHILD: I know. But I wouldn't let him. If we all react unfavorably it will be very embarrassing. I, for my part, will not be able to pretend to like them.

TURID: *(Covering her face with her hands)* I don't know what to do. It would seem like murder to touch or destroy those poems.

SVANHILD: Strong love should be able to do strong things. Only a weak love can fail. No love is worth anything if one couldn't commit a crime for its sake.

TURID: But there must be another way! This seems so hard—*(Her voice breaks.)*

SVANHILD: If it is too hard—if it is impossible for you, then you must not do it. I have simply told you what I would do—the decision for Ivar's good must rest with you. His future is in your hands one way or another. *(She goes to the window and looks out.)*

TURID: *(Half to herself as though trying to convince herself)* I know you are right—after all, you must be right.

SVANHILD: It seems as though the wind were blowing a thousand miles an hour. How wonderful it is! Like great, strong hands dragging its fingers across the face of the earth. *(She turns and looks at TURID.)* Well, there's nothing more to say. I'll see you at dinner. I must go first up to my lighthouse—on a night like this I must be sure that the light is burning strong and straight.

(She goes out. TURID sits with her face buried in her hands. Then slowly she raises her head. She takes the envelope and with closed eyes holds it to her. Tears roll down her cheeks. Then with a sudden, impulsive gesture she rises and flings it into the fire. As the flames catch it, she sinks on her knees and sobs.)
Curtain

Part 3

Two hours later. DOCTOR KJELLAND *and* SOPHIA *enter the room.* SOPHIA *pulls a chair up beside the table and adjusts the lamp so she can see better. She picks up some sewing off the table and begins to sew.* DOCTOR KJELLAND *kneels and pokes the fire. There is a minute of silence, then he turns, lights his pipe and stands before the fire looking at* SOPHIA.

DOCTOR KJELLAND: I don't know how you feel, but I am glad that dinner is over. For some unaccountable reason I have seldom felt more uncomfortable.

SOPHIA MUNK: It's the night and the storm. I dreamed about a storm like this not long ago. It rained and howled just the way it is doing now. Then out of the darkness I made out a huge black horse ridden by a white angel—at least I suppose it was an angel because he had great shimmering wings—they gleamed like frosted lilies, and he had a blazing sword in his hand. As he passed, the storm subsided and I was conscious that some beautiful and marvelous change had taken place. It's silly to tell about—no one else ever gets one's feeling of a dream. It left a curious impression on me.

DOCTOR KJELLAND: *(Laughing)* I should think you would be used to your dreams by now. You have so many—you should have written them down in a book all these years. Like a diary. A dream diary.

SOPHIA MUNK: Yes, but it's only certain ones that mean anything to me. Only certain ones that I consciously know mean something—I'm never wrong about them.

DOCTOR KJELLAND: That poor little Turid looked so nervous all through dinner. It seemed to me that she had been crying. I am beginning to think she is a bad match for Ivar. He should marry a woman with balance. One neurotic person in the family is quite enough to deal with.

SOPHIA MUNK: I thought, too, that Turid had been crying, but I wasn't sure. Certainly it can't be anything that Svanhild has done or said. She seemed amazingly sweet to Turid. I must say she never ceases surprising me. She never does what one expects her to. I was worrying that she would be rude to Turid, and now it turns out that Turid and she seem to have a sort of understanding between them.

DOCTOR KJELLAND: Turid didn't eat anything. She never touched her food. Neither did Ivar.

SOPHIA MUNK: He is probably nervous about reading his poems.

DOCTOR KJELLAND: I must say that I am, too. I hope they will be good. It will be so damn embarrassing if they are not. It will be difficult to know what to say. I don't know what we will say.

SOPHIA MUNK: They must be good or else a publisher would not have accepted them.

DOCTOR KJELLAND: Heavens, if that were a way of judging we would be spared a lot of bad books!

SOPHIA MUNK: Well, it's time Ivar got *some* encouragement. You know I think I will say they are good whether they are or not.

DOCTOR KJELLAND: Oh, you had better say what you think. If we are going to have artists in the family at least we must judge art impersonally. It's a rotten trick to lie to anyone about their work.

SOPHIA MUNK: Well, I hope we won't have to lie. It will be peaceful and happy if we can all sincerely admire them. As for Turid, he might have done much worse. I rather like the child. He might have been taken in by a much older woman, or a divorcee, or an actress—and given us no end of trouble. I must say I'm really relieved to find her so harmless, and to find Svanhild taking to her!

DOCTOR KJELLAND: Yes—that is luck. After all our worry, in the end, we may be able to say "and they all lived happily forever after!"

SOPHIA MUNK: What do you suppose those children are doing? Why don't they come in here?

DOCTOR KJELLAND: They are probably still sitting around the table settling the great problems of life. I'll call them. *(He goes to the door and calls.)* Ivar! Turid! *(IVAR'S VOICE is heard offstage answering, "What is it?")* Come in here. We are waiting for the reading.

(SVANHILD and TURID enter, followed by IVAR and OLAF HALVOR-SEN. OLAF is speaking as they enter)

OLAF HALVORSEN: I don't pretend to understand art, although my father has squandered a very big fortune on collecting old masters and rare books. I always felt he bought them as sort of a defense rather than from any love of them.

IVAR: You can't squander money on art. There is no such thing.

OLAF HALVORSEN: Well, I think there is. Money is money and squandering is squandering.

SVANHILD: Oh, what difference does it make? Why anyone wants to load themselves down with a lot of possessions just because they have money value, I never could see. I can understand wanting to own one beautiful rare painting that one really loved—even that, one shouldn't own—great art should belong to everybody.

SOPHIA MUNK: Well, then, I should take good care not to have any in my house. I shouldn't wish to have a lot of strange, probably dirty people prancing into my house just because I happened to have a work of art on my walls!

SVANHILD: *(At the window)* It's still blowing furiously. I wish I were up in the crow's nest of a ship tonight!

TURID: I'm glad I'm not. The sea frightens me.

SVANHILD: You should make the sea your friend.

OLAF HALVORSEN: *(Laughing)* There's another idea. You do say funny things, Svanhild.

SVANHILD: You are mistaken if you think the elements cannot be our friends or our enemies. I know differently.

DOCTOR KJELLAND: Isn't Ivar going to read us his poems? *(TURID looks up quickly and with terror. She looks at* SVANHILD, *who turns away and lights a cigarette.)*

SOPHIA MUNK: Yes—where are the poems, Ivar? I can't tell you how impatient I am to hear them.

IVAR: That's sweet of you, Auntie. I hope you will like them. I'm afraid they will bore everybody.

OLAF HALVORSEN: *(On the verge of yawning and sinking down into a chair)* I shall be delighted to hear them—if I can understand them. At any rate, I will close my eyes.

SVANHILD: *(Laughing)* So we can't judge whether you are listening or sleeping!

SOPHIA MUNK: Now, Svanhild—

IVAR: *(Standing in the center nervously and interrupting)* You can sit where you are, Auntie. *(To* KJELLAND*)* And would you mind sitting there? It would make me nervous to read if you were standing. I couldn't do it. *(With agitation he pulls up two chairs beside each other.)* And you, Turid and Svanhild, can sit in these two chairs. I will sit here. No, I think here instead. The light is better. Sit down, Svanhild—what's the matter? *(*SVANHILD *sits, throwing her head back and blowing the smoke up into the air.* TURID *stands trembling.)* And what's the trouble with you, Turid? Here, pull the chair this way. It will be easier for me not to be conscious of your face. Now, are we ready? Oh, by the way, where are the poems? Have you got them, Turid?

TURID: *(Standing rigid and white)* No, Ivar.

IVAR: "No, Ivar." What on earth are you talking about?

TURID: I—I haven't got them, Ivar.

SOPHIA MUNK: But you said this morning you had them in your bag.

IVAR: Have you gone mad, Turid?

TURID: No. Oh, Ivar—Ivar darling—try and understand—

IVAR: *(Going white)* Understand? Understand what? *(With terror)* You haven't lost them? You haven't lost my poems?

TURID: Ivar! Ivar!

DOCTOR KJELLAND: What's the matter, Turid? There's some misunderstanding. Where are the poems?

TURID: *(With difficulty)* I—I—burned them.

IVAR: *(With a cry of anguish)* Burned them! *(He rushes and seizes* TURID *by her two arms, peering into her face.)* Is this your idea of a joke? Do you know what you are saying? Burned them!

TURID: *(Sobbing)* I did it for you, for your good.

SOPHIA MUNK: *(Rising)* Turid—Turid—are you ill?

IVAR: *(Springing back from* TURID *and raising his voice hysterically)* Where are my poems? What have you done with them? I don't believe you have destroyed them! I will kill you if you have—if you have ever dared touch them! *(He looks wildly and with sudden hatred at* TURID.*)*

DOCTOR KJELLAND: *(Placing his hand on* IVAR's *arm)* Quietly, Ivar—quietly. There must be some mistake—no one burns poems for nothing. Give Turid a chance to tell us what has happened.

SOPHIA MUNK: *(Putting her arm around* TURID*)* What happened, Turid?

TURID: *(Sobbing)* I burned them to show—to prove that I love Ivar—

DOCTOR KJELLAND: *(Stepping between* TURID *and* IVAR*)* Wait a minute now. Have you really burned them, Turid, or is this just an idea? Don't tremble like that, just answer me quietly—it must be a mistake—isn't it?

TURID: *(Hysterically)* I burned them there in that fire before dinner.

IVAR: *(Pushing* DOCTOR KJELLAND *aside and facing* TURID. *He becomes completely beside himself.)* You burned my poems? *My* poems. My God, my God, what are you saying?

TURID: I knew they were not good. I did it to save you the disgrace of having them published.

IVAR: *(Hardly able to speak with emotion) You* knew they were not good! *(Shrieking)* Since when do you know anything about poetry?

SOPHIA MUNK: *(Wringing her hands in despair)* Ivar—Ivar dear— don't speak that way—(DOCTOR KJELLAND *motions her to be quiet.)*

SVANHILD: *(Rising)* What you say is right. She doesn't know any- thing about poetry except what I told her.

IVAR: *(Turning on* SVANHILD*)* You told her? So it's you! What did *you* tell her?

SVANHILD: That your poems were no good. That you would be a laughingstock if they were published. That is why she burned them. It's very simple.

IVAR: *(In a low voice, trying to control himself)* Simple! And you, how did you see my poems when only Turid had them in her posses- sion?

SVANHILD: Turid gave them to me to read because I asked her to do so.

IVAR: *(To* TURID*)* How dared you show my poems!

TURID: I did it for your good—for your sake.

IVAR: *My good.* Do you know what you have done to me? Do you know that you have sold me—sold me to this sister of mine who hates me—who knew my poems were good and used you to destroy them. You stupid fool—you—you worthless—

TURID: *(Screaming)* Ivar, Ivar, don't look like that! Don't talk to me this way!

IVAR: Talk to you! I never want to talk to you again.

TURID: *(Shaking violently)* Just for some words on paper, would you throw away my love like this?

IVAR: *(Passionately)* Words on paper? Do you call my poems words on paper? Three years of work you call words on paper. Thoughts and dreams that I have carried within myself and which have finally crystallized and taken form—that I have torn out of myself in pain and joy—that have meant my life—that are my life—my life's blood. Those poems were my soul—those poems were my soul. The depths of me. Get out of my life! I never wish to see your face again!

(TURID sways a second as though she was going to fall, then she dashes to the garden window, tears it open and before anyone has time to stop her, she rushes out.)

SOPHIA MUNK: *(In terror)* Go after her! Go after her, someone! For heaven's sake!

(OLAF HALVORSEN struggles with the wind and the door and rushes out after TURID. IVAR makes a gesture as though to strike SVANHILD, instead his hand drops to his side and he flings himself on the chair with his head in his hands sobbing wildly. SOPHIA puts her arms around him. She touches his hair and tries to calm him. SVANHILD hesitates a moment as though she had something to say to IVAR, then she quickly leaves the room. DOCTOR KJELLAND sighs, shakes his head and goes to the window peering out for sign of TURID. IVAR continues sobbing.)
Curtain

Part 4

Half an hour later.

SVANHILD's *room in the lighthouse. The room is octagonal with the walls in oak. The ceiling is low. There are three small windows with the glass panes curving out, such as used in lighthouses. A small wooden spiral staircase comes up through the floor along the upstage left wall and continues through the ceiling to the floor above where the light is kept burning. There is a large working table directly to the left upstage, with a chair behind it. On it are writing materials, a lighted lamp and books piled up. To the right, directly upstage, there is a small wooden bed with a little table beside it with some books and a small lamp on the table. There is nothing else in the room except one soft chair, an early American rug on the floor, and on the walls on both sides, framed glass cases are hung, each one filled with hundreds of feathers.* IVAR, *very white and tense, is sitting on the soft chair with his head thrown back and his eyes closed.* SOPHIA, *endeavoring not to appear agitated is walking about. Once or twice she looks out the window, from time to time she looks at* IVAR, *then goes over and tenderly smooths his hair on his brow. The storm continues outside.*

SOPHIA MUNK: *(After a long silence)* I do wish you would lie on the bed. I'm sure it would rest and relax you more. It's no good sitting there all tense and tight.

IVAR: Sitting or lying, it's all the same thing—what difference does it make?

SOPHIA MUNK: Well, I think it does. I think it always helps one's nerves to stretch out a bit.

IVAR: Sitting or lying doesn't help to get my poems back again. Nothing helps to do that. If I could only remember a few of them. Even that would be something, and might comfort me a little.

SOPHIA MUNK: They will come back to you when you are less agitated. Try not to think about them now. Try to forget them.

IVAR: It's easy enough to say—

SOPHIA MUNK: I know.

IVAR: If you had children whom you loved, whom you thought were beautiful, whom you believed might have contributed even some small beauty to life—it wouldn't be easy to forget them—it wouldn't be easy to forget that they were burned. *(With a sudden overwhelming pain)* Burned! Good God! Good God! How am I going to bear to think about it?

SOPHIA MUNK: I know there is nothing I can say—*(A long pause)* Do you remember last winter we were talking about Carlyle? How he started all over again after his first manuscript on the French Revolution was burned?

IVAR: French Revolution—yes. Data, facts! He had data, facts to start over with, but I have nothing. Fleeting dreams, vaporous fantasies, the shadow of a mood that may never in a lifetime reoccur again—those are the slender threads which have vanished from me, leaving no record that I may recapture them with.

SOPHIA MUNK: And I was so happy at the thought of your coming home. If I had ever dreamed that anything as terrible as this could have happened.

IVAR: Home! Svanhild and I can't share the word "home" either in reality or in speech.

SOPHIA MUNK: I've forgiven Svanhild many things, but I'll never forgive her this.

IVAR: I'll never forgive Turid.

SOPHIA MUNK: I'm only thankful that your mother didn't live to see this unnatural feeling between you and your own twin sister. It would have broken her heart. She always dreamed that you would both go through life meaning everything to each other.

IVAR: Everything to each other! Svanhild hates me. She has always hated me. I must remember that and hate her, too—go on hating her—go on hating—*(His voice trails off into a sob.)*

SOPHIA MUNK: Oh, don't say such things! *(Trying to change the subject)* I wish Olaf would come back and tell us that he has found Turid. It terrifies me to think of her out in that storm. No matter what the poor child did, my heart aches for her.

IVAR: I never want to see her again!

SOPHIA MUNK: That is very hard and unlike you.

IVAR: I never want to see her again!

SOPHIA MUNK: Whatever she did, she did it because she loved you. Anyone could see that, no matter what her mistake was. The poor little thing undoubtedly felt she was helping you.

IVAR: Helping!

SOPHIA MUNK: You'd be wise to try and appreciate the value of real love. Turid loves you—you shouldn't throw her love away.

IVAR: A strange way of showing real love.

SOPHIA MUNK: It is real just the same and so precious that anything done for its sake must be accepted and if necessary—forgiven. I know that now after nearly a lifetime. I wish I had had someone to make me realize it when I was your age. I wish I had had the gentleness, the fineness, the vision to have recognized real love. We think we can afford to pass it—that it will come over and over again—but it doesn't. Then, too, I believe there is a law in life that will not allow us to break a heart without in turn having our hearts broken, too. Turid loves you. Forgive her for, and because of, that love. I think there must be a holiness that goes with forgiveness toward one who loves you much, and who perhaps has blindly done wrong, only because of love's sake.

IVAR: I cannot talk about Turid. She has betrayed me.

SOPHIA MUNK: You are wrong. You are betraying yourself if you hold back your forgiveness from her. *(Another silence)* After they find Turid tonight, I think the best thing for you to do is to marry her in the morning and then leave here. Go on the continent and travel—you will soon begin to write new poems—even the old ones may come back to you. Before you know it, you will have enough for another volume.

IVAR: I will never marry Turid. I know now it was wrong from the beginning—I regret ever meeting her—*(From the bottom of the stairway* OLAF HALVORSEN'S VOICE *is heard.)*

OLAF HALVORSEN: Who is up there? Is Kjelland there?

SOPHIA MUNK: *(Leaning over the stairway)* No—only Ivar and I. Come up. Have you found Turid? *(*OLAF HALVORSEN *appears. His clothes are wet.)*

OLAF HALVORSEN: No—I couldn't find her. I have looked all over. Around the house, on the rocks round the lighthouse, on the beach. I tried to call her but the wind is so strong that I could barely form her name and then it could not be heard, I'm sure. It's pitch black, and in the blinding rain I could not see a foot before me. Holding a light is absolutely out of the question—it's no use, it can't be seen. I must admit I'm worried about her—it's very easy to slip on these rocks. She might easily break her leg or something worse.

SOPHIA MUNK: Oh, dear, oh, dear! Whatever shall we do?

OLAF HALVORSEN: I want Kjelland to come out, too, and look for her with me. She can't have gone far; there is no doubt of that. It's impossible to make headway in the wind. And anyone as frail as she could hardly move. I am convinced she is somewhere sheltered by the house. Poor darling—what madness for her to have run out like that—tonight of all nights. Sandvik says it's the worst storm in years.

IVAR: He says that about every storm.

SOPHIA MUNK: *(Touching* OLAF*)* You should put on a rubber coat. You are soaked through and through. The next thing you'll be ill— there is no point in catching your death. I'm afraid this night will have had enough consequences as it is.

OLAF HALVORSEN: I couldn't have believed that Svanhild could do such things—that she would have made so much trouble. Where is she?

SOPHIA MUNK: I haven't got the remotest idea. Nor am I concerned about her.

OLAF HALVORSEN: I can't help feeling there is some mistake— Svanhild must have had some sound reason—*(*DOCTOR KJEL- LAND *appears from below and interrupts his speech.)*

DOCTOR KJELLAND: Have you found Turid?

OLAF HALVORSEN: No. I came back to see if you would come out and help me look for her. I thought we could each go in opposite directions.

DOCTOR KJELLAND: Certainly I'll go. It's odd you didn't find her.

OLAF HALVORSEN: It would be hard finding anything in this storm. *(To* IVAR*)* I agree with Sandvik—it *must* be the worst in years.

IVAR: I suppose you two think I'm a cad not to go out and help you look for Turid, too.

DOCTOR KJELLAND: No, indeed. You've had enough for one night. Olaf and I are quite capable and ready to do the searching ourselves. I think you'd better lie down.

SOPHIA MUNK: That's just what I advised—but he won't do it.

DOCTOR KJELLAND: Come on, Olaf. I don't think we should waste time. While there can't be any actual danger—still it worries me to think of that child roaming around in such a storm.

SOPHIA MUNK: You both put on rubber coats and hats. You'll find them in the cupboard in the hall.

DOCTOR KJELLAND: Thanks—we will.

SOPHIA MUNK: Olaf is already soaked to the skin. If Turid doesn't catch her death in that thin dress, it will only be because she must be under some divine protection.

DOCTOR KJELLAND: When we find her, you can put her straight to bed. You've brandy in the house—haven't you?

SOPHIA MUNK: Yes.

DOCTOR KJELLAND: Well—that's good. On our way, Olaf? *(He turns to go down the stairs, followed by* OLAF *just as* SVANHILD *comes up.)*

SVANHILD: *(To* OLAF*)* I thought you were out looking for Turid.

OLAF HALVORSEN: I have been, but I couldn't find her. I came back to get Kjelland to help me.

SOPHIA MUNK: *(With a nod of her head at* IVAR*)* I think you had better stay away from here, Svanhild.

SVANHILD: I came to talk to Ivar.

SOPHIA MUNK: Let's not begin anything else tonight.

OLAF HALVORSEN: *(As though taking* SVANHILD*'s side)* Svanhild may have some explanation to make to Ivar.

SOPHIA MUNK: I can't keep her out, but I disapprove of Ivar being upset any more tonight.

DOCTOR KJELLAND: Yes, Svanhild. Sophia is right.

SVANHILD: I simply want a few words alone with Ivar—it's important that I should have them.

DOCTOR KJELLAND: Come, Olaf—we have *our* job.

(He and OLAF *go down the stairs.* SOPHIA *hesitates a moment, she looks at* IVAR *who does not move; remaining with his head in his hands.)*
SOPHIA MUNK: Oh, very well.
(She follows the other two down the stairs. There is a long pause before IVAR *looks up.* SVANHILD *lights a cigarette and throws the match away; she does not move from her standing position.)*
IVAR: *(Looking up defiantly)* I can't see that we have anything to say to one another.
SVANHILD: Ah! I knew it. I *knew* those would be your first words. I heard you saying them before I came up. *(She imitates him.)* I can't see that we have anything to say to one another.
IVAR: You are always so clever. If you know what I am going to say, why bother to come and hear me say it? I didn't ask you to come and talk to me. In fact, I think it rather bad taste on your part to do so.
SVANHILD: *(Softly)* At any rate, I didn't come to quarrel with you. You should know that—I think you do.
IVAR: *(Bitterly)* Why should you quarrel with me? Unless you don't think you have created enough havoc for one evening.
SVANHILD: I don't know. There are some situations which create themselves, over which we have no control. *(She puts out her cigarette and throws it away.)*
IVAR: It's odd to hear you admit that—you, who always seemed to have perfect control over everything.
SVANHILD: It's only your way of looking at me. I know, too, you think I have never suffered.
IVAR: Have you?
SVANHILD: I think so. More perhaps than you would know or understand. Only I treat suffering the way I face a strong wind. The way I would face this storm if I were out in it tonight. I would throw my head back and go out into it and through it. It would beat and sting and toss me about, but it would exhilarate me, too.
IVAR: It's a proof you don't really suffer. You dramatize your suffering and it leaves you with no scars.
SVANHILD: Not all of us show our scars. Sometimes our wounds are so deep that the surface heals over them, leaving no apparent scars—underneath, they remain open. These are the worst wounds of all—the ones that have seemingly healed well. The air or light never gets them—no one knows about them—one simply bears them in silence, that's all one can do.
IVAR: I don't want to talk to you. I might regret my words—I—

SVANHILD: *(Interrupting)* Why should you regret anything? I've always felt that has been the real difference between us. You, who have always regretted every step of your life—I, who never regret anything.

IVAR: You have been too fortunate to have to regret anything.

SVANHILD: No—no—no—that isn't so—besides, nothing is really as dreadful as you think it is—all this, for instance—

IVAR: *(Breaking in)* Is that what you came to tell me?

SVANHILD: In a way. Not exactly to tell you in so many words, but to show you. To begin with, I shouldn't worry about Turid if I were you. They are sure to find her, and a little wind and rain can't harm anyone. If so, I would have been harmed long ago. I live out in storms all winter. Then when they find Turid you should forgive her for everything. She has nothing to be blamed for. You would naturally not expect her to attach the value to any poems that you and I would, or that any poet would. Then, too, you should remember she did only what I told her to do. I am the only one to blame.

IVAR: If Turid came and prostrated herself before me, I would never forgive her. She has gone out of my life tonight as truly as she went out into that storm. As for your part in all this, it should not have surprised me only—only—*(He puts his hand to his brow in a gesture of suffering and despair.)*

SVANHILD: Only what?

IVAR: Nothing you could understand—nothing I want you to understand. You have succeeded in taking everything from me. I suppose that was what you wanted. I have nothing left.

SVANHILD: Nothing has really been taken from you. It is you who have taken from me. Always—always. But *that you* would not understand.

IVAR: *(Bitterly)* No, nothing has been taken from me! You, of course, would call my poems nothing. They were little to you—but they happened to be everything to me.

SVANHILD: *(Sadly)* So little to me, Ivar, that I could not bear another woman to have them. That is why I took them away from her.

IVAR: *(Fiercely)* Burned them, you mean!

SVANHILD: No—took them away. *(She goes to the desk, opens the drawer and takes out an envelope.)* Here are your poems, Ivar. They were never burned.

IVAR: *(Springing up)* Are you tricking me? *(SVANHILD shakes her head.)*

SVANHILD: You can see for yourself.

(She walks over and hands him the envelope, which he snatches from her. Frantically and hungrily he takes out and goes through his poems, counting them, fingering them lovingly and passionately.)

IVAR: Good God! I must be mad.

SVANHILD: No. You see, I merely put blank sheets in the envelope I returned to Turid. I was certain she would do just as I told her. I was equally certain she would not look at them before burning them. *(Tenderly)* They are beautiful—so beautiful. So much more beautiful than anything I have ever written—than anything I could ever write. Sensitive and beautiful like you, Ivar. You are the poet, a great poet, a genius, I think. I have always known that—always. Long before you wrote anything that mattered like these. But you would not have been so great if you had not *(She changes her tone, defiantly using the word.)* hated me so much. *(For a full minute they stand and look at each other, neither one moving, barely breathing. Then* IVAR *jerks himself around, afraid to longer look at* SVANHILD.*)*

IVAR: You have given me back my poems. It is too late to do anything about Turid.

SVANHILD: I meant it to be too late. That is why I did it. Did you ever really want her? *(*IVAR *does not answer.)* Were those poems written to her?

IVAR: *(He hesitates then he speaks low and muffled.)* No—

SVANHILD: *(Barely making a sound)* Ah—

IVAR: *(Still in a low voice)* What right had you to try and separate Turid from me?

SVANHILD: She was not strong enough for you—not wild enough. *(Triumphantly)* You could not hate *her*!

IVAR: *(At first fiercely, then working himself into a passionate rage)* How dare you try to wreck my life? How dare you interfere in my life? What fiend are you that you should want to crucify and torture me?

SVANHILD: If those poems were not to her, nothing you say can matter. If you cannot hate her, nothing matters. Nothing but those two things matter to me.

IVAR: *(He speaks with difficulty and with passion.)* But I hate you. Hate you.

SVANHILD: *(Throwing back her head and stretching wide her arms. She speaks low but triumphantly and also passionately.)* Ah, how I have wanted you to say that! All these years I've longed to hear you say that.

IVAR: *(Without moving a step, but trembling)* Hate you—*hate you*—
hate— *(Before he finishes,* SVANHILD *drops her arms to her side
and lowers her head. For a full second they look at each other. When*
IVAR *speaks again, his voice is hardly audible.)* Love you—

SVANHILD: *(Ecstatically)* And I love you—love you—have always
loved you—

(As though lifted beyond herself SVANHILD *seizes* IVAR *in her arms.
They kiss on the lips deeply, violently, passionately—clinging to one another. Suddenly their arms fall to their sides, there is a dead and tense silence, neither of them move. Then* IVAR *sways and sinks on the chair,
beating his fists against his brow.)*

IVAR: *(Hysterically)* God! Good God! What are we saying? What are
we doing?

SVANHILD: Why not? We have always known it. It has been beautiful in my life. Like an exquisite sharp pain. I have waited for you
to have the courage—

IVAR: Stop! Stop! You don't know what you are saying. You're mad!

SVANHILD: Are you so afraid of words? Is it only their power that
makes you shrink? Didn't you feel always another divine power—
a power that bound us together the way the sand is bound to
the sea?

IVAR: You don't know what you are saying—what you are doing. You
have taken the last thing from me. The power to hide from you
how I felt; the power to hide my love in my hatred.

SVANHILD: Hide. Hide. That's how it always has been. All our lives
we have hidden from one another—from our real selves—until
now they have grown so strong that they broke through and would
not be hidden any longer.

IVAR: *(Almost insanely)* We cannot both go on living with this—this
openly between us.

SVANHILD: You could live when you held our love secretly to
yourself—when you held it in darkness and closed up within
your own heart. To me it has become more beautiful now that
we can hold it between us—not in pretend hatred, but as it is—
like a dark light.

IVAR: *(Wildly)* You are mad! You are mad, I tell you! You live so
much here alone with your crazy feathers and wild sea that you
have lost the touch of the world—you cannot see things as other
people see them—you can't understand—

SVANHILD: *(Sadly)* You think the light from my lighthouse has
blinded my eyes.

IVAR: Something has blinded you.

SVANHILD: I think rather that it has been I who have seen. You have tried to blind yourself with a false love for Turid.

IVAR: I have tried to protect myself with Turid. To cure myself of you.

SVANHILD: No. I will tell you what you have done. Do you remember the time I saved your life and dragged you out of the sea? Then afterwards you lay in my arms and cried like a child. I had to lay your head on my lap and stroke your eyes and touch your face to reassure you that you really were saved and to drive out that momentary fear of death that you had experienced. I had to talk courage into you—give you my strength. And so I dragged you back to life lending you my vitality—my force. After that you admired me with a furtive, hidden admiration. The kind of admiration the weak have for the strong—not even strong enough to be frankly weak in admitting their admiration. I became more of a truth to you than you were to yourself. Without admitting it, you began to draw on me for everything. I charged your brain with a desire to live, to work, to write. You walked beside me day by day pretending to hate me but in reality leaning on me, drinking in my thoughts, becoming inwardly little pieces of me. And I, I was aware of it all—utterly conscious of it. Every word I said, every thought I thought, I said and thought consciously to give you a pillar to lean upon—a step to stand upon. The very poems I thought to write—those poems maybe—I transferred in thought to you. With my own personality, I gave you a personality until you were able to stand upon your own feet. It was then you left me—but you had already written those poems—your best poems, here in this house close to me. You left me, but you couldn't get on without me, so you tried Turid as a substitute—or a protection, as you put it. But in some mysterious way the source of your inspiration seemed to dry up—you need me again and so you came back. You came back to drink again from my hands. But what you do not realize is that you and I are twin shoots that spring from the same stem—you could not tear yourself away from me without wounding us both—you as well as I. We were twins in much more than flesh and blood—in the spirit of complementing each other— you lacking what I have—I lacking what you have. But you cut yourself loose too soon, before your shoot had grown roots of its own. You were not as ready for freedom as I was because you had not yet learned how to find joy still having pain and loneliness in your heart. I know now it is this which you must learn—you must learn to become—as strong, as happy as I. You could learn it with me, if together we could face our love. If we cannot be together—if life has deprived us of that—you can and *must* learn it without me.

IVAR: *(In spite of himself)* How beautiful you are! Like some strange secret of the wind which you seem part of. I have fought against you. I couldn't help that—have held this thing more precious than myself hidden—as you say—in darkness. Have held it so deep in me so that I might never hear it saying "I love you"—so that I might never hear it crying out "I love you." I have held it to me as though it were something of which to be ashamed—as though my poems—my love poems to you were something of which to be ashamed, because I didn't realize until now that love is like a white flower and can be beautiful no matter how or where it grows. *(Frantically)* And yet, we cannot live and face this! We must give each other up—never see each other again. Tomorrow I will go away—never, never to return. I wish I had the courage to kill myself. If I only had!

SVANHILD: *(Looking at him with tenderness and compassion)* You must not kill yourself. Only those must kill themselves who have gained the thing they wanted most. *(She throws back her head and laughs.)* Only those who can go out laughing on a high note.

(She repeats the same gesture as she made in the first part. They stand looking at each other as though some terrific force were drawing them together. Then slowly SVANHILD backs toward the stairs but as she does so it seems as though she were drawing closer to him instead of further away. Never once do her eyes leave his face—as though she were pouring herself into him—giving herself to him. Then suddenly she turns and quickly runs up the stairs. IVAR stands as though rooted to the spot, then he crumples up and sinks down upon the chair. He is sitting like this when SOPHIA appears from below.)

SOPHIA MUNK: *(Anxiously)* Ivar, is anything the matter? I said you should not have seen Svanhild alone. Did you two quarrel? *(IVAR, as though hardly hearing her, shakes his head in the negative.)* Well, anyway, they found Turid, thank heavens! She was trying to walk into the town, poor child. She was, of course, wet to the skin. I gave her some brandy and put her to bed. She fell asleep at once, so that is something to be thankful for. *(She goes over and picks up the poems, which are lying on the table.)* What are these papers?

IVAR: *(Still as though he were hardly conscious of anything outside himself and answering mechanically)* My poems.

SOPHIA MUNK: Your poems? What do you mean? What poems?

IVAR: The ones that were supposed to have been burned but were not.

SOPHIA MUNK: *(With joy but still incredulous)* Not burned!

IVAR: No. There were only blank sheets in the envelope that Turid burned.

SOPHIA MUNK: What a miracle! How wonderful! Why, then, everything is all right. Turid has been found, and the poems are not burned. There is nothing more to worry about! *(OLAF'S VOICE can be heard coming up the stairs.)*

OLAF HALVORSEN: Svanhild! Are you there? *(He appears.)* Oh, I thought Svanhild was here. Where is she, do you know?

SOPHIA MUNK: No, I haven't got the slightest idea. Have you heard the wonderful news?

OLAF HALVORSEN: No—what?

SOPHIA MUNK: The poems were not burned at all. Here they are— Turid only burned blank sheets.

OLAF HALVORSEN: *(To IVAR)* Oh, I am so glad! And we've had all this fuss about nothing!

SOPHIA MUNK: Svanhild's idea of a joke—no doubt. *Disgusting*!

OLAF HALVORSEN: The most amazing thing has happened. Her light has gone out. I happened to look out of the window and noticed it wasn't flashing any more. *(IVAR leans back and closes his eyes.)*

SOPHIA MUNK: Nonsense. It never goes out.

OLAF HALVORSEN: I'll look again, but I know that I am right. *(He goes to the window and looks out.)* It *has* gone out. It's totally dark out there—no reflection whatsoever.

SOPHIA MUNK: How very extraordinary!

OLAF HALVORSEN: Where can Svanhild be? She is not downstairs. *(DOCTOR KJELLAND comes upstairs, OLAF turns.)* Have you heard the wonderful news? The poems—*(He stops as he sees DOCTOR KJELLAND's face, which is white and full of alarm.)*

DOCTOR KJELLAND: *(To SOPHIA)* I have some bad news.

SOPHIA MUNK: *(Catching the terror in his voice)* What? What's happened?

DOCTOR KJELLAND: It's—it's Svanhild. She—she fell from the top of the lighthouse—

OLAF HALVORSEN: *(With a cry)* Svanhild!

DOCTOR KJELLAND: *(In a low voice)* Killed—*(SOPHIA closes her eyes and nearly collapses. DOCTOR KJELLAND puts his arm around her and steadies her. They remain like that a second, clasping one another. In their sudden grief, they are nearer than they have ever been in all their lives.* IVAR *is the only one who remains as he was, without moving a muscle.)*

DOCTOR KJELLAND: Sandvik found her where she had fallen. He rushed in for me, but it was too late; her head had struck a rock—I think she was killed instantly.

OLAF HALVORSEN: *(With a sob)* God! Svanhild dead! *(He runs down the stairs.* DOCTOR KJELLAND *pauses a moment, still holding* SOPHIA, *then he, too, goes quickly down the stairs after* OLAF.*)*

SOPHIA MUNK: *(Putting her hand to her heart as though the pain was more than she could bear. She weeps and her voice chokes.)* The—last—words—I—said—to—her—were—unkind—*(She goes brokenly and slowly toward the stairs, then suddenly she remembers* IVAR. *She turns and pauses as though hesitating between going to* SVANHILD *or remaining with* IVAR.*)*

IVAR: *(Without moving)* I'm all right, Auntie—you can leave me alone.

*(*SOPHIA *turns and slowly goes down the stairs, sobbing. For an instant* IVAR *remains motionless, then quickly he sits very straight—he throws his head back with a characteristic gesture of* SVANHILD*'s. He looks suddenly like her—as though he were very strong, and no longer afraid—as if her spirit had suddenly entered into him. A curiously exalted light illuminates his face.)*
Curtain

Illusion
A Play in Six Parts

The Characters
MAGGIE
"MAMA"
NINA
MIKE
JOE
HUNT ASHLEY
NORA SUMNER
MRS. ASHLEY
ETHEL DIKE
STEPHEN DIKE
HARVEY OLIVER
DOCTOR ROBB
CLAIRE OAKLEY
ERIC FRAZER
TOM BODLEY
A MAID
FORBES, *a butler*
A SKIPPER
1ST SALVATION ARMY WOMAN
2ND SALVATION ARMY WOMAN
A SALVATION ARMY MAN
A CARPENTER
A DOCTOR
A POLICEMAN
GANGSTERS, LONGSHOREMEN, SAILORS,
SOLDIERS, PROSTITUTES, POLICEMEN,
CURIOSITY SEEKERS,
SALVATION ARMY FOLLOWERS,
SOCIETY GIRLS,
SOCIETY MEN, ETC.

Part 1
Time—*The present.*
A rough cabaret dive in Vancouver, frequented mostly by seamen. It is after midnight but still too early for the place to assume any life. The room is

rather small with a low ceiling. Directly right upstage there is a swinging door, such as used in the old-time saloon. This door opens onto an alleyway. Almost to the middle of stage, directly upstage but a little to the left, there is a bar. In the corner to the left there is a platform. On the platform is a piano, three chairs and two music stands. The middle of the room is left empty, as though for dancing, but around to right and left there are small tables and chairs. The tables and chairs are in disorder; some chairs are piled up on the tables, as though the place was not yet ready to be used. There are no windows in the room, and it should give a feeling as though it might be underground. It is lighted by gas and a few swinging oil lamps. A small straight staircase runs directly upstairs on the left with a door on the top that obviously opens into rooms for prostitution. The whole place gives a sordid atmosphere.

*As the curtain rises, "*MAMA*" is cleaning glasses behind the counter. She is a fat, old German with her face hardened by her life, although in spite of it there is something kindly about her and underneath her rough exterior one detects a certain gentleness. She has been in America more than thirty years but still retains a strong German accent.* NINA*, a half Russian, half Persian girl, is sweeping up the old dirty sawdust off the floor and sprinkling down new. She is small and scrawnily thin. She is shabbily and untidily dressed and does her work in a lazy and indifferent manner.*

In the beginning of the scene, neither of them speaks for a few minutes. When NINA *has finished with the sawdust, she slowly begins to arrange the tables and chairs around the center of the room, leaving the dance floor in the circle in the middle.*

MAMA: Gott, yer a lazy goil, ain't no wonder, that Armenian give yer the air from sellin' rugs for him.

NINA: He ain't Armenian—I told yer that before—he's Persian.

MAMA: A lot of difference that is! It's one and the same ter me—all dark and greasy, the same as Dagos. We'd scrub the whole crowd of yer up in Germany and if yer didn't clean up, we'd boil yer fer grease-fat. If it ain't been fer Maggie yer'd have a swell chance keepin' yer job here.

NINA: If it ain't been fer Maggie yer'd have a swell chance getting' customers here or anyone—yer would. Do yer think all them sailors would run here the minute they puts their foot on land, if it ain't fer them wantin' ter see Maggie? I'm Maggie's friend and I guess I stays here as long as I like.

MAMA: Yes—yer will—yer lazy good-fer-nothin' Russian. Russians is all lazy.

NINA: I'm half Persian.

MAMA: One and the same to me I told yer—all dark and greasy like
Dagos.

NINA: *(Mimicking a grand voice)* Me father was a Persian poet and
me mother a Russian princess.

MAMA: Yer do yer work—that's what!

NINA: *(Disgusted and bored)* Ach! *(Two* AMERICAN SAILORS *come
in. They sit down at a table upstage right.)*

1ST SAILOR: *(To* NINA, *in an Irish accent)* Say there, skinny-flint,
where the hell is the life round this dump? Who's croaked that it's
all sittin' empty-like, as though the crowd had gone fer a joy ride
ter the cemetery? *(The* 2ND SAILOR *laughs.)*

MAMA: This joint don't open so oily—this is a respectable place.
(With a smile) We don't start rough music until them what don't
like it is asleep, so they can't hear it. You sea boys ain't got the delicate feelin's of land folks so yer can't appreciate that there is hours
for everything. *(Both* SAILORS *laugh, in which* MAMA *joins.)*

2ND SAILOR: Well, maybe it's the hour for a drink! A couple of brandies, kid. *(*MAMA *pours them out two brandies.* NINA *serves them.*
2ND SAILOR *lifts his glass to* MAMA *and* NINA*)* Here's to you!

1ST SAILOR: *(Holding up his glass to* MAMA*)* Luck to youse!

MAMA: Thanks.

(They drink. Various types begin to stroll in and sit around. Three FRENCH
SAILORS *come in with a* CHINESE GIRL. *Four* LONGSHOREMEN, *all
drunk, come staggering in and fall leaning up against the bar. They call
for drinks.* MAMA *serves them. A rough-looking* TOUGH *that might be a
stoker comes in with a* GIRL *who is dazed with dope. They sit at a table
to the left, the* GIRL *looks straight before her as if she were not conscious
of her surroundings. The* TOUGH *takes out a mouth harmonica, tips his
chair back and begins playing a melancholy tune. Two* LONGSHOREMEN
collapse down on chairs at a table.)

1ST LONGSHOREMAN: Christ, what bloody bad whiskey—worse
than last month.

2ND LONGSHOREMAN: Hey, Mama—what are yer puttin' in the
drinks nowadays?

1ST LONGSHOREMAN: Tastes like as yer were usin' a little rough-on-
rate with a dash of vitriol.

MAMA: I serve the best stuff round here, and if yer don't like it yer
can get the hell out.

2ND LONGSHOREMAN: Well—well, it don't matter as long as
Maggie's here.

1ST LONGSHOREMAN: *(Coming to life)* Where the hell is Maggie?
Got a present fer her. *(He takes a soiled piece of paper out of his*

pocket, unwraps it and shows a cheap little silk purse. Both MEN
bend over it and examine it. A ROUGH LOOKING MAN *comes in
dressed in a sweater with his cap pulled over his eyes and stands by
the bar.)*

MAMA: What's on yer mind, Joe?

JOE: Goin' ter see some fun here ter nite.

MAMA: Fun?

JOE: *(Chewing and spitting)* Yer—fun. That slick dude what's ben
hangin' round Maggie is back agin.

MAMA: Well, what of it? You mind yer own business.

JOE: Yer, I knows—but what about Mike? "I'll blast the bloody head
off that guy if he comes around Maggie again," is what he said. Yer
heard him say it.

MAMA: He better not start a row down here, if he knows what's good
fer him. Besides, that guy's a nut anyway, if he wasn't he wouldn't
be hangin' round here.

JOE: Well, I'm only tellin' yer. I saw him comin' along with some slick
dame. *(He makes fun.)* Showin' her the sights as how the under-
world lives!

(He turns to the bar and drinks, talking to MAMA *in an undertone.* NINA,
*lazily dragging her feet, goes from one table to the other serving the men.
The* STOKER *continues playing the harmonica, monotonously repeating
"Bye Bye Blackbird" over and over again.* HUNT ASHLEY *and* NORA
SUMNER *come in.* HUNT *is good-looking and very much an individual.
In spite of the fact that he is still a young man, he at once gives the impression of having seen much of life and of the world—although he still retains
much idealism, and by the sensitiveness of his face one can see he could
easily border on fanaticism and follow blindly and passionately a person
or a cause in which he believed.* NORA SUMNER *is older than* HUNT;
*she is distinguished and rather beautiful for her type. She is dressed in a
dark tailor-made suit. They come forward and sit at the table directly to
the right of the stage. During their conversation everyone else continues
talking to each other with various business. Their voices, however, should
not interfere with* HUNT *and* NORA*'s conversation, nor distract from it.
The harmonica continues playing. Various people continue coming in—
some* MEXICANS, *a few* SOLDIERS, *a few* STREET WALKERS, *etc.)*

HUNT: I hope you won't be angry with me, Nora, for bringing
you here.

NORA: How foolish of you to think that. It's a great lark for me; I've
never been in a place like this.

HUNT: I'm afraid we'll have to order something to drink. What
would you like?

NORA: I don't care—a whiskey and soda perhaps.

HUNT: *(To* NINA*)* Two whiskies and sodas! *(*NINA *goes to the bar for the drinks and during their conversation brings them to the table.)*

HUNT: I suppose you thought it was odd my wiring you like that to San Francisco, and asking you to change your plans.

NORA: Why no. I was flattered you wanted to see me. It was just a question of changing my tickets. I have nothing definite to hurry back to New York for, and I was rather pleased to come this way. I've never been here before. I must say the scenery along the way is marvelous.

HUNT: Well, you were sweet to pay attention to my wire. I just sent it on a chance of catching you. You are always such a sport, Nora.

NORA: *(Pleased)* Oh, I don't know.

HUNT: But I do. What other woman in the world, at the last minute, would have chucked all her plans the way you did, and leap on a train going in an entirely different direction and then be met by a wild man like myself, and before you hardly have a chance to clean up, be brought down to a dump like this? And you haven't even murmured a word of protest!

NORA: *(Laughing)* Well, if you insist upon making me the angel-heroine I'm quite willing, Hunt darling. Incidentally, I'm a little curious to know why you sent for me and what's up and all that. *(Putting her hand on* HUNT*'s)* I hope the black sheep of the Ashley estates hasn't been getting into any grave trouble.

HUNT: *(Covering her hand with his)* And if he has, will Nora—the world's most extensive traveler—help him out? *(They both laugh.)* Just because I sent for you, why should you think I'm in trouble?

NORA: Only judging from the many other S.O.S. calls of our past friendship.

HUNT: It's true. I've always run to you with all my troubles. This isn't exactly a trouble—

NORA: *(Breaking in)* Ah! Nora sighs relief!

HUNT: I'm going to draw a deep breath—count three, and then break the news to you.

NORA: All right! *(*HUNT *straightens up and draws breath.* NORA *counts.)* One—two—three—

HUNT: I want to get married!

NORA: A vagabond like you marrying? I can't believe it.

HUNT: It's true.

NORA: But why did you send for me, and why rush down here to this place?

HUNT: I sent for you because I want your help, and brought you here because the girl I want to marry lives here.

NORA: *(Horrified)* Lives here?

HUNT: Well, comes here—dances here.

NORA: You can't be serious, Hunt. God knows you've been wild all your life—

HUNT: *(Interrupting)* That's just it, and now I want to settle down. I *am* serious, Nora—desperately serious.

NORA: I'm really speechless—but you might as well tell me everything before I begin protesting, because protest I will—you must expect that.

HUNT: I'm prepared, but I think you will understand a little of what I see and feel—about Maggie, I mean.

NORA: Maggie? *(She laughs.)* I actually think you've lost your sense of humor, Maggie Ashley! Oh dear—oh dear, I can see your mother and your sister's face. *(She laughs again and wipes her eyes.)*

HUNT: Oh, laugh if you like—

NORA: *(Controlling herself)* Hunt—I really think you *are* serious. *(She takes his hand again.)* Tell me about it.

HUNT: You know as well as I do the way I've wasted my life—squandered money—drifted—been engaged to decent women—kept endless mistresses—vagabonded—traveled—and where has it all led me? What have I got from it all? Nothing but discontent and restlessness.

NORA: But you never wanted to lead a conventional life. Why haven't you settled down and married some nice girl?

HUNT: Settle down with some tiresome nice girl of my own class, who in the end would bore me to death, and I her—and what then? Divorce, and much more misery than if one had never gotten into it. No, thanks—besides I've never found anyone I wanted to really marry until now—

NORA: You've always been self-willed, Hunt, so I don't suppose anything I would say would change you—but your Maggie can't be different from any other girl that has led this type of life—Oh, it isn't that I don't believe she may be many of the things you think—

HUNT: *(Interrupting)* Well, you see that's just what I don't do—Maggie is the first woman I have ever met in my life that I don't think about and analyze. At least, I don't think about her the way you mean. I "feel" her in my brain rather than "think" her. She's

the kind of person that could do anything right before my eyes—
she could steal before me, and yet somehow I'd know she wasn't
stealing—something about her would convince me she wasn't a
thief. It's like that about her life—call her—call her, anything you
like—bring me evidence and I'll admit it, but I won't admit that
Maggie is really like that or that it touches her. Besides, can't you
see what it will mean for me—what it will do for me? Why you've
always wanted me to have a job—Well, what could be a better job
than developing and helping Maggie—showing and giving her
things that she's missed and never had a chance to see or know?

NORA: Do you think you really love her, or isn't this just another
adventure? Do you think you could really love a—a—*(Hesitating)*

HUNT: *(Quickly)* A prostitute? I wouldn't dream of using the word—
I—*(Again interrupting)* But I would. It's rather wonderful in con-
nection with Maggie. It's like someone showing you something
black, then with your own sleight of hand turning it white—
because, of course, it's only a trick and it really has been white
all the time.

NORA: Well, you see Hunt, what really worries me is—the exagger-
ated colors you see it in. I know you have always been sort of a
fanatic on any fancy that's happened to hit you—you've lacked dis-
cipline. But, after all—as long as you don't object to the word—she
is a prostitute—a prostitute in a low dive—in a low life—

HUNT: I suppose if she was a prostitute in high life it wouldn't
matter.

NORA: Oh, come now, why split hairs? A prostitute is a prostitute,
and I can't see a man of your breeding, your intelligence, or your
position marrying her. To me it's utter madness no matter what
her qualities may be.

HUNT: Sometimes mad men see further than sane men.

NORA: Perhaps in their own eyes—not always in other people's.
How did you ever meet this girl? What made you first come to
this place?

HUNT: I didn't meet her here, but I always came afterwards because I
knew I'd see her if I did. As a matter of fact, our first meeting was
rather a strange one.

NORA: In what way?

HUNT: She more or less saved my life. I was walking along the docks
late one night—you know the fascination water has for me—I was
very intent, looking out into the blackness of the sea and not noticing anything around me. Quite suddenly and before I could do
anything about it, three men jumped upon me, seized me, and

pinned me down to the ground. I, of course, struggled violently while they tried to take my money; one of them beat me on the head with a club. I don't remember much after that, until I came to, and found Maggie bending over me, bathing the wound in my head. She happened to come along while the men were attacking me and rushed upon them, beating them off me with her fists and screaming. They evidently were afraid her screams had been heard and so they all quickly ran off. When I was able to sufficiently pull myself together and manage to keep the blood out of my eyes, I went back to Maggie's room with her where she bandaged my head with a piece of the only sheet she had. I offered her money for saving me but she wouldn't take it.

NORA: That was nice of her, but I still don't think it makes her any more marriageable. What can a woman like that really be to you?

HUNT: A little bit my child—a little bit my mistress—a little bit my wife—and perhaps very much my job—

(Suddenly a POLICEMAN*'s whistle is heard, the sound of running feet down the alleyway, and the door is burst open. A* SMALL MAN *rushes in and, like a cornered rat, looks frantically from right to left.* MAMA *leans over, grabs him by the collar and lifts him over the bar concealing him at her feet behind the bar. It all happens in a flash and just as two* POLICE-MEN *enter.)*

1ST POLICEMAN: Hey there, all of youse—where's that thief? *(The* CROWD *shifts, but no one answers until* MAMA *speaks.)*

MAMA: Ack, now, officer, quit yer givin' us a scare. We ain't seen no thief here—don't allow them in my place—but if it's a drink yer after and using a poor thief fer an excuse! *(*EVERYONE *laughs.)*

1ST POLICEMAN: Cut it! *(To the other* POLICEMAN*)* Go look upstairs. *(He goes up.)*

MAMA: Come now, officer, have the courage to have a drink—as long as yer protect my booze so kindly—*(The* POLICEMAN *reappears.)*

2ND POLICEMAN: No one there.

1ST POLICEMEN: *(Tossing off a drink* MAMA *hands him.)* Well, seein' it's you, Mama, I won't bother to search further, but if I catch that pimp and he's been down here—

MAMA: And quite right, officer. *(The* POLICEMEN *go out, and the* CROWD *laughs.* MAMA *drags the* THIEF *out.)* Now yer get out and stop puttin' me in these risks—*(She gives him a shove. He rushes up the stairs and disappears.* MAMA *speaks disgustedly.)* The courage of a sewer rat—he'll hide there all night and day—

NORA: Well, I'm glad the place wasn't raided. Probably one of Maggie's friends, Hunt—a common thief!

HUNT: Well, that's what's pathetic about him, because he is a common thief.

NORA: There's no use arguing with you. As for Maggie, I wonder what your family will do about her?

HUNT: They won't matter. After all, I am the black sheep.

NORA: You've made yourself that. You know your mother adores you. She would give her soul to have you home.

HUNT: The funny part is that now I want to go home. I want to take Maggie back there. I want you to help me to make my family like her.

NORA: When is she coming?

HUNT: She should be here any minute. She always comes with the musicians.

NORA: Couldn't we get a little air until then? It's so warm and stuffy here.

HUNT: Of course. Come out and we'll come back after. *(Before they go out,* HUNT *speaks to* NINA *and indicates he wants the table reserved for them.* NINA *turns down the chairs against the table. They go out.)*

MAMA: *(To the man with the harmonica)* Say, for God's sake, are yer ever going to stop that music?

SAILOR: Music! Christ, that's a good line! Say, I'll blow him to a drink if you'll throw a knockout drop into it. *(They all laugh.)*

AN ENGLISH TOMMY: *(In a Cockney accent)* Blow me—when the hell is the real music coming? *(At that moment an* AMERICAN SAILOR *with bright red hair rushes in.)*

SAILOR: *(Excitedly)* Here comes Maggie now sure. *(The* SAILORS, *the* SOLDIERS, LONGSHOREMEN, *and* TOUGHS *all let up a shout.)*

CHORUS OF VOICES: Maggie—Maggie—hurrah for Maggie!

*(*MAGGIE *enters, surrounded by several* ROUGH TYPES, *a few* SAILORS, *a* PRIZE FIGHTER, *and the* MUSICIANS, *who carry their instruments and mount the platform. There is something at once arresting about* MAGGIE, *something wistful and tremendously appealing about her. She is frail and seems delicate—almost ill—her eyes are large and sad, although she offsets their sadness by a curious nervous vitality which might pass for gaiety. Her face is pale and contrasted to the bright rouge on her lips. Her clothes are shabby and cheap with a pathetic attempt to be a la mode. She wears a hat at a rakish angle.)*

MAMA: As usual, Mag, they are all waiting for yer.

1ST LONGSHOREMAN: *(Very drunk and from the table)* We thought youse was never comin'—then in youse comes with the band.

MAGGIE: *(Blowing him a kiss)* Trust Maggie to come in with the
band. I say if there was more music in the world there would be
less doctors. Music I say for health and happiness!

OLAF, A SWEDE: *(Putting his arm around* MAGGIE *)* You're always
right, Maggie, so here's a drink for you.

(He hands her a drink. MAGGIE *tosses it down.* MIKE, *a rough-looking
loafer, comes in and stands by the bar looking at* MAGGIE. *)*

A SAILOR: *(Calling out)* Say, Mag, look out. Mike's got the evil eye
on you again.

*(*EVERYONE *laughs.* MAGGIE *snaps her fingers and turns to the bar with
the* SWEDE. *The place begins to fill more and more. Several* WOMEN
NEGRO PROSTITUTES, *a few more* CHINESE *in native costume and
more rough-looking* "GANGSTERS" *come in. The music, which consists of
a piano, violin, saxophone, accordion, and a drum, begins playing jazz. A
number of* COUPLES *get up and begin dancing. They dance holding each
other closely round the necks and moving slowly. The room becomes thick
and heavy with smoke, there is much boisterous and coarse laughter and
drinking. Occasionally a* COUPLE *go up the stairs and disappear into the
rooms. As the jazz stops,* MIKE, *who has been watching* MAGGIE *all the
time, goes to the table directly upstage to left. He tips his chair back and
puts his feet up on the table.)*

MIKE: *(Calling to* MAGGIE *)* Coming to have a drink with me, Mag?

MAGGIE: *(Turning and coming to the table)* Sure thing—didn't I
promise you?

*(During the following scene, the accordion and violin play very low. They
play cheap sentimental but emotional music, occasionally a dreamy waltz,
then slow melancholy music. No one dances, most of the couples sit huddled
together, some drinking, some touching each other or kissing, others silent.
A* LONGSHOREMAN *and a* GIRL *have fallen asleep, drunk, across a table.
Occasionally a rough or a shrill laugh rings out and then is quickly sub-
dued. The atmosphere grows bluer and denser with smoke. Nothing, however, that takes place among the* CROWD *should distract from* MAGGIE
and MIKE*'s scene.)*

MIKE: Yer're different again ter night.

MAGGIE: *(Lighting a cigarette and coughing slightly)* Why should I be?

MIKE: *(Leaning forward and speaking vindictively)* 'Cause that gentleman nut is hangin' round here again. Oh, I seen him all right as
we came along, and so did yer. Got a dame with him, too. I suppose he brought her along to make yer jealous, or maybe to hide
behind, so I wouldn't push in his bloody nose. *(Leaning back and
laughing mockingly)* Or maybe she's his real sweetheart and he's
givin' yer the chuck, Mag.

MAGGIE: It don't make no difference to me.

MIKE: *(Grabbing her wrist and speaking angrily)* Yer lie and yer knows it, yer change when he's around.

MAGGIE: Let go my wrist. *(MIKE lets her wrist go.)*

MIKE: *(His voice softening)* Mag, what's he ter yer?

MAGGIE: Nothing.

MIKE: Yer're different with him—something different between yer—creepy like—yer ain't like yer are with any of us.

MAGGIE: Why should I be? He ain't like us.

MIKE: Then what in hell's he doin' round here? This ain't a hangout joint for sight-seein'.

MAGGIE: *(Teasingly)* He ain't sight-seeing, unless yer call me a sight.

MIKE: Oh, I know he comes to see *yer* all right. Can't miss that, by the way he leers at yer—he wants yer all right.

MAGGIE: *(Angrily)* Cut it!

MIKE: He's got the price all right—more than all of us put together.

MAGGIE: *(Banging the table)* Cut it, I said!

MIKE: *(Softening again and trying to touch her hand)* Maggie, yer ain't gone on him—are yer?

MAGGIE: Ah, gee, of course not.

MIKE: Would yer go with him?

MAGGIE: *(After a pause)* Maybe.

MIKE: *(Bitterly)* Money?

MAGGIE: Nope.

MIKE: Then what fer if yer ain't gone on him?

MAGGIE: You wouldn't understand.

MIKE: Try me. Why would yer go with him if it ain't fer money or love?

MAGGIE: *(Slowly and thoughtfully)* To find something—something like I can't explain—something I can't find here—

MIKE: Holy Jesus—gone cracked?

MAGGIE: I knew you wouldn't understand.

MIKE: I likes ter hear yer speel yer thoughts just the same.

MAGGIE: Not much thoughts, just—romancing maybe, like in the movies. Dreaming maybe, and thinking.

MIKE: About what?

MAGGIE: He's higher up than we are—cleaner—better. Maybe him and the people he goes with is nearer the something I'm looking for.

MIKE: That dame?

MAGGIE: Maybe. She's higher up. If you're higher up, you must know more—if you know more you must be nearer decent things—

nearer God. *(Sighing)* Kings is lucky. They are so high up they must be awful near to him.

MIKE: Kings is boobs. Yer come one night ter my I.W.W. meetin', they'll tell yer what stuffed prunes kings and queens is. It's men like me and women like yer, too, that's the backbone of a country.

MAGGIE: *(Shaking her head, unconvinced)* We're too far from God.

MIKE: Oh, nuts, Maggie. I—

(He stops suddenly as HUNT and NORA come in. They make their way through the crowd and sit at the table to the right again. MAGGIE has her back to them, but you see at once she is aware of their presence. She does not turn, however. NORA faces her, HUNT faces the audience.)

HUNT: The one with her back to you, that's Maggie.

NORA: I wish she would turn around. I can't see her face.

MAMA: *(Behind the bar and banging on it with a hammer)* Maggie— time to dance! *(A chorus of voices and hand clapping)* Maggie's dance—Maggie's dance!

(The music begins a very sensual and primitive jazz. MAGGIE rises, takes off her hat and tosses it on the table. EVERYONE shifts their positions to watch her. They crowd around the circle of the room. She begins to dance a slow rhythmic jazz, moving her whole body. She dances with extraordinary grace and seduction; as the music grows faster, she becomes wilder and more passionate. As the music stops with a crash, she looks at HUNT for the first time, then looks away. There is a wild burst of applause and cheers amid general confusion. A DRUNKEN SAILOR grabs MAGGIE, but she pushes him violently away. Finally the piano is pushed out into the middle of the room with cries of "A song, Maggie, a song." The PIANIST sits down and begins to play a few bars; then MAGGIE joins in and sings. She sings a popular tough song. At the end, the CROWD joins in the chorus. When the song is over, they cheer MAGGIE. She sits at a table with some SAILORS. Gradually the CROWD begins to go out and also the BAND.)

NORA: They all seem to be going.

HUNT: No, they just move next door. This bar closes, so they won't get raided. But Mama keeps next door open until early in the morning. *(While he is talking, the muffled sound of jazz in the distance next door can be heard)* There's the band now.

NORA: I'm tired, Hunt—will you take me home?

HUNT: You haven't met Maggie—

NORA: Perhaps tomorrow—give me time.

HUNT: Very well—after all I've said, the joke may be on me, perhaps she won't marry me.

(NORA rises, HUNT follows her, MAGGIE only turns her head slightly as he passes. Gradually the place is nearly empty except for MAMA cleaning

up behind the bar, a SAILOR *sitting with* MAGGIE, *and* MIKE *standing sullenly by the bar drinking. As* HUNT *passes out, he spits on the floor after him.)*

SAILOR: Comin', Mag?

MAGGIE: Nope—Tired—*(She yawns and stretches. She slowly starts to go upstairs.)*

MIKE: Have one smoke with yer, Maggie?

MAGGIE: *(Indifferently)* For ten minutes, if you like—

(She goes up. MIKE *follows her.* NINA *cleans up. The last* SAILOR *flings his money down on the bar and goes out.* MAMA *turns out the gas and leaves only the lamplight.)*

NINA: Yer can go along—I'll clean up.

MAMA: God—what's struck yer!

NINA: I ain't always lazy—

MAMA: Glad ter hear it from yer own lips.

NINA: Waitin' fer the small guy; have a hunch he's comin' back ter see Maggie. Thought I'd stick about ter git Mike out.

MAMA: Oh—*(She goes out.* NINA *pours herself a drink, then sits at a table with her head in her arms. The music still goes on faintly playing.)*

Curtain

Part 2

(Upstairs. A small, cheaply furnished room with soiled, torn wallpaper on the wall. A bed in the corner, opposite it a wash stand with basin and bowl. A table in the middle of the room with an overhanging gas lamp with a dark red shade on it. It casts its light down in a circle over the table, leaving the rest of the room in semidarkness. MAGGIE *is sitting at the table, manicuring her fingernails. She has taken her dress off and is in a dressing gown. The light shines down full on her.* MIKE, *slightly out of the circle of light, is sitting smoking. He watches* MAGGIE *in silence.)*

MAGGIE: *(After a few minutes)* That's your third cigarette. I told you you could come up for a smoke but not to burn up a tobacco factory.

MIKE: I'm on me way—*(*MAGGIE *gathers up the manicure things and sets them aside.)*

MAGGIE: Well, supposing you start—

MIKE: Yer haven't answered my question.

MAGGIE: Which one? You ask me so many.

MIKE: *The* one. Why yer and me ain't the same anymore.

MAGGIE: I didn't notice we wasn't.

MIKE: Yer know we ain't—Yer changed and it's that swell guy.

MAGGIE: I told you to cut it. I'm sick of that. He don't even notice me. Did he notice me tonight?

MIKE: No—'cause he was with a swell dame—that's what makes me sore.

MAGGIE: *(Dropping her head in her hands dejectedly and wearily)* Well, she's probably his wife or his sweetheart—Maybe he won't come back no more.

MIKE: *(Furiously)* He'll come back all right. He's after one thing— I've seen it in his cursed face—he'll come back with his filthy money—*(There's a knock on the door.)*

MAGGIE: Who's that? *(NINA opens the door and peers in.)*

NINA: Mama wants ter talk with Mike. Says it's important.

MIKE: Ah, hell!

MAGGIE: You were going anyway. I'm tired.

MIKE: *(To NINA)* Well, gas it, I'm comin' ter her in a minute.

NINA: All right. *(She closes the door. MAGGIE gets up. MIKE rises, too, and puts his hand on her arm.)*

MIKE: Mag. I can't get over bein' stuck on yer. Can I come back ter night?

MAGGIE: No. *(MIKE tries to take her in his arms.)*

MIKE: *(Passionately)* I love yer, Mag.

MAGGIE: *(Pulling away)* I told you I was tired—

MIKE: I want yer altogether, Mag—all of yer—the way we used ter be—my gal. That swell only wants yer body—somethin' he can get fer money.

MAGGIE: I haven't noticed he even wants that—

MIKE: *(Breaking in excitedly)* Yer lie! Yer know that's what he's hangin' around fer—I'll smash—*(NINA opens the door again.)*

NINA: Mama wants yer, Mike—

MIKE: Oh, Christ, ter hell with that old harpie! *(He goes out. NINA closes the door and puts her finger to her lips.)*

NINA: I wanted ter git rid of him. The rich guy, he wants ter see yer!

MAGGIE: *(Terrified)* No—no—no. Mike will kill him. I don't want to see him.

NINA: No fear. They won't run into each other. Look what he give me—a ten spot. *(She holds up the money.)*

MAGGIE: I won't see him!

NINA: He only says fer ten minutes—oh, hell, why not? What's the matter with him? He looks healthy enough. Besides if yer don't, I won't have earned this ten spot. Promised him yer'd see him.

(MAGGIE hesitates. Then, unconsciously and instinctively, she rushes to the mirror and puts rouge and powder on her face. NINA goes out. In a

second, HUNT *comes in. He closes the door behind him. They stand and look at each other. There is an awkward pause.)*

HUNT: Good evening—or—rather almost—good morning—it's late—

MAGGIE: *(Slowly and disturbed)* It's no use—I—I ain't doing business tonight. I told Nina I didn't want to see you.

HUNT: Business? Oh—eh—I didn't come for that. *(Another long pause,* MAGGIE *looks down at her hands.)*

MAGGIE: *(Laughing nervously)* Gee—it's sort of funny. You always make me uncomfortable—whenever you're in the room.

HUNT: I'm sorry.

MAGGIE: Oh, no offense. I didn't mean it that way—it's something—something I can't explain. Maybe it's because—because you're educated—higher up—you know—grander than me.

HUNT: Grander than you? That would be difficult. *(Another pause, then* MAGGIE *goes quickly over and locks the door. She turns.)*

MAGGIE: You see, I'm afraid of Mike—if he found you here, he'd kill you.

HUNT: I'll take my chances. Besides he can hear our voices through a locked door.

MAGGIE: You might be any other man—

HUNT: I'd forgotten—it's not a very pleasant thought—

MAGGIE: *(Almost childishly)* You get used to it.

HUNT: Not with you, Maggie.

MAGGIE: *(Brightening)* Didn't you come—for that?

HUNT: No. I came to ask you a great favor.

MAGGIE: Me? A favor!

HUNT: Yes—

MAGGIE: What could I ever do for you?

HUNT: I want to ask you if you will marry me, Maggie.

MAGGIE: *(A little hurt and disappointed)* You're making fun of me—pulling a joke on me.

HUNT: *(Coming close to her)* It isn't a joke, Maggie. I mean it. I want to marry you and take you away from here.

MAGGIE: *(Sinking down on the chair)* What a joke! *(Looking up quickly and intensely)* Don't say these things to me. It ain't fair. I never guyed *you*—seriously.

HUNT: I'll marry you tomorrow!

MAGGIE: *(With a gesture to the room)* Knowing this?

HUNT: You're better than I am. I've had chances and what have I made of them? Every chance in the world. Have you?

MAGGIE: Chances?—me chances? I don't know—

HUNT: Will you do it, Maggie?

MAGGIE: *(Bewildered)* But what—what do you get out of it? I don't understand—you're a rich guy—swell people and all that—whereas me—

HUNT: *(Interrupting)* Do you believe in love?

MAGGIE: Yes—maybe not your way of believing—

HUNT: You're going to do something for me that no one else has ever done. Will you take a chance?

MAGGIE: Gee—where will you take me to?

HUNT: East. To my home.

MAGGIE: With grand people?

HUNT: If you call them that.

MAGGIE: *(Thinking)* Listen. I want you to know something. I ain't doing it for money—I don't think I exactly love you neither—I don't know—leastways not—

HUNT: It doesn't matter.

MAGGIE: It does—we've got to start right—

HUNT: Why are you doing it, then?

MAGGIE: It's harder even to tell you. I didn't care if he laughed—

HUNT: Who? Mike?

MAGGIE: Yes—*(Hesitating)*

HUNT: Go on—

MAGGIE: *(With great difficulty)* I once went to a Salvation Army meeting—You know—it was nice to hear them sing and beat tambourines—Well, they got me thinking—about getting higher up—maybe with people, with people like you, you're higher up—it may be easier to find—

HUNT: What?

MAGGIE: I don't know—a better life—happiness, maybe—Your kind—they must be straight and grand—Gee, they'll teach me!

HUNT: We'll try and make a go of it, darling! *(He takes her hand and kisses it.)* I'll come for you tomorrow. *(He unlocks the door and goes out.* MAGGIE, *still bewildered, looks at her hand that he has kissed incredulously.)*

Curtain

Part 3

Two months later.

The library of the Ashleys' house on Long Island. The room is very beautifully furnished. The walls are paneled in green Queen Anne old paneling with books set in, ranging high up and all around. There is a glass door directly upstage left, which opens onto a terrace—this door is closed. To the extreme right upstage there is a door which leads out of the room. This door is also closed. Also upstage right there is a very beautiful Queen Anne mantel with an old portrait hanging over it. A fire is burning in the fireplace. Soft chairs and one or two tables are placed about with lamps upon them. There is a large comfortable chair before the fireplace upon which HARVEY OLIVER *is sitting. He is a man about forty, shrewd-looking but not an unpleasant face. He is talking to* DOCTOR ROBB, *who sits in a chair near him.* DOCTOR ROBB *is older, he has a genial and kind face. Both men are in dinner coats and are smoking.*

HARVEY OLIVER: Heaven knows I always knew that Hunt would end by doing something utterly wild. I predicted it even in his college days. There's a decidedly unbalanced streak in him somewhere.

DOCTOR ROBB: Oh, perhaps a little eccentric—I'm fond of the boy, though, even if he did inherit much of the old boy's wildness. *(He points up to the portrait.)*

HARVEY OLIVER: Grandfather, isn't it?

DOCTOR ROBB: Yes. Hunt is a case of history repeating itself. His grandfather ran away and married a dancer. It shocked everyone, but it turned out happily for him. Let's hope for the same thing in this case.

HARVEY OLIVER: I know, but Hunt might at least have thought of his family, of his mother and sister. I never even knew of his marriage until I arrived from Europe last week. Mrs. Ashley didn't have the courage to cable me, in spite of the fact that I've been an old friend for so many years. It's amazing that she accepted this girl.

DOCTOR ROBB: Oh, that's not very amazing. After all, Hunt is her weak spot. She has always adored him in the most pathetic manner imaginable. His wanderings and adventurings have caused her, I know, many sighs and heartbreaks. Her one desire in life has been to have him home safe again with her. When he wired that he was married and would come home only on condition that he could bring his wife, she, of course, seized the opportunity to get him home at any cost, and accordingly opened her arms to them.

HARVEY OLIVER: I suppose one must compromise with oneself for one's only son. Did she actually know what—what class the girl was?

DOCTOR ROBB: Oh, I don't know. I think she accepted her as being a chorus girl. I think it rests there. I've not discussed it with her.

HARVEY OLIVER: It must have been a difficult pill for her and Ethel to swallow.

DOCTOR ROBB: In a way—but worse for Maggie. She's the one I'm sorry for.

HARVEY OLIVER: *(Throwing back his head and laughing)* Every time you say that name it makes me laugh. A "Maggie" in the Ashley family is something to laugh at. It must make Ethel wince. Why did your Maggie disappear as soon as dinner was over?

DOCTOR ROBB: She'll be down again, I suppose, although I must say she manages to keep a great deal to herself, except for Hunt, of course. She seems genuinely to love him and he's certainly mad about her.

HARVEY OLIVER: Aren't the family staying rather late in the country this year?

DOCTOR ROBB: Yes—between you and me—they are rather in hopes of keeping Maggie down here. Oh, I suppose just until the curiosity about her dies down, you know what the papers are and all that sort of thing. *(He looks at his watch.)* Ethel and Mrs. Ashley certainly ought to be back from town soon. It's odd they didn't come back for dinner. Mrs. Ashley usually does even when Ethel remains in town. I think there must have been a mistake about Mrs. Ashley not being here to meet you.

HARVEY OLIVER: Possibly, possibly. It doesn't matter. Ethel, as usual, was vague on the telephone about what night I should come down, said it didn't matter, so I simply picked tonight. She's certainly upholding *her* end of the family, marrying Steve Dike. I hear he has all the money in the world—and a trifle dumb. Convenient for Ethel.

DOCTOR ROBB: I haven't seen much of him. He always seems overpowered when Ethel's around.

HARVEY OLIVER: She never lacked the possessive spirit—even as a child. She always wanted what she wanted and managed to keep it regardless of anyone else's feelings.

DOCTOR ROBB: Well, she manages, I think, to make life pretty difficult for Maggie. If you get a chance to talk to her, I wish you would try to make her nicer to Maggie. I feel awfully sorry for that poor child no matter what she may be. There is something very sad about her—oh, not outwardly—outwardly she is gay enough— but inside I seem to feel her searching for something she can't find, something she seems to miss.

HARVEY OLIVER: Heaven knows, I should think she would be contented enough in a home like this after what she must have been used to.

DOCTOR ROBB: Yes, you would think so. But that's just where

Maggie's different. These things don't seem to mean anything to her at all. After all, we both know Ethel married for money. I don't believe Maggie did.

HARVEY OLIVER: Strange—

DOCTOR ROBB: I am doubly worried about her because I don't think she's well. *(While they are speaking, HUNT comes in. He, too, is in a dinner coat.)*

HUNT: I'm sorry to appear so inhospitable as to leave you two alone. Maggie would have it that you wanted to be by yourselves or at least that *she* was in the way—thought you had things to talk about or something—so I stayed with her. I don't like to leave her too much. It's a little lonely for her here. I imagine she had never been in the country before she came here.

DOCTOR ROBB: A real city urchin—eh? Well, we had nothing to talk about that she couldn't hear. I hope she didn't get that impression at dinner. We'd be glad to have her with us.

HARVEY OLIVER: Yes, call her down. She mustn't get silly notions like that.

HUNT: All right. I'll call her. *(He goes out.)*

DOCTOR ROBB: You see, she's oversensitive. It makes it difficult, you know.

HARVEY OLIVER: It's nice in her just the same.

(HUNT re-enters with MAGGIE. MAGGIE is dressed in an evening dress that is covered with spangles. She gives the impression of being overdressed. Her hair is done differently, which rather changes her from part 1. She appears self-conscious and a little awkward and appears to choose and weigh her words before she speaks. She overenunciates and makes a visible effort not to use slang.)

DOCTOR ROBB: You silly child, you shouldn't run off and leave us like that. Mr. Oliver and I have known each other too long to have any secrets.

MAGGIE: Knowing each other so long I thought you would have lots to say, private like. *(Quickly)* Privately, I mean. I thought maybe you wanted to talk about me.

HARVEY OLIVER: *(Laughing)* I see you are like all women, they always think men are talking about them. As though we had nothing else in the world to talk about!

MAGGIE: *(Also laughing)* Oh, I wasn't handing it to myself, *(Correcting herself again)* flattering myself, I mean. I wasn't flattering myself that you had anything much to say about me—just talking me over, maybe, with Mr. Harvey. He's just come from Europe and, and didn't know about me and Hunt marrying, maybe.

HARVEY OLIVER: Well, now that I do, I hope we are going to be friends.

MAGGIE: Thanks. A kid maybe needs one here. I mean, it's sorta lonely in the country. You see, my old life was much gayer.

DOCTOR ROBB: *(Interrupting)* Oh, the country's gay enough, Maggie, in the summer. Naturally, in the autumn it's a little dreary, but you'll be going to town soon so it won't matter.

HUNT: Maggie only told me yesterday that she would be glad to stay down here all winter with me.

MAGGIE: Yes, I did. I did say that.

DOCTOR ROBB: Good. You see, that's what it means to be in love. *(FORBES, a butler, enters. He addresses HUNT.)*

FORBES: The motor is coming up the drive, Sir, with Mrs. Ashley and Mrs. Dike. I thought you might like to know.

HUNT: Thanks, Forbes. I'll go out and meet them. *(FORBES and HUNT go out. HARVEY OLIVER goes to the glass door and looks out.)*

HARVEY OLIVER: Yes, here they come. I'll bet Ethel has been buying up all the clothes in New York. I've never yet decided which was a worse year for her bills, the year she goes to Paris or the year she remains home.

DOCTOR ROBB: I'm worried about your cough, Maggie. If it doesn't get better, we'll have to do something about it.

MAGGIE: Thanks, you mustn't bother—

DOCTOR ROBB: And you must get over also thinking so little of yourself. Assert yourself more, Maggie, especially with Ethel.

MAGGIE: You don't know me, Doc—Doctor. I think a lot of myself— that's why maybe I don't bother much about Ethel. You see, I used to think that girls like her would be different. I thought they knew so much that they would have to be different. I thought being higher up their ideas, or their hearts would be higher, too. I'm beginning to know now I was wrong. I guess, after all, it don't matter how you're born. I guess what makes you higher up and bigger is how much you've suffered and how you've taken your suffering, whether it's left you gentle and kind or not, how much you've learned from it.

DOCTOR ROBB: I think you are right, Maggie.

(There is a commotion outside. HARVEY OLIVER turns from the window. MRS. ASHLEY, ETHEL and HUNT enter from the other door. They are followed by FORBES and a MAID, who removes MRS. ASHLEY's coat. MRS. ASHLEY is a handsome woman of about fifty. ETHEL is about twenty-four; she is blond and a typical so-called "modern" girl. She

seems a good deal older than her age and at once gives the appearance of being worldly wise. They are both dressed in town clothes. The MAID *goes out.)*

MRS. ASHLEY: My dear Harvey, how disgraceful that I didn't know you were coming down tonight! Of all nights that I should have stayed in town so late!

HARVEY OLIVER: *(Taking her hands)* It doesn't matter. I've had a very pleasant time.

MRS. ASHLEY: Ethel only told me as we came into the gate that you might be here.

ETHEL: *(Giving her hand)* Hello, Harvey. You'll have to forgive me. I can't be expected to remember everything, you know. As it was, I don't believe I forgot one box out of all the things I bought, and that's doing very well for me.

DOCTOR ROBB: Miracle of miracles! I'll wager you'll forget the bills the beginning of the month.

ETHEL: Not anymore, Robbie. I've got a husband to hand them to, now. I just sit back comfortable and hand them to him.

MRS. ASHLEY: How are you, Maggie! *(She goes forward and not unkindly, although a little formally, she kisses* MAGGIE.*)*

MAGGIE: Thank you, Mrs. Ashley. I'm great—feeling awful good.

MRS. ASHLEY: Ethel, have you seen Maggie?

ETHEL: I'm not blind! *(Turning from* MAGGIE *indifferently and lighting a cigarette)* Hello. *(*MAGGIE *does not answer.* HUNT *quickly breaks in.)*

HUNT: I'm glad you're back, Mother. Not like you to stay away for dinner. I was getting worried as you had not telephoned.

ETHEL: You didn't need to. I guess Steve and I are capable of taking care of Mother.

HARVEY OLIVER: Oh, is your husband with you? I'm glad, because I want to meet him.

MRS. ASHLEY: Yes, he went upstairs to wash up. I must, too. *(To* FORBES *who is hovering about)* What is it, Forbes?

FORBES: Will you care for dinner, Madame?

MRS. ASHLEY: No, thanks, we had it in town.

FORBES: Very good, Madame. There was a message for you, Mrs. Dike. Miss Oakley telephoned to say that she and a number of other young ladies and gentlemen were coming over here tonight with a band. She told me to say that she had hired the "divine" Negro band that you liked so much.

ETHEL: Heavens above! Why didn't you tell me at once? What time did they say they were coming?

FORBES: Miss Oakley said she and the other guests would be here about ten.

MRS. ASHLEY: Ethel, I won't have another one of these noisy rough parties that last until the morning. I simply *won't* have it. I consider it a great piece of impertinence for Claire Oakley to consider that she can arrange a party in my house like this without having the manners to ask my permission. I object to her, anyway—anyone can see she is full of drugs.

ETHEL: She wasn't looking at it from the angle of *your* house. She was probably considering it mine and she knew I'd love it. We had already arranged it, although I didn't know it would be tonight. We had arranged it when someone who is a mutual friend of ours could come down and stay with her.

MRS. ASHLEY: And who is that, if I may ask?

ETHEL: Oh, just someone I don't think you even know. Anyway, why waste time? It must be nearly ten now. Open the ballroom, Forbes, and see that everything is arranged. Sandwiches and salad and cake and *plenty* to drink.

FORBES: I have already done so, Madame, as I was afraid you would arrive too late to give the orders.

ETHEL: And open two or three dozen bottles of champagne.

MRS. ASHLEY: Ethel, you will not have champagne. I refuse to squander my champagne on all your friends.

ETHEL: I'd like to know why not, when the whole cellar is filled with it! Don't be so stingy, when it gives out we can always get more. You actually talk as though there wasn't a drop of liquor in this country and as if every bottle we consumed was our last. Very unpleasant feeling.

MRS. ASHLEY: *(Despairingly)* Well, I give you up. Hunt and Steve can fight it out with you. *(As she says this,* STEVE *comes in. He is good-looking but a rather dull young man. His face shows weakness.)*

STEVE: What can I do, Mrs. Ashley?

MRS. ASHLEY: Cope with Ethel. After a day of shopping, such as we've had, she now is preparing to keep the whole house awake all night with a jazz band.

HARVEY OLIVER: *(extending his hand to* STEVE*)* I'm glad to meet you, even through the battlefield smoke of a family fight. My name's Harvey Oliver. *(They shake hands.)*

MRS. ASHLEY: Forgive me, of course—you know everyone else, Steve—Doctor Robb.

STEVE: *(Shaking hands with* DOCTOR ROBB*)* Of course. Hello, Hunt, and Maggie. *(He shakes hands with* MAGGIE.*)*

MAGGIE: Hello, Steve.

MRS. ASHLEY: Well, I'm going upstairs and I don't intend to come down again tonight. But I still maintain that it's an outrageous piece of impertinence using my house as though it were a cabaret or a roadhouse. *(To* HARVEY OLIVER *and* DOCTOR ROBB*)* You both come upstairs to my study. We at least can have some privacy up there. I'll change my clothes first.

MAGGIE: I'll come with you and help you, Mrs. Ashley.

(MRS. ASHLEY, MAGGIE, OLIVER, HARVEY, *and* DOCTOR ROBB *go out.)*

ETHEL: Your wife always acts as though Mother didn't have a maid.

HUNT: Oh, I don't think that. Maggie simply likes Mother. It wouldn't hurt you to give her a little of the same attention.

STEVE: I must say I wish all these people weren't coming. I thought we were going to have a quiet time by ourselves, Ethel.

ETHEL: *(Ignoring* STEVE*'s remark and continuing to* HUNT*)* I do wish you'd do something about that dress, Hunt. I must say it's pretty terrible, all those glittering spangles and everything. Rather like the window of a ten-cent store in a small town.

HUNT: You mean Maggie's dress?

ETHEL: It's clever of you to get the inference! Naturally I meant that, and I wish she hadn't put it on tonight with all these people coming. Why she should have bought a dress like that I can't imagine, when all the smart cloths now are as simple as possible.

HUNT: She hasn't had your chances nor your experiences in shopping. If you took a little more interest in her you probably could help her get the clothes you consider the right thing. As far as I'm concerned, it doesn't make the slightest difference to me.

STEVE: *(Interrupting)* Maggie looks pretty whatever she wears.

HUNT: That's the way I feel. She's so much more beautiful than anyone else it doesn't matter what she's got on and unless you really want to help her, Ethel, forgive me for saying in a brotherly fashion, that you had better mind your own damn business.

ETHEL: *(Suppressing her temper)* I won't argue with either of you. *(She gathers up her things and goes out of the room, almost colliding with* MAGGIE, *who is entering. There is a moment's awkward silence.)*

MAGGIE: I hope you two weren't quarreling about me.

STEVE: Eh—why, no—no. *(He goes to the door leading to the terrace.)* Heavens, here are a lot of motors coming now!

(While he is speaking, a number of motor horns can be heard. HUNT *goes over and kisses* MAGGIE*'s hand. At that moment, a number of* YOUNG

MEN AND WOMEN *bang loudly on the glass door,* STEVE *opens it, and they crowd into the room. The* WOMEN *are all very smartly dressed in evening clothes, the* MEN *in dinner coats.)*

HUNT: Hello, Claire. What made you come in this way?

CLAIRE: *(A very pale, neurotic-looking girl. She speaks excitedly and without pausing)* To get in before the others. They have all gone around the front way and the band, too. Isn't it exciting my getting the divine Negro one Ethel wanted. Where is Ethel?

STEVE: Gone up to dress. She'll be down in a minute.

CLAIRE: *(To* STEVE*)* You know everyone, don't you?

STEVE: Yes. *(He shakes hands with several* GIRLS *and exchanges greetings with some of the* YOUNG MEN*.)* You all know Hunt, and this is his wife. *(One or two of the* MEN *advance and shake* MAGGIE*'s hand.)*

CLAIRE: Hello, Mrs. Ashley. I haven't seen you for two weeks. Where do you keep yourself? I thought you'd at least appear at some of the hunts.

MAGGIE: No—no, I haven't. *(A little awkwardly)* I've never seen a hunt. I don't know much about them; besides, I should feel so sorry for the poor little animal, or whatever it is you hunt.

CLAIRE: It's a fox, and I'm sure they don't mind being killed. They have such a glorious race for their life, or death, whichever way you want to put it. *(She laughs.)* Can we go and take our things off, Hunt?

HUNT: Of course, of course.

STEVE: Let me do the honors.

*(*EVERYONE *follows him out of the room. They are all talking.* CLAIRE'S VOICE *can be heard saying,* "There's the divine band now tuning up." *Accordingly, the* BAND *can be heard tuning up. A second later, it begins to play jazz, playing through nearly all of the act, except during pauses between dances. It, however, should not be heard too loudly so as to drown conversation.)*

MAGGIE: *(Putting her hands to her ears)* Gee, jazz brings things back.

HUNT: *(Laughing and taking her hands from her ears)* I thought you weren't going to say "Gee" anymore.

MAGGIE: Oh, I forgot again!

HUNT: I don't care, darling. I was only teasing you. You can say anything you like. *(He looks at her.)* Anyone as beautiful as you should have all the privileges.

MAGGIE: *(Pleased)* Do you really think I'm beautiful when you have all those girls to judge from?

HUNT: I should think so. *(He takes a letter out of his pocket.)* See, I've had a letter from Nora Sumner, see what she says, "give my love to your beautiful wife and God bless you both." I'm grateful to her, Maggie, because she gave me courage by going with me that night I asked you to marry me.

MAGGIE: And I'm grateful to her, too. You haven't said anything about my new dress, Hunt.

HUNT: I told you, you looked beautiful.

MAGGIE: I'm glad you like it. I thought it was beautiful, too. It shines so gloriously. Do you know, it's the kind of a dress I always dreamed about when I used to pretend things to myself? I never dreamed I could ever own one. It's like a dress in a fairy story, don't you think?

HUNT: *(Putting his arms around her)* Everything about you, Maggie, is like a fairy story. *(He kisses her passionately.)* I love you so much.

MAGGIE: And I love you. *(After a pause)* Hunt, if anything should ever happen between us, you must never think I haven't been grateful for—for everything.

HUNT: Heavens! What a way to talk. Which reminds me. Doctor Robb has an idea that you look unhappy lately. I think it's true, too.

MAGGIE: You mustn't think that! I suppose it's because it's all strange to me. Then, too, it's different than what I thought it would be. The people are different, oh, not you, Hunt—although I did think even *you* would be a little different. Oh, darling—not really—you're wonderful, I know—I wish I could explain—don't be offended—I don't know exactly what I mean.

HUNT: What do you mean—about me, Maggie?

MAGGIE: You see—I thought you'd be doing something—something big. I thought your life would give you such big chances. You see, back there in my life I always thought people loafed and were bums and got in trouble because—because they didn't have chances.

HUNT: *(Half-hurt—half-jokingly)* Thanks for calling me a loafer—

MAGGIE: Not really a loafer—at least, I suppose, not in your life. In mine a man who didn't work *was* a loafer, or a bum, or something.

HUNT: I've always been a loafer, Maggie. A loafer and an adventurer. No one has ever been able to make anything out of me.

MAGGIE: Silly, you must do that yourself, but I didn't say you were a loafer, Hunt, no, really—*(She puts her arms around him.)* I think you're wonderful. You must be to have married me.

HUNT: *(Putting his hand over her mouth)* Now you're the silly. Will you come and dance?

MAGGIE: *(Shaking her head in the negative)* I'd rather not. I'm scared

of all those people. Let's just watch. (ETHEL *comes in with a*
YOUNG MAN.*)*
ETHEL: Oh, I didn't know you two were in here.
MAGGIE: We were just going out.
ETHEL: I don't think you know my brother, Mr. Frazer, and this is
my sister-in-law, Margaret.
ERIC FRAZER: Happy to meet you.
MAGGIE: But my name's Maggie. I used to be called Mag, anyway—
just Maggie. We're going to watch the dancing. (HUNT *and she go
out.* ERIC FRAZER *bursts into laughter. He shows that he has been
drinking.*)
ERIC FRAZER: My word, you are funny, Ethel! That girl has got char-
acter, Maggie, of all names! *(He laughs again.)*
ETHEL: I don't see the huge joke. Would you mind going out and
finding Claire? I want to speak to her.
ERIC FRAZER: Certainly. *(He goes out.* ETHEL *lights a cigarette and
walks about impatiently. In a moment,* CLAIRE *enters alone.)*
CLAIRE: I wanted to get you alone, but I never could get a chance.
ETHEL: Well, what happened? Why didn't Tom come? You knew it
was the only reason I wanted this party.
CLAIRE: Yes, of course, I know, and everything would have been all
right if he hadn't had too much to drink at dinner. I was afraid to
bring him along for fear he would talk. But I've arranged just the
same, so don't worry. This is my plan. In about an hour and a half,
I will pretend to get very ill and you must insist on coming home
with me. When we get home, you can telephone that I'm too ill
and that you are going to spend the night with me. Tom will be
sobered up by then, and you and he can take my car and motor
up to town for the night just as you did before. No one else will be
any the wiser for it. I can lend you clothes, and when Steve calls
you up in the morning, I can say you are asleep and can't be disturbed. You can be back yourself before twelve, and even my servants won't know you haven't spent the night in the house. If your
maid comes over in the morning with your clothes, she can leave
them downstairs. When you come back, you can come in the side
door and no one will ever see you.
ETHEL: That sounds all right.
CLAIRE: Of course it is. (*A number of* YOUNG MEN AND GIRLS
come in.)
1ST GIRL: What are you two doing in here with that marvelous jazz
going on?
ETHEL: We are coming now.

(She and CLAIRE *go out. The* OTHERS *remain. A* BUTLER *comes in with champagne on a tray. They all take a glass, lounging about and smoking. One or two of them obviously have had too much to drink.)*

2ND GIRL: I'm glad at last to see the new sister-in-law. Isn't she terrible? *(They all laugh.)*

3RD GIRL: What a dress!

1ST YOUNG MAN: She's prudish enough, won't even dance. These chorus girls always amuse me when they marry well. My God, they always become such perfect ladies that they would give anyone a pain! *(They all laugh.)*

2ND YOUNG MAN: Yes, they always give up their liquor and drink tea with their little finger up, like this. *(He gives an imitation. They all laugh again and suddenly stop as* MAGGIE *comes in with* ERIC FRAZER, *who now is quite intoxicated.)*

MAGGIE: No, I told you, Mr. Frazer, I don't want to dance. *(On seeing everyone in the room,* MAGGIE *stops and appears shy.)*

A YOUNG MAN: Come in, Mrs. Ashley. Here's a chair and some champagne.

ERIC FRAZER: Won't take any champagne for me, won't dance, but I tell her jes' same, she's the most beautiful girl here—Maggie or no Maggie. And what's—the matter—with Maggie for a name? That's what I'd like to know. *(*MAGGIE *sits down, and he looks around.)* That's what I'd like to know.

2ND YOUNG MAN: Oh, all right, Eric, don't bother us. Claire will be looking for you soon. See, I was right, here she is. *(*CLAIRE *enters.)*

CLAIRE: I was looking for you, Eric. I merely turned to say something to Hunt when you disappeared.

ERIC FRAZER: Disappeared with a damn good-looking girl—beats the whole crowd of you!

CLAIRE: Well, come back and finish the dance. *(She takes his arm.)*

1ST GIRL: I love your dress, Claire.

CLAIRE: Do you? That's good.

2ND GIRL: It's terribly smart.

3RD GIRL: Frightfully, my dear. *(*CLAIRE *and* ERIC FRAZER *go out.)*

1ST GIRL: I hope I won't choke on that lie.

2ND GIRL: *(Laughing)* It looks like an old table cloth! *(They all laugh.)*

1ST YOUNG MAN: Poor old Claire. She has certainly got it badly on Eric. Let's dance! *(A* GIRL *and he go out and are followed by the* OTHERS, *until they have all gone but* MAGGIE *and two* GIRLS.)*

1ST GIRL: Have a cigarette, Mrs. Ashley?

MAGGIE: I wish I could, but I've got such a cough. *(Changing her mind)* Oh, I think I will anyway. *(She takes one and lights it.)*

1ST GIRL: And why not some champagne. *(Finishing a glass herself.)*

MAGGIE: *(Embarrassed)* Well, to tell you the truth—I—I was a little afraid of drinking at such a swell party—I didn't think you—you'd all drink so much. *(Both GIRLS scream with laughter.)*

2ND GIRL: We can manage it all right. Have a glass. It will cheer you up.

MAGGIE: *(Hesitating, then she finally drinks a glass of champagne.)* It's good.

1ST GIRL: That's better.

2ND GIRL: Be careful of Eric, Mrs. Ashley.

MAGGIE: *(Laughing)* In what way? What do you mean?

2ND GIRL: Oh, just don't give him any money to invest for you.

MAGGIE: That's easy. I haven't got any. What's the matter with him?

1ST GIRL: He has a trick of investing money and, and—well, let's call it, losing it. I only tell you as you are a stranger here and you might be taken in by him.

MAGGIE: But if he's crooked—why does Claire like him and why isn't he copped—I mean arrested?

2ND GIRL: *(Laughing)* Arrested! A Frazer! Do you know the power that's behind his father? Eric just does that sort of thing because he can't help it, not because he needs it, but it's not very pleasant if you happen to be the one he does it to. Why, if he wasn't a Frazer he would probably be called a common thief—some people call him that anyway. *(She gets up. The orchestra is playing the same tune that MAGGIE sang in part 1. She hums it a second, then sings a snatch of it.)* Isn't that a wonderful song? Do you know it, Mrs. Ashley?

MAGGIE: *(Reluctantly)* Yes—

2ND GIRL: *(Jazzing and snapping her fingers)* Well, that jazz is calling me. I'm going back to dance.

1ST GIRL: I'm coming, too.

(They go out. MAGGIE is left alone. She begins to cough, then throws her cigarette away. She moves the big chair and sits before the fire. She is almost hidden from view. After a minute's pause, a MAN looks in the glass door and then opens it. He enters the room, swaying a little on his feet. MAGGIE looks around and then suddenly rises to her feet. They face each other. The MAN looks incredulously at her and then rubs his eyes.)

TOM BODLEY: I knew I was drunk, but I didn't know I was as bad as this. Am I seeing things? Are you Maggie, or aren't you?

MAGGIE: I'm just as much Maggie as you are Jack Davis, unless you go by a different name here.

TOM BODLEY: You guessed right. I go by my right and own name here, Thomas Bodley.

MAGGIE: I thought you wouldn't be traveling under the same name as you did out there.

TOM BODLEY: God's name, how did *you* get here? Wait—*(He sways again and tries to pull himself together.)* You aren't Ethel's chorus girl sister-in-law?

MAGGIE: I'm Ethel's sister-in-law, but I never said I was a chorus girl.

TOM BODLEY: *(Bursting into laughter)* Let me have a laugh! Maggie Ethel's sister-in-law! *(He laughs again and steadies himself with a chair.)* Well, they think you were a chorus girl and I certainly won't tell on you as long as you keep your mouth shut about me.

MAGGIE: What are you doing here?

TOM BODLEY: Wouldn't you like to know? Oh, well—we're pals, so I'll tell you. I'm here because I like Ethel. She and I are just about the same as you and I were, only her tastes are more expensive. Oh, not in money—just in the way I have to do things for her. *(He laughs.)*

MAGGIE: You lie! Ethel's married to a decent man. She's a decent girl.

TOM BODLEY: I didn't say she wasn't—that's your interpretation. Just because she is going—well, just because she's going with me isn't anything against her, I hope.

MAGGIE: *(Passionately)* Ethel's straight. No decent woman would give herself to you.

TOM BODLEY: You're rather hard on yourself, aren't you?

MAGGIE: I have no illusions about myself.

TOM BODLEY: Well, that's a good thing, at least. It so happens, however, that Ethel's going into town to spend the night with me to-night as she has before. I tell you simply because I know you won't say anything considering what I could tell about you around here, if you tell on me or on Ethel either. As far as Ethel's marriage goes, she only married that stupid man for money. She loves me, but I, as usual, am not overstocked with the golden coin.

MAGGIE: Ethel will not go to town with you tonight. *(While they are speaking, ETHEL comes in. On seeing TOM she rushes forward, at first not noticing MAGGIE.)*

ETHEL: Tom! What are you doing here? You will spoil the plan. *(She sees MAGGIE.)* Oh, I didn't know you knew each other.

TOM BODLEY: We didn't. I came in this door and we just happened to speak.

MAGGIE: That's a lie. I knew him well three years ago.

ETHEL: *(Frigidly)* Indeed. That's interesting.

MAGGIE: Ethel, the things he has been telling me can't be true.

ETHEL: *(Apprehensively, looking from one to the other)* What things?

TOM BODLEY: Ethel, I forbid you to listen to that girl. I know what she is. You shouldn't even be speaking to her.

ETHEL: Since when have you the right to use the word forbid to me? Since you two know each other so well—

MAGGIE: *(Breaking in)* Ethel, I don't care what you think of me, or what you say to me, but you can't go into town tonight with this man.

ETHEL: *(Amazed)* He told you *that*!

TOM BODLEY: I tell you not to listen to her, Ethel—oh, when I first came here I was drunk—I didn't know what I was saying.

MAGGIE: He wasn't any more drunk than he is now—he told me that you had spent the night with him before—

TOM BODLEY: *(Frantically)* Can't you see that she is jealous? She's making every word up to take you from me. Do you think that kind of a woman would think of anything else? You told me she was a chorus girl. I'll tell you what she was—just a common prostitute in a low dive.

ETHEL: *(Angrily)* You have no right to speak that way. After all, Maggie's my brother's wife.

TOM BODLEY: Yes—but living under false pretenses. Ask her to deny it.

MAGGIE: *(Courageously, yet rather sadly. She speaks low and quietly.)* I don't deny it.

ETHEL: *(Horrified)* So that's what you were—that's why Hunt was so mysterious about you. A prostitute!

MAGGIE: And what are you?

ETHEL: How dare you!

MAGGIE: What are you? What are you? It is true I was a prostitute. I earned my living. What excuse have you?

ETHEL: I won't lower myself by talking to you.

MAGGIE: I don't want you to talk to me—I only want to prevent you from disgracing yourself when you are married to a nice clean man like Steve.

ETHEL: Heavens! Must I listen to you moralize? It's amusing at least to hear a—a harlot moralize.

MAGGIE: If it wasn't for Hunt and your mother, I wouldn't care what you would do.

ETHEL: I don't see why you should worry about Hunt, he wasn't par-

ticular about his wife, so why should he be about his sister? Oh, I
suppose now that he's married you that makes you quite all right
in your own eyes.

MAGGIE: It's more than you will be able to say of your marriage.
Prostituting yourself in marriage hasn't got the virtue of hon-
esty that at least the lowest girl in the street has. Your marriage is
prostitution—even your lover says you married for money—only
you haven't got the decency to admit it.

TOM BODLEY: Don't listen to her, Ethel, she'll only lie about me. I'm
ashamed I ever knew the girl. I'll explain to you about it tomorrow.

ETHEL: Yes, I'm tired of listening to her now—you'll *need* to explain.
(To MAGGIE*)* In the future, conduct your own moral campaign
but not mine. I'm quite capable of managing my own life. *(To*
TOM*)* As for you—I'm not used to men who tell. *(Defiantly and
sarcastically)* I at least still have a code about that! *(She goes out.)*

TOM BODLEY: You have done for me now with Ethel. Well, I at least
have done for you, too. I don't think either of us had better stay
round here much longer.

(He goes out the glass door onto the terrace and disappears. MAGGIE *sinks
down despondently onto a chair. The music has stopped.* STEVE *comes in
looking very gloomy. On seeing* MAGGIE, *his face brightens a little.)*

STEVE: I'm glad you're alone, Maggie. I'm so tired of this party.
Thank heavens they are all leaving, they are going on to someone else's house to dance until morning.

MAGGIE: You look tired, Steve.

STEVE: I was just going to say that about you. Do you know, Maggie,
there is something about us that is rather alike? Neither of us
seems to fit into this sort of thing very well. Oh, heaven knows
I've had it all my life. Born, I suppose you would say, with a
golden spoon in my mouth—endless money—opportunities—
everything that one would think would make a chap happy. Somehow, I never have been happy. I know I'm not very clever—rather
dull, in fact, I expect—but lately I've been doing a lot of thinking.
I've been thinking there must be a better life somewhere that I'm
missing. Have you ever thought of that, Maggie?

MAGGIE: A better life—yes. Why, yes, I left my old life for this
because I thought it would be better.

STEVE: Is it?

MAGGIE: *(Shaking her head sadly)* No. I'm beginning to think now
my old life was better.

STEVE: Ethel doesn't understand these things. I've tried to explain
to her, but I'm afraid she just thinks I'm stupid. I've felt so much

lately that she and I could be happier if we had less money, if we went with simpler and humbler people. I've somehow come to think lately that people lower down in life must be nearer God.

MAGGIE: That's funny.

STEVE: *(Rather hopelessly)* Well, maybe I don't know. It's all rather mixed up anyway, isn't it? I mean life. It's hard for a chap to know what to think. I suppose I should be grateful and happy marrying a wonderful girl like Ethel. *(HUNT enters.)*

HUNT: Oh, there you are, Maggie darling. Nearly everyone has left. If you don't mind, I'm just going to run Cynthia and Kay over to their house. I'll be back in a few minutes.

MAGGIE: No, I don't mind. *(HUNT goes out again. STEVE rises.)*

STEVE: I think I'll go to bed. Good night, Maggie, pleasant dreams to you. You should go to bed, too.

MAGGIE: I'll go when Hunt comes back. *(He kisses her hand.)* Good night, Steve.

STEVE: Good night.

(He goes out, MAGGIE turns her chair to the fire. She throws a log on it and sinks back in the chair with her feet on the fender. She coughs and then relaxes, closing her eyes. She falls asleep, the stage grows dark, then one by one the people of her dream appear in a dim shaft of light. They should give the confused feeling of a dream. They walk stiffly and move like marionettes. Two POLICEMEN come on with ERIC FRAZER hand-cuffed between them; he is dressed in convict clothes.)

1ST POLICEMAN: You don't get away with that sort of thing here.

2ND POLICEMAN: We knowed yer fer all yer swell clothes. As soon as we ripped *them* off, stripes was the color of yer skin.

1ST POLICEMAN: And handcuffs for party gloves—a common thief.

(They both laugh a weird, hollow dream laugh, and all three disappear into the darkness. CLAIRE comes in dressed in an old table cloth, it hangs in a long train behind her. SECOND GIRL follows her.)

2ND GIRL: You have no idea, Claire dear, how becoming that table cloth is to you. I've never seen you look more beautiful.

CLAIRE: Table cloth? Why, you must be raving, this is the latest thing from Paris. I had it in one of the boxes that I didn't lose on the way from New York. *(ETHEL comes in. She is dressed in MAGGIE's clothes of part 1. As she strolls on, she sings MAGGIE's song.)*

ETHEL: Isn't that an amusing song? Do you know it?

CLAIRE: *(Drawing her train aside)* My dear, she's a prostitute and all the time she has been pretending to be a real lady.

(They both rock with laughter, but no sound comes from their lips. Sud-

denly a wild jazz band begins playing, very much out of tune. It plays very fast and loudly. They all three dance off very slowly and out of time with the music. The music breaks off unfinished. From the darkness STEVE'S VOICE *can be heard.*

STEVE'S VOICE: Maggie, where are you? I can't find my way. *(There is a sob and anguish in his voice. He enters groping his way. His eyes are blindfolded.)*

STEVE: Maggie—Maggie—where is there a better life? Take my hand, Maggie. *(He stumbles.)* You see I'm so stupid.

(Six YOUNG SOCIETY MEN *enter, walking two and two. They are dressed in dinner coats, but wear gangster and longshoremen caps pulled toughly over their eyes. The first two carry a big sign which reads "To the City of The Golden Spoon." They walk very slowly.)*

STEVE: *(Unhappily and trying to untie his bandage)* I hear steps— help me see—*(He gives up struggling with his bandage and begins again to grope.)* Lower life, Maggie—nearer God—

(He touches the last two MEN, *who quickly seize him and they all go rapidly off, dragging* STEVE *with them. His voice can be heard, crying "Maggie," "Maggie." As it fades off into the distance, it changes into* HUNT'S VOICE. *The lights come up as* HUNT *enters calling "Maggie." He does not perceive* MAGGIE *behind the chair. At the same moment,* MRS. ASHLEY *comes quickly into the room. She is dressed in a dressing gown. She looks disturbed and worried.)*

MRS. ASHLEY: I wanted to see you. I've been waiting for you to return.

HUNT: *(Surprised)* What's up?

(At the sound of voices, MAGGIE *gradually awakens. At first she seems dazed, then as the significance of the conversation dawns upon her, she sits slightly forward, tensely listening. She seems torn by a desire to let them know that she is there. Then, as she hears the purpose of the conversation, she is unable to move, shrinking back into the chair, deeply wounded and stunned.)*

MRS. ASHLEY: *(With emotion)* I've just had a very distressing thing told to me and I want to know whether it is true or not.

HUNT: *(Alarmed at the tone of her voice)* Heavens, Mother—

MRS. ASHLEY: *(Interrupting and slightly hysterical)* I've heard that you have deceived me about Maggie. After the struggle I had with myself to make allowance for her being a chorus girl, I now find that she is—that she is—oh, I *can't* say the word, Hunt, is it true?

HUNT: You've been listening to gossip.

MRS. ASHLEY: I've been listening to what your sister told me and which has been told to her upon good authority from a man who knew Maggie in former days; a man who unfortunately came to the house, brought by some of these wild, impossible guests. Ethel had never met him before.

HUNT: Why should Ethel tell you a thing like that?

MRS. ASHLEY: If it is true, she did quite right in telling me. Stop evading! Is it true or not?

HUNT: I refuse to classify Maggie. I love her and I know she is what I want her to be—that's all that matters.

MRS. ASHLEY: Perhaps for you. You don't take into consideration your sister's and my reputation—the value of decency for your mother's home. God knows I've loved you, Hunt, and put up with more from you than most mothers would. When you brought Maggie here, with all her crudeness, with all her faults, I welcomed her for your sake, in spite of the fact she was not one of us. I—

HUNT: (Breaking in) You welcomed her for her own sake. You told me you liked her.

MRS. ASHLEY: Yes, I did. That has nothing to do with the fact that you deceived me—that you both deceived me. That you brought a woman to my home that you know does not belong here—that you thought so little of me and of your sister as to allow a woman like that to come under my roof.

HUNT: Maggie may be in name what you think, she is not so in heart. What right would I have had to have branded her? What chance would you or any of you have given her if you had originally known the truth? Now you know Maggie—as she really is—you say yourself you like her—Ethel's not liking her is merely jealousy.

MRS. ASHLEY: (Beside herself, but not unkindly) I don't know what to do! I love you, Hunt—I can't forget that—but I *know* it's wrong of me to let this girl remain here. It can do no good, only bring evil.

HUNT: If Maggie goes, I'll go, too. Never to return.

MRS. ASHLEY: Don't say that! (Despairingly) Hunt, why have you done this? Can't you see it's impossible? Give Maggie up quietly—I'll settle anything you want on her. Do it before this all gets around—before it's too late. She will ruin your life.

HUNT: Never. You must be mad. I'll take Maggie away tomorrow—you needn't worry, you'll never see either of us again.

MRS. ASHLEY: Don't Hunt—I can't live without you. I'm getting old—you'll break my heart.

HUNT: And my heart?

MRS. ASHLEY: You are young—all your future to look forward to. I have really only you. Ethel was never as close to me as you.

HUNT: I can see no solution, unless you accept Maggie.

MRS. ASHLEY: She won't remain true to you. Those women never do. It will bore her here, and she, of her own accord, will want to leave you. She'll go back to her old life.

HUNT: Never.

MRS. ASHLEY: I'm sure of it. You'll see.

HUNT: *You'll* see, but that doesn't solve it for now. What do you want me to do? It rests with you.

MRS. ASHLEY: *(Weakly)* Oh, Hunt, I can't let you go. I—I—will pay any price to get rid of that girl. *(She cries.)*

HUNT: You are unstrung, Mother. Go to bed—we'll talk about it tomorrow.

MRS. ASHLEY: Darling, let her go. They can't run straight, those women—I'm sorry for her, but you should think of me—she will ruin your life and mine.

HUNT: *(Angrily and determinedly)* I won't discuss it any more tonight. You can tell me what you want me to do tomorrow. The decision is in your hands. Come to bed. *(He takes her hand and they go out.)*

*(*MAGGIE *sits for a minute without moving. Then slowly she passes her hand over her eyes. She rises, clenches her hands together, emits a slight sob, then goes to door; she opens it and passes out onto the terrace. After a minute,* HUNT *returns, he stands before the fire. In a minute,* MAGGIE *reenters.)*

HUNT: I've been looking for you. Where have you been?

MAGGIE: Outside.

HUNT: Is anything the matter? You look—

MAGGIE: I want to tell you something.

HUNT: Why, what is it, darling?

MAGGIE: I've had a dream. I seen them—I mean I saw them as they really are—then something else—I've decided something, Hunt.

HUNT: What? You've been dreaming? *(Laughing)* I hope not out in the cold garden.

MAGGIE: *(Hesitating)* It's difficult, Hunt—difficult to tell you.

HUNT: Something Ethel has said to you! Has she hurt your feelings?

MAGGIE: No—it isn't Ethel. It isn't anyone—just me—in here—*(She places her hand to her heart.)*

HUNT: *(Alarmed)* What is it?

MAGGIE: *(With deep feeling)* Oh, don't be hurt with me—don't think I'm ungrateful for all you've done—

HUNT: *(Interrupting and alarmed)* What is it, Maggie?

MAGGIE: I'm going back.

HUNT: Back? Where?

MAGGIE: Where you brought me from.

HUNT: You're ill. *(He steps toward her, but she evades him.)*

MAGGIE: No. I'm serious. *(Tenderly and pathetically)* Oh, darling—understand—*understand*. I *can't* stay here. It's killing me—it isn't what I thought—

HUNT: *(Very low and with terrific pain)* You want to leave me?

MAGGIE: No, no, not you. You know I love you. But even for you I can't stay here. You come with *me*, Hunt. Away from all this.

HUNT: But it's my home—the life I've already too long neglected.

MAGGIE: Come back with me to my life—I think now it was better than this.

HUNT: Are you asking me to sink to a life I raised you from?

MAGGIE: But I know now I didn't rise. I thought I would—I know now—all of a sudden like—tonight like a flash it come to me. I know now my old life was truer, at least for me. That is the only thing we can go by—what is truest to ourselves. We must seek and find our own truth—each one of us perhaps. If this is truer, for you—then you're right, too—only—only we'll have to part—oh, Hunt—

HUNT: *(Taking her in his arms)* Maggie, you are talking nonsense—don't you know I love you—madly, passionately—you love me—How could we part?

MAGGIE: I do love you—oh, Hunt, *so* much. So much that I must keep something in me right—straight. No matter what else happens. I came with you to this life because I thought it would be different—I thought I would get away from all those things in my life. But they are the same here—there isn't any deep down difference. Show me one person that's better or finer here than all those people I knew. The only real difference is that there, they live openly what they are; here, through wealth and what you call the decencies of society, they manage to conceal what they are most of the time from other people, and even part of the time from themselves. Your sister shudders at prostitutes, yet she is kept by a husband she doesn't love—takes his money—the protection of his name and yet deceives him with lovers. And your friends—a man like Eric Frazer—isn't he just a thief?

HUNT: Maggie, you mustn't talk like that about people.

MAGGIE: Why not, if I am talking the truth? You've told me yourself about men. I've sat at your dinner table with politicians—
lawyers—you've told me they were cheating the government—
defrauding their clients—using pull to make money. And look
at the women who come here to this house—who were here
tonight—who take dope and drink and gamble and debauch
their lives away. I'm not holding out against them—it's only that
I belong where I can live really as I am—amongst people who are
really what they are.

HUNT: *(Bitterly)* And what of our love?

MAGGIE: It couldn't survive here. Can't you feel that? You, always
trying to forget my past; I, always trying to be something I'm not—
seeing other people through my own eyes and not theirs—eyes
that are strong because they have faced life—eyes that have seen
suffering and struggle—but have not had the price with which to
buy glasses that might have made them see life colored more rosy
like, but perhaps less clearly.

HUNT: You would make no sacrifice for me and my life?

MAGGIE: Sacrifice? Maybe I'm making more sacrifice than you
think. It ain't so easy to give up luxury and the soft things of life—
nor to give you up.

HUNT: You asked me to go with you.

MAGGIE: Yes—but I shouldn't have. You must stay here with—your
mother—*(Sadly)* with your life. You made a mistake in marrying
me, Hunt.

HUNT: I did what I wanted.

MAGGIE: *(As though not hearing him)* We can each only find our
own way. I must go back. Whatever I am, I can be myself there.
That must be what counts most.

HUNT: You're quite mad. Do you think you could go back to that
life after having known this? You don't realize yourself how much
you've changed. I'm not going and I'm not going to let you go
either.

MAGGIE: Don't make it harder for me. Nothing will change me. I'm
going to leave this house and motor up to New York tonight.

HUNT: There is something back of this—you made up your mind so
suddenly.

MAGGIE: Something—something made me realize it all in a flash.

HUNT: I *won't* let you go.

MAGGIE: Oh, darling—you can't keep me—it's useless—Can't you
see that?

HUNT: Listen to reason!

MAGGIE: Reason comes from the brain—this is coming from something stronger than even myself.

HUNT: And your heart! Your heart!

MAGGIE: *(Brokenly)* With you, Hunt.

HUNT: I don't believe it. It's a put-up job to leave me—even Mother said—

MAGGIE: Don't say that, Hunt! Don't say anything you will regret.

HUNT: *(Angrily)* It's you that will regret—it's heartless of you—you're going back to someone—you never would do this to me otherwise—someone you can't live without—you're going back to try and find him—some old love.

MAGGIE: *(Wearily)* To find myself, Hunt. I told you that night you asked me to marry you what I was seeking, you didn't understand me then, you won't understand me now.

HUNT: I understand perhaps too well. I won't try and hold you either—nor grovel at your feet. I might have known what I was warned of is true.

MAGGIE: I don't know what that was, but I *must* go.

HUNT: *(Beside himself)* I'll tell you what it was—*(He approaches her, shaking)* once a prostitute, always a prostitute! *(*MAGGIE *raises her hand as though to ward off a blow, then drops it helpless and lowers her head. She turns and quickly leaves the room.)*

HUNT: *(With a cry)* Maggie . . . *(As she does not return, he sinks on the chair with his head in his hands.)*

Curtain

Part 4

Ten days later. The scene is the same as part 1. It is again very late at night. NINA *is cleaning up before closing. The sound of jazz in the dive next door can again be heard.* NINA *is alone on the stage when the curtain rises. After a minute, she goes up the stairs and disappears. The stage is left empty a few seconds when* MAGGIE *comes in; she enters slowly and hesitatingly and walks as though she is exhausted and weak. She is dressed in the same clothes as in part 1, but they seem even shabbier and as though they had lost their attempt to be a la mode. Her face seems thinner and she looks ill and changed. She stands silently looking about like one in a daze, then she sinks down on a chair. She takes her hat off with a weary gesture and drops it on the floor beside her. She coughs, then sits without moving, staring vacantly before her.* NINA *appears again; as she descends the stairs, she sees* MAGGIE.

NINA: *(With a cry of joy)* Maggie! *(She runs quickly down the stairs.*

MAGGIE *starts, makes a visible effort to pull herself together.* NINA *rushes forward and takes* MAGGIE*'s hand. With alarm in her voice)* Maggie—where have yer come from? What's up?

MAGGIE: Back again. *(She smiles.)* Like the old penny that always turns up.

NINA: But we thought yer was out East—happy—rich!

MAGGIE: I know—well, you see now I'm not.

NINA: And I picturin' yer all dressed in oimine and swell clothes.

MAGGIE: Well, you can see how swell I am. Left all the grand clothes behind—luckily I had kept these. I thought *they* were grand once—now I know different. Gee, I must look a mess in these!

NINA: Same as yer always did.

MAGGIE: Sure—I know that.

NINA: *(Looking hard at* MAGGIE *)* And yet yer seem different—same hat—same coat—but somethin' changed. Yer look ill, too.

MAGGIE: *(Looking up and smiling weakly)* Hungry—I guess.

NINA: Hungry!

(She runs to the bar, she gets some sandwiches and something to drink and places them before MAGGIE. MAGGIE *eats and drinks ravenously;* NINA *kneels beside her without speaking until she has finished eating.)*

MAGGIE: *(Rather pathetically)* Better now.

NINA: Where did yer come from? And we all thinkin' yer was with that swell guy.

MAGGIE: Not much to tell. Couldn't find it there—

NINA: Find what?

MAGGIE: What I was looking for—

NINA: Didn't he treat yer right?

MAGGIE: *(Shaking her head sadly)* Yes—it wasn't him. I'd have stayed if it had only been for him.

NINA: *(Exasperated)* What made yer leave?

MAGGIE: They didn't want me. You see his mother found it out—about me, I mean. I heard her talking to him one night—when I heard what she said I knew she was right. I hadn't ought to have married him. Leaving was best for him. Then something in here made me leave—something in here . . . *(She puts her hand to her breast.)* I thought I was nearer, back in this life—but when I got here—back in these clothes—it seemed changed. Somehow I couldn't be like I used to—for three nights I've tried to come here—my money gave out—

NINA: Where have yer been?

MAGGIE: *(Dazed)* Just wandering round—dozing here and there—in

the park—on the docks—where no one would see me—then I got
so weak and hungry—I had to come—

NINA: Well, yer ain't too complimentary.

MAGGIE: *(Without hearing but looking around)* It's changed here,
too—all changed.

NINA: There ain't one thing changed.

MAGGIE: I had remembered it larger—more space—cleaner. Not all
cramped and kinda—kinda dirty like.

NINA: Say, this is the best joint round here—yer forgettin' that!

MAGGIE: Maybe—but I had remembered it differently. *(She suddenly
seizes* NINA*'s hand and speaks intensely)* I don't believe I *can* go
back to the old life—out East I thought I could—I thought this
was better than that—but now *this* has changed—

NINA: *(Looking suspiciously at* MAGGIE*)* Say—yer ain't been takin'
dope? *(*MAGGIE *shakes her head in the negative.)* You're changed,
Mag. It's *you.* Yer're cracked or somethin' or else how could yer
have given up that swell life?

MAGGIE: *(Shuddering again)* I'm afraid.

NINA: Yer certainly have changed. Yer that was never afraid of nothing'. How are yer goin' ter live if yer ain't got no money?

MAGGIE: Would Mama take me back just to dance—and pay me for
that? Just to dance and sing?

NINA: Say, Mag, yer ask Mama yerself. Yer were always a favorite of
hers. *(She goes to the door and calls.)* Mama! Mama! A surprise fer
yer! *(*MAMA *comes in; on seeing* MAGGIE, *she gives a shout of joy
and rushes to her. She violently embraces her.)*

MAMA: If it ain't my Mag. If it ain't the only goil that kept my
business safe and sure! Only tonight a traveling salesman what
says he knows you, didn't want ter stay with you gone. "Come for
Maggie," he says—wouldn't spend a penny otherwise. I've been
trying to cheer him up next door. Gott! All them sailors will be
glad to see yer. I'll spread the good news—

MAGGIE: *(Seizing her hand and detaining her)* Mama, can I dance
here again? Dance and sing for money?

MAMA: Can yer dance here again? Say, what yer think?

MAGGIE: Not like before—just dance and sing for money—nothing
more. Will you pay for that?

MAMA: *(Puzzled)* What's up?

NINA: *(Winking to* MAMA*)* Mag's changed.

MAMA: *(Throwing back her head and roaring with laughter)* Yes—
swell chance she's got to change. Yer kind don't change, Maggie.

I'm willin' ter take that chance on that. Yer can dance all yer like and fer money—sure I'll pay yer—*(She laughs again.)* Yer'll pay me in the end—yer always did. *(She goes out, almost running. Her voice can be heard off stage, calling, "Maggie's back," "Maggie's back." MAGGIE remains without moving, gazing before her.)*

NINA: Cheer up, Mag. Everyone will be glad ter see yer.

(A roar and wild cries can be heard outside when suddenly SAILORS, GANGSTERS, PROSTITUTES, LONGSHOREMEN, etc. all burst into the room, led by MAMA. They gather around MAGGIE, seize her chair and lift her high in their midst, cheering loudly. MAGGIE makes a faint effort to respond. When they lower her again, two SAILORS grab her; one finally flings his arms about her and kisses her on the lips. MAGGIE struggles and pushes him violently away, beating him with her fists.)

SAILOR: Steady Mag, what the hell's the matter with yer? Can't a feller give yer a welcomin' kiss?

MAMA: *(Laughing)* Mag's changed—only wants ter make her money dancin' now. She's gone cold on all yer fellers since she's knowed a gentleman. *(They all laugh.)*

VOICE IN THE CROWD: Mag ain't changed. She's still our Mag.

2ND VOICE: Three cheers for Mag.

CHORUS: Mag! Long live Maggie!

MAMA: I'll blow yer all ter drink Maggie's health.

(Cheers. MAMA goes to the bar and pours out drinks. NINA helps her and hands them around. There is general confusion. A SAILOR lifts MAGGIE onto the table. They all lift their glasses and cheer. Someone puts a glass in MAGGIE's hand.)

A VOICE: Speech from Maggie!

CHORUS: Speech! Speech!

MAGGIE: *(Lifting her glass)* Here's—to—you—all—*(She drops the glass from her hand. It falls with a crash to the floor. The CROWD all shout again.)*

VOICES: A dance from Maggie! Maggie's dance!

MAMA: *(Clapping her hands and shouting wildly)* Maggie will dance. Clear the way.

(The CROWD falls back. Someone rushes to the piano and begins playing jazz. A LONGSHOREMAN lifts MAGGIE off the table. She stands a minute as though bewildered, then mechanically begins to dance. She dances as she danced in part 1, but without fire or spirit. As the music grows faster she tries to dance wildly, then suddenly she stops absolutely still. Her eyes are wild, her voice shaking and uncontrolled.)

MAGGIE: *(Wildly and seemingly crazed)* You can't get me. I've gone away from you, I tell you. I was a fool—a *fool* to come back. I hate you all—*hate* you! You and this place! ·

MAMA: *(Running forward and seizing* MAGGIE *by the wrist. She shakes her.)* Say, don't pull any of that grand stuff here.

A VOICE: She's gone nuts. *(The* CROWD *laughs rather hysterically.)*

A WOMAN'S VOICE: She's got too swell fer us. *(More laughter)*

LONGSHOREMAN: *(Very drunk)* Think—yer all right—jus' same— 'Mire a gal with yer nerve.

MAMA: Hate this place—do yer? Well, see what other place will take yer in. Ain't goin' ter have no more fellers?—Maybe they won't have yer—Mike got another girl soon enough. He didn't croak fer love of yer. Cut it, Mag, the straight and narrer is a hungry road.

LONGSHOREMAN: Hard to—walk on—when—yer—drunk.

(More laughter. MAGGIE *sinks on a chair and stares before her without moving. The jazz in the other dive gradually attracts the crowd.)*

SAILOR: Follow the music—Mag'll come round all right—probably ben hittin' it up too much out East on good liquor. Champagne maybe ain't good fer little gals.

(More laughter, then they all begin to go out, finally no one is left but MAGGIE, *who remains without moving, and* MAMA *who washes and dries glasses behind the bar. After a long silence,* MAMA *speaks.)*

MAMA: Better pull yerself tergether and get over them high guy notions. Don't want yer here no more while yer have 'em. No gloom boids wanted here.

*(*MAGGIE *still does not move. A breezy and cheap* TRAVELING SALES- MAN *enters. On seeing* MAGGIE, *he stops and appears a little self-con- scious before* MAMA. *She, however, pays no attention to him and goes on cleaning the glasses.)*

TRAVELING SALESMAN: Heard you had come back, Maggie—but could hardly believe my luck—*(*MAGGIE *jumps as though startled and looks slowly at him.)* Mighty glad—*(*MAGGIE *does not answer.)* Remember me? Sure you do. Over a year ago I told you I'd come back. Don't have to be on my way until eight tomorrow morning and my pay's here in my pocket—good money, too—*(Still no an- swer from Maggie)* I'm no cheapskate, you know that—not a travel- ing man for nothing—paid you well last time—remember? *(He laughs a trifle nervously then speaks coaxingly.)* Come on, Maggie. You'll feel better after a square meal and in a warm bed. *(*MAGGIE *rises as though still dazed. She shudders slightly, then stoops and picks up her hat.)*

MAGGIE: *(Half to herself and hopelessly, despairingly)* Guess people like me never fit anywhere—it can't matter—much—

TRAVELING SALESMAN: *(Taking her arm) Come on*, Maggie. You're wasting my night, Kid. *(He leads her out.)*

MAMA: *(Looking after Maggie)* Changed! Hm—swell chance—*(She continues drying glasses.)*

Curtain

Part 5

Three months later. A landing on the waterfront. It is night and very cold. To the left there is a shed with two windows in it and a door facing out. The door is closed. A sign is hanging on the door which reads: "Meeting here at 9:00 o'clock tonight—all are welcome." To the extreme right there is a board fencing with some old and torn sign posters on it. In the middle is sort of a dock or landing which looks out over the water. The water and the sky give a sense of bleakness and blackness. There is snow on the ground and on the shed.

As the curtain rises, an old SKIPPER *is kneeling against the shed braiding a piece of rope by the light of a coal fire, which is burning in a tin pail. The funnel of a small tug can be seen against the landing. He drops down onto the tug, busies himself on it a minute or two, then hoists himself onto the landing again. Except for the light cast by the flame of the fire, the stage is almost in darkness.*

MAGGIE *appears from the side of the boards. She is dressed in the same clothes as before, which now are utterly worn and ragged. On seeing the* SKIPPER, *she tries to hold her thread-worn coat close to her, and shivers with the cold. The* SKIPPER *does not see her, she advances timidly towards the fire. As the light strikes her face, she looks pinched and desperately ill. She coughs slightly, the* SKIPPER *jumps.*

SKIPPER: God bless us, young woman, you scared me—and I'm not one easily to be scared!

MAGGIE: I'm sorry—

SKIPPER: Never saw you comin'—like a ghost you sneaks up—walks right into my thoughts like. Sorry—it ain't no use, young woman, you're wastin' your time with me.

(He goes on busying himself and turns his back on MAGGIE, *who does not move. Then he jumps down onto the tug again. Timidly* MAGGIE *draws towards the fire and warms her hands. As the* SKIPPER *pulls himself up again, she draws back.)*

SKIPPER: *(Kindly)* Go ahead now, warm your hands. Glad to lend you a little warmth, you look mighty cold.

MAGGIE: *(Shivering)* I'm awful cold—

240

SKIPPER: What's the idea comin' down here? You won't get much business down here. You don't exactly pick a very gay beat. 'Fraid of the cops?

MAGGIE: I come here because I thought there was going to be a Salvation meeting in the shed there.

SKIPPER: *(Laughing)* So that's it! Trying to pick 'em off the Lord?

MAGGIE: You haven't got my number—I come—well—to see if maybe they will pray for me—Something I want. Will there be a meeting tonight?

SKIPPER: Sure thing. At nine o'clock—they'll be comin' along soon. Sorry I got you wrong.

MAGGIE: *(Coughing)* It don't matter.

SKIPPER: Here, while you're waitin', put on this muffler. *(He takes a muffler off and winds it round* MAGGIE.*)* It's too cold for the likes of you a night like this.

MAGGIE: Thanks awful much. Maybe when they come it will be warm in the shed—if I dare go in.

SKIPPER: Yes—they light a stove. Why shouldn't you go in? I often think that lots of them go in to get warm more than to get religion. Then sometimes they dole out coffee, too. Good blokes, them salvationers—I ain't got no kick against them if I ain't one much for religion.

MAGGIE: I used to follow them for their singing—then I got wise that their prayers maybe would have more influence than mine.

SKIPPER: What you prayin' for? Wealth, and to be the Queen of England?

MAGGIE: Praying to bring my husband back to me—Guess my prayers could never do it—Only a miracle I guess can do it.

SKIPPER: Want him as much as that? That's funny.

MAGGIE: Haven't you ever wanted something terribly—so it hurt?

SKIPPER: Yes—long ago—but not no more—I'm wiser now. I know now that most everything you wants turns out the same way.

MAGGIE: How?

SKIPPER: Illusion. That's the joke life's got on us. Everythin' real—everythin' we think real is just an illusion. God! Did I ever want anythin'? I remember wantin' the sea until I was sick from wantin' it. That was long, long back when I was a kid. You wouldn't believe it to smell the stink of the sea in my blood now, but I was born inland—a farmer's kid—never even had a sight of the sea until I was twenty. Worked on the farm—ploughed and tilled the land—but always dreamed and wanted the sea. When I was stackin' the hay, I used to think of the sea and imagine ships with white sails

and white salt spray breakin' over their decks. I cursed and hated
the soil because I pined to stand on a ship and feel the rockin' and
tossin' of the sea's restlessness beneath my feet. I used to cry and
grew ill and I told my mother I would never find happiness unless
I went to sea. Then I ran away to the coast and shipped as a second mate on a tramp boat carrying iron to South America. And
ever after I've been on the sea—tied to it like bein' tied to some
kind of a mistress that held me on a chain.

MAGGIE: But you found your happiness?

SKIPPER: Illusion. The sea was a dream, an illusion to me—what
the land became afterwards. Many a night I lay in my bunk and
cursed the sea and craved for the soil—craved to be pushin' a
plough again along the soft fresh earth in springtime. Craved to
feel again the sweat of the oxen toilin' over the land—to smell the
odor of the manure piled up in the barn. So the earth then—as the
sea had done—became my illusion of happiness. And these
salvation guys—these God-hunters—that's their happiness and
ain't it an illusion? Who really knows about God or heaven, or
hell, or death? Ain't they maybe all illusions? Maybe birth is death
and death life—who's to know or say?

MAGGIE: And love?

SKIPPER: Blast me! The greatest illusion of all! Ain't it a proof that
it's an illusion—our *own* illusion—'cause don't we always think the
one we love the grandest and swellest of them all? And if they *was*
the swellest and grandest why wouldn't everyone else be gone on
them? It's just because it's our way of lookin' at it—our illusion, I
say. Happiness! Ain't happiness just an opinion? But I say the secret is to *keep* your illusions. Fool life at its own game! (*In the distance,* VOICES *can be heard singing "Onward Christian Soldiers."*
MAGGIE *gets up rather slowly as though it were difficult for her to
rise.*)

MAGGIE: They're coming.

SKIPPER: I'm glad—so as to get you warm. Christ, you look all in!
(*He puts his hand out to steady* MAGGIE, *who sways.*)

MAGGIE: Thanks—I'm, all right. (*The singing grows louder. A* SALVA-
TION ARMY MAN *appears with a lantern in his hand.*)

THE MAN: Good evening, sister and brother. Come in and get warm.
(*He unlocks the shed and goes in. Through the window he can be seen
lighting a gas lamp, then lighting a stove and throwing coal into it. At the
same moment two* SALVATION ARMY WOMEN *appear followed by a
small group of poor-looking* MEN AND WOMEN. *They continue singing*

and enter the shed. One of the WOMEN *closes the door. Their singing can still be heard but only faintly through the closed door. Then it stops. Through the windows, the* GROUP *can be seen praying with lowered heads.*)

SKIPPER: You'd better go in.

MAGGIE: (*Faintly*) I'm scared—

SKIPPER: Scared?

MAGGIE: They—they seem so good.

SKIPPER: (*Gathering up his things*) Well, I guess you're just as good.
If you don't go in, they won't pray for you.

MAGGIE: I'm going. Here's your scarf.

SKIPPER: You keep it—as a souvenir.

MAGGIE: Thanks—it's soft.

SKIPPER: You go in and get warm, then you go home—You need
lookin' after. So long!

MAGGIE: Good-bye—

(*He goes off. She takes a step towards the door, then she leans against the shed. She passes her hand over her eyes. The voice of the* SALVATION ARMY MAN *can faintly be heard reading. He says,* "Come unto me, all ye that labor and are heavy laden, and I will give you rest . . . Take my yoke upon you, and learn of me; for I am meek and lowly in heart; and ye shall find rest unto your souls . . . For my yoke is easy and my burden is light." MAGGIE *moves forward, then limply drops to the ground. Inside they begin to sing another hymn. A* MAN *enters, he is about to go into the shed when he stumbles on* MAGGIE'*s body. He stoops and lifts her then he bangs violently on the door. Someone opens it—the light falls on the* MAN *holding* MAGGIE. *The* SALVATION ARMY WOMEN *run to* MAGGIE—*the crowd gathers in the doorway.*)

1ST SALVATION WOMAN: (*Feeling* MAGGIE) She's fainted!

THE MAN: She's numb with cold!

SOMEONE IN THE CROWD: Bring her inside! (*A man pushes forward.*)

MAN: I know her, it's Maggie. She don't live far from here. I'll carry
her home.

ANOTHER VOICE: I'll get a doctor.

1ST SALVATION WOMAN: You're right. It would be wiser to take her
home, she should be put to bed.

ANOTHER MAN: (*Leaning over her*) A drop of brandy would do
her good.

1ST MAN: Let me have her—I'll take her home. (*He gathers* MAGGIE
in his arms. The FIRST SALVATION WOMAN *takes her cloak off
and wraps it around* MAGGIE.)

1ST SALVATION WOMAN: I'll go with you. *(They go off. One or two*
 PEOPLE *following. The* REST *enter the shed again and close the*
 door. They begin singing again.)
Curtain

Part 6

The same night. MAGGIE*'s lodging room. The room is small and dingy*
and gives the feeling of desperate and sordid poverty. Directly upstage, a
small window is high up in the wall, with one small pane of glass, broken;
a piece of newspaper is stuck in it to keep out wind and storm. The snow
outside, lodged in the corners of the window, is visible. From the window
to the right, the ceiling slopes down, forming an eave. Under this eave an
iron bed is placed, which extends out from the wall. A grey torn blanket
and a dirty pillow are on the bed. Near the bed and almost at the foot a
small table stands with a green-shaded oil lamp burning on it. There is
very little oil in the lamp, so it burns very low, although it casts strange
great shadows on the wall. This is the only light in the room. To the left
upstage there is a little coal stove with a broken wooden chair placed before
it. Under the window there is a washstand with a broken pitcher and a
basin standing on it. There is nothing else in the room except a torn piece
of rag rug on the floor and a small worn Bible on the table beside the lamp.
A door, which is closed, leads out to the extreme left; there is another door,
also closed, to the right.

 As the curtain rises, NINA *is bending over the stove, heating something*
in a saucepan. From time to time, she also warms her hands over the stove.
She shivers and appears cold. After a few minutes, there is a sharp knock
at the left door. NINA *appears startled, then cautiously she opens the door.*
As she does so, it is pushed open and HUNT ASHLEY *comes in. He wears*
a heavy coat and soft hat.
NINA: Christ! Where did yer drop from?
HUNT: Where is Maggie, Nina?
NINA: Where do you think at this hour of night?
HUNT: Where?
NINA: *(Imitating "grand" voice)* Why, taking her exercise on the
 streets, of course! Trying to reduce her figure. *(Seriously)* Rotten
 luck she'll be having on a cold night like this!
HUNT: *(Taking off his hat and flinging it on the chair. He sinks onto*
 the bed with his head in his hands.) God!
(NINA *shrugs her shoulders, then goes on cooking. There is a long silence.*
HUNT *remains with his head in his hands, then suddenly he jumps up*
and speaks wildly and passionately.)

HUNT: I followed her, Nina—I followed her. I couldn't stick it back there without her. I thought I should stick out my own life—but when she left, the truth of it seemed to go, too. There was nothing left after Maggie left—no truth or anything.

NINA: Why didn't you come sooner? You might have helped three months back, now—

HUNT: Three months back I thought I was right. I thought I was right and she was wrong. The night she left I thought that she was betraying me to go back to a life of looseness. I almost hated her that night, I think.

NINA: What changed yer way of thinkin'?

HUNT: The truth that went out of my life when she left. It was like having held a coin in your hand all your life, thinking it was gold, then suddenly to open your hand and find only mud. Listen, Nina, I've seen that my life was wrong—what Maggie said was true, it was filled with sham, hypocrisy, and lies—this life as she said may be truer, but it's wrong, too. *Good God, it's terrible. (His voice breaks.)* I come here to follow her, to find her, and you talk of her on the streets. *(Wildly and distractedly) On the streets,* as though it were nothing to walk the streets and fling one's body to anyone for fifty cents. *(He approaches* NINA *and takes her roughly by the shoulders.)* Listen, Nina, listen, do you hear? My life may have been wrong and all that, but hers is wrong, too. But what does that matter? Why must people be classed in any definite life? I've been doing a lot of thinking since Maggie left and I know now that love is the only thing that really matters. If you *really* love someone, you're happy in any kind of life. If Maggie loves me, why can't we make a life of our very own—somewhere away, away from both our lives?

NINA: If yer only could. If it only ain't too late.

HUNT: Not if she loves me. *(*NINA *regards him silently, then returns to the stove and continues warming her hands.)*

NINA: Bitin' night—God, I'm cold! This would be a swell hangout for summer—"swept by ocean breezes" and all that—ain't so good fer winter. Ain't had our storm shutters put up yet. *(She looks at the window and laughs.)*

HUNT: *(Taking off his coat)* Here, put this around you. I'm not cold, burning fire within, I guess. *(He wraps his coat around her.)*

NINA: Thanks.

HUNT: I'm going out to look for Maggie. Where can I find her?

NINA: God knows. I don't. It won't do no good looking for her, nei-

ther. If she don't—well, if she don't have no luck, she'll come home
here; if she does have luck, yer won't find her anyway, or maybe—

HUNT: Maybe what?

NINA: She might bring her luck back here.

HUNT: *(He looks about and shudders.)* God—here!

NINA: Sure, it's her home, ain't it? Leastways for guys that ain't
particular.

(HUNT *sinks down onto the bed again and rocks to and fro, holding his
head between his hands. Inaudible moans and words come from him.*
NINA *wraps herself in the coat and sits as close to the stove as possible.
There is another silence.)*

NINA: Speaking of "fires within," I guess if it ain't been fer that, Maggie
would have croaked long ago—it's that what's kept *her* goin'.

HUNT: *(Without looking up)* Tell me about her, Nina.

NINA: What's to tell? What beats me is how she ever had the nerve
to leave the life yer offered her ter come back ter this. Cracked,
that's what—nothing bad in Maggie—straight stuff as far as she
sees it—lookin' fer God, she says. Plain cracked. "Lookin' fer God!"
I guess he don't come here in our lives. *"Lookin' fer God"* in a place
like this and her spittin' blood most of the time.

HUNT: Spitting blood? *(He looks up.)*

NINA: Yep. A lunger I guess, although she ain't had no doctor. Says
she must suffer and pay in suffering—head filled with a lot of
damn stuff by those Salvation Army prunes—same ones what play
the band and sings, same ones what gave her that book. *(Hunt
picks up the Bible off the table.)*

HUNT: A Bible.

NINA: Yep. That's what she says, although she don't know much
what's in it. Just says it's holy. Sorry I can't offer yer nothing to
eat—bad times, these.

HUNT: *(Springing up)* I don't want anything, thanks. It's you that
must need it. Here, take this. *(He hands her money.)* Get something
to eat when Maggie comes. Don't leave me until she does.

NINA: *(Taking the money)* Gee—thanks. Yer always was generous.

HUNT: *(Walking about impatiently)* God, when *is* she coming? My
nerves are all on edge.

NINA: *(Listening)* I hear someone coming up the stairs now. *(She
looks apprehensive.)* It ain't Maggie, the step is too heavy.

HUNT: God, if she's bringing a—*(His words are interrupted by a loud
banging on the door.* NINA *opens it hastily.* JOE *enters, out of breath
and excited.)*

NINA: Say, what's bitin' yer?

JOE: It's Maggie. They're bringin' Maggie. I beat it ahead ter tell yer.

HUNT: *(Alarmed)* What happened to Maggie?

JOE: She done a pass-out act—carpenter found her—comin' now.

(He goes out the door, HUNT *follows him.* NINA *wrings her hands, then spreads the blanket on the bed. Voices and approaching feet can be heard on the stairs. The* MAN *enters carrying* MAGGIE; *a very poor looking and shabbily dressed* DOCTOR *carrying a black bag follows. The* SALVATION ARMY GIRL *is close behind, also* JOE *and* HUNT. *A few* POOR TYPES *off the streets who have followed for curiosity crowd in. The* MAN *places* MAGGIE *on the bed. Her face is deadly white and her eyes closed. Her hair has fallen and hangs about her. She suddenly looks like a little small child.* HUNT *and* NINA *tenderly wrap the blanket round her,* HUNT *puts his coat over her. A* POLICEMAN *breaks through the crowd.)*

POLICEMAN: Say, what's the row? I followed this crowd—

DOCTOR: *(Interrupting)* No trouble, officer. This fellow here—

(Pointing to the MAN *who carried* MAGGIE*)*

MAN: A carpenter by profession, sir.

DOCTOR: *(Continuing)* As I understand it, this fellow here found this girl in the snow, and—

CARPENTER: *(Interrupting)* I didn't find her—she fainted outside a prayer meeting—

SALVATION ARMY WOMAN: *(Breaking in)* Outside our meeting— another man—*(She looks about.)* he isn't here—Well, he stumbled over her. This gentleman here—this carpenter said he knew her and was kind enough to carry her home. We picked the doctor up on the way.

DOCTOR: I live a few doors down, and happened to just be coming in from a sick call.

POLICEMAN: *(To the* OTHERS*)* And all these—just idle busybodies and butt-ins. Out with youse all! *(He pushes them out. Everyone leaves except* HUNT, NINA, THE DOCTOR, THE CARPENTER *and the* SALVATION ARMY GIRL.*)* And these? *(To* HUNT *and* NINA*)*

CARPENTER: Nina's Mag's friend.

POLICEMAN: *(To* HUNT*)* And you?

NINA: He's a friend, too.

POLICEMAN: *(Looking at* MAGGIE*)* She ain't dead, is she?

DOCTOR: No.

POLICEMAN: Well, then, I'll be going on.

CARPENTER: Me, too—unless you need me, Nina. *(*NINA, *still bending over* MAGGIE, *nods her head in the negative. The* CARPENTER *and* POLICEMAN *go out.)*

SALVATION ARMY WOMAN: Shall I stay?

HUNT: *(Feeling* MAGGIE*)* She is coming around, she seems a little warmer. You needn't stay—thank you so much. *(The* SALVATION ARMY GIRL *goes out.)*

(The DOCTOR *takes out instruments, places them to* MAGGIE*'s chest and listens to her breathing. Then he feels her pulse and places a thermometer between her teeth. They all stand silently.* NINA *rubs one of* MAGGIE*'s hands. Finally the* DOCTOR *looks at the thermometer.)*

DOCTOR: Um—

HUNT: It's not high, is it? Nothing really wrong?

(The DOCTOR *goes to his bag, takes out a small bottle and pours a few drops into a glass before answering. He manages to pour the few drops down* MAGGIE*'s throat. He then takes out a little bottle of tablets and puts them on the table.)*

DOCTOR: She will probably come round in a little while when those few drops get down. When she does, give her two of those tablets with a quarter of a glass of whiskey, here it is. *(He takes a small flask out of his bag.)* The whiskey and the tablets will make it easier—easier for her going off.

NINA: *(With a cry)* Going off?

DOCTOR: Just a question of a few hours. I can do nothing more than just make it easier.

NINA: *(With a sob, sinks on her knees beside the bed and drops her head.)* Maggie—Maggie—

HUNT: *(Stunned)* What—what's the trouble, doctor?

DOCTOR: Lungs—last stages and then she's got—

HUNT: What?

DOCTOR: *(Kindly)* Oh, it doesn't matter, young man, it doesn't matter what she's dying of, she'll go just the same. *(He looks at* HUNT.*)* Better take a little of that whiskey yourself. *(He closes his bag.)* I'd stay if I could help—but I can't, I must go to a case where I'm really needed—If it will make it any easier for you both, I'll come back in an hour or so. *(*HUNT *still stands dazed.)* Good-bye.

HUNT: *(Weakly)* Good-bye. *(The* DOCTOR *goes out.* HUNT *looks after him, then slowly turns and gazes at* MAGGIE. *Then quite suddenly he speaks with an excited voice of hope.)* Nina—Nina— get up—get up! After all, what can a doctor like that know? He's just a poor, probably very bad doctor. He may be quite wrong. Listen, run and find a taxi and then go to this address. *(He takes a little book from his pocket and writes. He tears the leaf from the book and gives* NINA *money.)*

HUNT: This is one of the best doctors, tell him to come at any price. If you can find a taxi, you should be back in less than an hour—if he should be out, go to the hospital right opposite and get any doctor you can.

NINA: *(Hurriedly)* Yes, yes, I understand!

(She seizes her shawl and goes out quickly. HUNT stands for a minute at the foot of MAGGIE's bed gazing at her, then slowly he kneels beside her. He touches her face gently and tenderly and smooths her hair back.)

HUNT: *(In an agonized and deeply emotional voice)* Maggie—Maggie. Speak to me. Speak to me, Maggie. You *must* hear me, I want you so to hear me.

(He drops down, kissing her hand, remaining with his face buried. Gradually, MAGGIE opens her eyes; at first she seems dazed, then her eyes fall and rest on HUNT's head and kneeling form. She lifts her right hand wearily and touches his hair.)

MAGGIE: *(Faintly and with a slight childlike smile)* You—

(HUNT lifts his head quickly, they gaze at each other, she still faintly smiling.)

HUNT: Maggie! *(At the sound of his voice, her smile slowly fades.)* Don't you know me, Maggie?

MAGGIE: *(Almost inaudibly)* Yes—now. At first I thought you were someone else.

HUNT: Oh, Maggie!

MAGGIE: No—one—to—be—jealous of—just—dreaming—I guess.

(She coughs. HUNT rises and gives her whiskey and tablets.)

HUNT: Take these, darling, the doctor said you should have them. *(He braces her while she drinks the whiskey. She sinks back and closes her eyes again.)*

MAGGIE: Better—now.

HUNT: *(Kneeling beside her again and taking her hands again)* Thank God. You are going to get well, darling. You *must* get well. I've come for you to start all over again. *(Quickly as she opens her eyes and looks at him)* You see, in the end I *had* to follow you!

MAGGIE: When I came back it was gone—it wasn't in your life—it wasn't here—I couldn't find it—I didn't seem to fit in—*(Her voice trails off.)*

HUNT: We must make a life of our own—just by ourselves. Both our lives are wrong—we just need each other—somewhere in a new country where we will be taken for just what we really are.

MAGGIE: I have been thinking sometimes—out there—when I've been walking at night, that maybe a great saint can easily be a great devil or a great devil, a great saint—maybe they're so near to each other—maybe they're so near to each other that the vast distance between them—only—only brings them closer.

HUNT: Oh, Maggie, my darling, you mustn't worry your head about these things.

MAGGIE: You—you—don't—understand—

HUNT: *(Passionately)* I only understand I love you—it's the only thing that matters. If you loved me, you would understand that, too.

MAGGIE: I do love you. I loved you when I left you, but I knew there was something else that mattered more.

HUNT: *(Passionately)* What else matters more than love? *(MAGGIE closes her eyes before she answers. There is a minute's silence, then she speaks slowly and almost to herself.)*

MAGGIE: Doing what you've got to do—straight—is greater than love.

HUNT: But you can love straight, Maggie.

MAGGIE: Yes, if that's what you're meant to do. *(Sadly)* Prostitutes maybe ain't meant for love—maybe they can be truer to themselves, truer to what they've got to be, without it. *(A silence)* Maybe it isn't what you are that matters—I guess it's only if you are what you are sincerely, that matters. I remember a kid once telling me, he was a soldier he was, remember him? The kid with the pretty hair and blue eyes. Remember how you—*(Her voice trails off as she makes an effort to remember.)* how you—the kid— and—and—and—remember how we used to sit around the old hangout before this one?

HUNT: I didn't know you then, Maggie.

MAGGIE: *(Looking at him searchingly)* That's true. Gee, that's funny. I thought you used to. *(A silence)* Maybe the whiskey's gone to my head—that would be funny, too—just that little bit gone to my head—the boys would laugh if they saw me—I used to drink eight glasses straight without winking an eye. *(She laughs.)* Long before you knew me—drank all the boys under the table—*(She pauses as though her brain is muddled. She puts her hand to her brow.)* Where was I?

HUNT: Don't talk so much, darling. You'll exhaust yourself.

MAGGIE: Oh, yes—I remember now—about the kid. He was a soldier. I remember once he told me about the army—he told me about spies. I remember his exact words. *(She pauses again and closes her eyes, opens them again and continues.)* "In war time," he said, "a spy must go out into the enemy's camp—often he is the guy through which a victory is gained." Then he said, "the penalty is death." I remember that specially—"the penalty is death." It got me thinking that—about the spy serving his army, I mean—and death. It got me thinking girls like me is like that—in the army of life—serving God, maybe—spies sent out so that some guy—or some nice kid, maybe—can resist us—maybe that glorifies him when he does—and girls like me get service stripes—for being the reason of making them resist, I mean—doing our job well— serving straight—*(Slowly)* I guess our penalty is death, too . . .

HUNT: Don't talk like that, Maggie. Try and rest. Nina's gone for a good doctor; she ought to be back soon.

MAGGIE: *(Faintly)* I feel fine, now—honest I do.

HUNT: Of course you do. You're going to be well in no time, and we won't separate again, I can tell you. We'll start again somewhere under blue skies—just you and I—*(Maggie touches his hair and smiles.)*

MAGGIE: Read me something, Hunt. Something in the book. *(She motions to the Bible. HUNT picks it up.)*

HUNT: Heavens, I haven't read anything in the Bible since I was a child.

MAGGIE: I couldn't make it out—you read it.

HUNT: All right—I'll just open anywhere—

(He opens at random and turns the pages slowly, casually looking at them. MAGGIE has sunk back, a strange look of exaltation upon her face. HUNT finds a passage and begins to read. He reads monotonously without any special feeling.)

HUNT: "Blessed are they which are persecuted for righteousness' sake; for theirs is the kingdom of heaven. Blessed are ye, when men shall revile you, and persecute you, and shall say all manner of evil against you falsely, for my sake"—*(He stops reading and looks at the lamp.)* I can't see, it's too dark. *(He rises and looks at the lamp.)* No wonder—there is only a drop more of oil—it's so cold here, too. I guess I'll sacrifice this chair for a little heat and light. *(He picks up the chair and begins to break it. MAGGIE pays no attention to his remarks or actions, she speaks to herself.)*

MAGGIE: He said that, did he? Blessed—when men shall revile you and persecute you—say evil against you . . .

HUNT: *(Still breaking the chair)* What, darling? *(He throws a few pieces of the chair into the fire.)* That won't do much, but it will do something. *(A faint flame flares up, casting HUNT's shadow against the wall and throwing a light on MAGGIE's dying face.)* I hardly realized how dark it was.

MAGGIE: *(Scarcely audible and with a transcended and exalted expression on her face)* Full of light to me—*(Her eyes close; her arm falls limp from the side of the bed.)*

HUNT: Well, that's a little better. *(He turns to the table and is about to pick up the Bible again when he looks at* MAGGIE. *At first his voice shows alarm, then a cry of anguish.)* Maggie! Maggie! *(He rushes and feels her and then shakes her. She falls dead and limp from his arms. He flings himself down beside the bed, gathering her frantically and frenziedly to him, despair and heartbreaking sobs burst from his lips.)* My darling—my darling—my Maggie—

Curtain

Robert A. Schanke is a professor of theatre at Central College, Iowa. He is the author of *Ibsen in America: A Century of Change* (1988) and *Eva Le Gallienne: A Bio-Bibliography* (1989). His *Shattered Applause: The Lives of Eva Le Gallienne* (1992) was a finalist for both the Lambda Literary Award and the Barnard Hewitt Award for theater research. With Kim Marra, he coedited *Passing Performances: Queer Readings of Leading Players in American Theater History* (1998) and *Staging Desire: Queer Readings of American Theater History* (2002). In addition to editing this collection of plays by Mercedes de Acosta, he has written her biography, *"That Furious Lesbian": The Story of Mercedes de Acosta* (2003). His articles on theater history appear in *Theatre Survey, Theatre Topics, Southern Theatre, Central States Speech Journal,* and *Nebraska History.* He has contributed to numerous reference books and anthologies, including *Women in American Theatre, Cambridge Guide to American Theatre, Cambridge Guide to World Theatre, American Theatre Companies, Shakespeare Around the Globe,* and *The Oxford Companion to the Theatre.* He serves as the editor of the international journal *Theatre History Studies* and edits Theater in the Americas, a book series published by Southern Illinois University Press, which includes the present volume.

THEATER IN THE AMERICAS

The goal of the series is to publish a wide range of scholarship on theater and performance, defining theater in its broadest terms and including subjects that encompass all of the Americas.

The series focuses on the performance and production of theater and theater artists and practitioners but welcomes studies of dramatic literature as well. Meant to be inclusive, the series invites studies of traditional, experimental, and ethnic forms of theater; celebrations, festivals, and rituals that perform culture; and acts of civil disobedience that are performative in nature. We publish studies of theater and performance activities of all cultural groups within the Americas, including biographies of individuals, histories of theater companies, studies of cultural traditions, and collections of plays.